Hollywood's
Hard-Luck Ladies

Hollywood's
Hard-Luck Ladies

*23 Actresses Who Suffered
Early Deaths, Accidents, Missteps,
Illnesses and Tragedies*

LAURA WAGNER

McFarland & Company, Inc., Publishers
Jefferson, North Carolina

LIBRARY OF CONGRESS CATALOGUING-IN-PUBLICATION DATA

Names: Wagner, Laura, 1970– author.
Title: Hollywood's hard-luck ladies : 23 actresses who suffered
early deaths, accidents, missteps, illnesses and tragedies / Laura Wagner.
Description: Jefferson : McFarland & Company, Inc., Publishers, 2020. |
Includes bibliographical references and index.
Identifiers: LCCN 2020000405 | ISBN 9781476678436
(paperback : acid free paper) ∞
ISBN 9781476638331 (ebook)
Subjects: LCSH: Motion picture actors and actresses—
United States—Biography—Dictionaries. | Actresses—
United States—Biography—Dictionaries.
Classification: LCC PN1998.2 .W33 2020 | DDC 791.4302/80922 [B]—dc23
LC record available at https://lccn.loc.gov/2020000405

BRITISH LIBRARY CATALOGUING DATA ARE AVAILABLE

ISBN (print) 978-1-4766-7843-6
ISBN (ebook) 978-1-4766-3833-1

Front cover: Publicity photograph of Mayo Methot (author's collection)

Printed in the United States of America

*McFarland & Company, Inc., Publishers
Box 611, Jefferson, North Carolina 28640
www.mcfarlandpub.com*

In loving memory of my aunt, Charlotte Rainey (1937–2013), a lady who taught me about strength, perseverance and the value of a great sense of humor

Table of Contents

Introduction and Acknowledgments

Centuries ago, a wise man set forth that industry, perseverance and frugality make fortune yield, and in most lines of work, that probably still holds true today. But not for actors and, especially, actresses in the Hollywood movie mills. When it comes to advancement, luck plays a vital role. And there are two kinds of luck. Many girls braved the movie capital, quickly found open studio gates and open arms, and embarked on careers both long and lucrative. But there were others less fortunate. As a wise movie character once griped, "Whichever way you turn, Fate sticks out a foot to trip you."

There have been many tragedies in Hollywood history. An ocean of ink has been spilled on the most famous of these ladies—stars such as Marilyn Monroe, Judy Garland, Natalie Wood, Sharon Tate, Jean Harlow, Thelma Todd and Jayne Mansfield—and with good reason. But what of those whose stories are less documented? Actresses who found it either difficult to navigate the rough waters of Hollywood or saw their dreams shattered by hard luck or, worse luck yet, an early demise? They never attained top stardom, but their stories, too, deserve to be told.

"Hard luck" is defined as "marked by, relating to, or experiencing bad luck or difficulty." There are degrees, of course. Although some may not consider alcoholism hard luck, it *is* a disease and in many cases intoxication caused actresses to do things they wouldn't do otherwise. These actions disrupted lives and careers. Also, the pressures of Tinseltown have been known to exacerbate a performer's drinking and/or her already fragile mental stability.

Within you will find 23 actresses who, for one reason or another, found their trips through Hollywood, and life in general, tumultuous, and are now better known for their show business exits than their entrances. There are those who suffered from mental illness, drug addiction and/or long, drawn-out declines; victims of accidents, apparent suicides, sudden deaths and even murder. You will also read about husbands who put the skids under the promising careers of their mates. It's almost a stereotype that actresses marry the wrong guys, but for stereotypes, there's usually a good reason.

There were few medical treatments for mental illness when each of these ladies strutted her stuff upon the soundstage, so victims of bipolar disorder (Lynne Baggett, Mary Castle, Mae Clarke, Mayo Methot, Rosa Stradner, et al.) found themselves on the road to ruin. With no medications to ease their pain, alcohol was their escape, and that created even more problems. If they weren't institutionalized, they were left pretty much on their own to wreak havoc. In this category, the poster child was poor Clarke, who went through hell with shock treatments and other horrors.

Then there were the ladies who suffered accidents that tested their courage and determination: Suzan Ball lost a leg to cancer; a hunting accident paralyzed Susan Peters; a car crash put Marjie Millar out of commission; a mysterious bump on the head threw Rita Johnson's life into chaos. Lynne Baggett and Helen Walker committed vehicular homicide and carried emotional scars to the finish of their short lives. Car crashes brought untimely ends to promising screen personalities Dorothy Dell and Judy Tyler. A cold that developed into lobar pneumonia robbed us of Helen Burgess.

If it weren't for hard luck, Sidney Fox, Mary Nolan, Peggy Shannon and Karen Verne would have had *no* luck, and all were apparent suicides. Susan Cabot was clubbed into the next world by her own son. Morphine addict Mary Nolan was in and out of hospitals, her problems wrecking the multiple chances given her.

Bad luck can also be a result of typecasting. Charlotte Henry could never shake her title role in *Alice in Wonderland* (1933). Others felt the sting of being hired by studios as "threats" to established stars whom they resembled, and career-wise they went nowhere; the classic example of this was Mary Castle, who was the spitting image of screen goddess Rita Hayworth. Along with a host of personal issues, Dorothy Comingore was ultimately done in by the Blacklist.

In each case, their path to possible Hollywood stardom was blocked. While many made the wrong decisions, others couldn't help what Fate had in store for them.

Researching these actresses, all of whom I have enjoyed immensely as performers, was an emotionally draining experience. I have tried not to be cynical or judgmental about them and their tribulations, instead approaching each as sympathetically and honestly as I could. You will find inspirational stories here and, maybe too, you'll get a bit angry at some of the ladies' inability to modify their self-destructive behavior.

While the bulk of the names might be unfamiliar, their stories are by turns shocking, painful, inspirational, sad—but always interesting.

◈ ◈ ◈

My research was done via newspaper archives, quotes from books and interviews with those closest to my subjects. You will notice that I use a lot of primary articles (and gossip columns) from the time when these ladies were active. I believe this gives a clearer and more accurate picture of how they were perceived at the time. All too often, writers write about their subjects the way they think it was, instead of how it really was.

If something I have written conflicts with information given elsewhere, it is because I have access to new data, including genealogy records. I have not relied solely on the Internet Movie Database for credits, and have added titles not listed on that site. My timeline in discussing these ladies' films is based on their shooting dates, not the release dates. A reference section, arranged by actress, follows the main text, and includes books, articles, interviews and other resources from which information was gleaned.

I am grateful for the following people for their friendship, support and help: Alisa Ann Armes, Michael Barnum, Peggy Biller, Lisa Burks, Diane Byrnes, Bob Fergusson, Eve Golden, Sandra Grabman, Ray Hagen, Frances Ingram, Scott Levine, James Robert Parish, Paul Petro, Karine Philippot, the late Ruth Prigozy, Tamera Rainey-Jordan, Christina Rice, the late Steve Tompkins, Bonnie Tone, Larry and Debra Vichnis, Barry Virshbo, Patricia Wagner and Archie Waugh.

I will always be indebted to Bob King for taking a chance on me in 1995 when I started writing for the magazines *Classic Images* and *Films of the Golden Age*. I had no experience and wasn't even very good (i.e., I was terrible). But he stuck with me and, if I do say so myself, I've improved a lot. In addition to allowing me to do articles on obscure actors, he gave me three regular columns, "Book Points," "Overlooked in Hollywood" (formerly known as "Forgotten Faces") and "Call Sheet."

His colleague Carol Peterson is one of my best friends. Not only is she indispensable to our publications' readers, she is indispensable to me, too. She is helpful, yes, but also fun to be around and a very caring friend who I love very much.

I would like to thank those who lent me photos for this book: Scott O'Brien, Tom Weaver, Greg Mank, Bob Burns, John Antosiewicz and C. Robert Rotter. I am particularly grateful to the latter, who went out of his way to scan many stills from his amazing collection. He runs the fabulous Glamour Girls of the Silver Screen site (http://www.glamourgirlsofthesilverscreen.com/).

It was Robert who aided me in locating Mary Castle's granddaughter, Cynthia Lee. I had long hoped to speak to a relative of Castle's, whose later years were never documented. Cynthia came through for me and I truly appreciate her honesty and insight. She also contributed two candid photos of her grandmother for this book.

Honesty marked my correspondence with Shannon Quine, Susan Peters' granddaughter. The story of the difficult childhood and adult life of Susan's adopted son Timothy has never been told, and I thank Shannon for sharing it with me. It could not have been easy.

Author Stephen D. Youngkin wrote the definitive book on Peter Lorre, *The Lost One: A Life of Peter Lorre*, and it was a great starting point for my research on Karen Verne. He also graciously took the time to answer some of my questions via email and shared with me his interview with Karen's sister.

Thanks, too, to author Michael Karol for asking Lee Tannen about the Lucille Ball–Suzan Ball connection; Jay Dee Witney for relating his memories of his dad, director William Witney, and also Mary Castle; and Michael Tierney for his intelligent, thoughtful response to my query about his uncle Lawrence Tierney's possible involvement in Rita Johnson's accident.

Tom Weaver helped with suggestions and information. Tom is one of the best writers on film, ever, and I trust his judgment implicitly. I am indebted to him for sharing with me his previously unpublished interview with Susan Cabot's ex-husband, Michael Roman. Mr. Roman's insightful, candid and heartfelt comments added so much to Susan's story and he cleared up a lot of misconceptions (and downright lies) about her.

My nephews, Jake and Luke Vichnis, continue to make me very proud. They have grown up to be terrific guys and are always surprising me with their talent. I will never forget introducing them to one of my favorite movies, *All Through the Night* (1942) with Karen Verne, and how they enjoyed it. I love them both with all my heart.

How I wish my late mentor, Doug McClelland, was here to read this book. He gave me a helping hand when I needed it most and shared with me a love of lesser-known actors and actresses. We had many wonderful conversations about some of these ladies, and he even gave me clippings on them. I cannot believe he's been gone 15 years already.

Melanie Young saved me from propagating misinformation. As far as I'm concerned, her ability to uncover facts is unparalleled, and she came up with some startling information for me. Without exaggeration, this book could not have been written without Melanie's valuable help. I appreciate her and her friendship very much.

As always, I must thank my wonderful brother, Tom Wagner, for standing by me and helping me when I needed it. I don't know what I did to deserve him, but I ain't complaining! I love him very much.

Jackie Jones is my rock, my biggest booster, my person, and my best friend. She's always there for me with an encouraging word and puts up with me when I babble on about obscure actors. I am lucky to have this great lady in my life.

My late mother Fran Wagner and aunt Charlotte Rainey were both big movie fans and were among the very few in my family who cared about what I wrote. Both gave me a good example to follow and they will continue to inspire me in the years ahead.

Lynne Baggett

For many in Hollywood, beauty invites trouble. You don't have to be a star to feel the pressures of Tinseltown. Lynne Baggett had a lot of promise when she started and with the right opportunities she could have advanced to bigger roles. A relationship with a powerful man, personal issues and some really hard knocks quickly smashed those hopes.

She was born Ruth Lynne Baggett on May 10, 1924, in Wichita Falls, Texas. According to Hollywood publicity, she came from a wealthy oil family, but in truth her father was a farmer turned auto mechanic, her mother a stenographer. She grew up in nearby Dalhart. There has been speculation that a childhood head injury caused many of the problems she faced as an adult.

In 1942, the pretty raven-haired 18-year-old was spotted in a Dallas department store by Warner Bros. talent scout Solly Baiano, and subsequently signed to a contract. During her four years with the studio, Baggett was seen almost exclusively in uncredited bit parts as nurses, chorus girls, salesgirls, waitresses, hostesses, party guests, etc. Columnist Hugh Dixon called her the "town's newest ah-h-h-h." She was linked romantically with the studio's head of publicity, Robert Taplinger.

In February 1944, newspapers reported that her father, stepmother and one-year-old stepbrother had died in an Arizona fire. In fact, while the latter two did perish, Lynne's father lived until 1952.

Her only credited role for Warners came in the Oscar-winning Don Siegel–directed short *Star in the Night* (1945). In this modern retelling of the Nativity story, Baggett plays pregnant Maria (aka Mary) who comes to the Star Auto Court with her husband José (Anthony Caruso) on Christmas Eve. While it was an important role in the story, it was also a small one with no dialogue. The drama centers on the auto court owner (J. Carrol Naish), who has his faith

Columnist Hugh Dixon called Lynne Baggett the "town's newest ah-h-h-h" (courtesy C. Robert Rotter/Glamour Girls of the Silver Screen).

restored by seeing how those around him become selfless when made aware of Maria's pending blessed event.

Although Baggett was a competent actress, screenwriter Peter Viertel told author Natasha Fraser-Cavassoni that she did not have a "come hither quality," adding a little unfairly, "There was no love affair going with her and the camera. None of the alchemy happened that actresses such as Marilyn Monroe would be capable of sparking."

When not "acting" in minimal, decorative parts, Baggett was doing publicity. She was a favorite of servicemen, named "The Serpentine Lady," "Cobra Girl" and the "Triple-A-Girl," the A's standing for "adorable, amicable and amorous." Meaningless titles, perhaps, but it helped get her attention.

In 1945, she met producer Sam Spiegel (aka S.P. Eagle)

An early Warner Brothers glamour shot (courtesy C. Robert Rotter/Glamour Girls of the Silver Screen).

while she was doing a screen test for his next movie, *The Stranger*. She didn't get the part but she got the producer: The two became inseparable. Spiegel secured for her a Universal contract, and she was cast in a major supporting part in Abbott and Costello's *The Time of Their Lives* (1946) as John Shelton's fiancée. It was her first and last for Universal, a shame since she showed potential to be an up-and-coming leading lady. After getting her the contract, Spiegel changed his mind: He did not approve of her continuing her career.

On April 10, 1948, 23-year-old Baggett wed 47-year-old Spiegel in Las Vegas, with director John Huston and his wife Evelyn Keyes as witnesses. Spiegel's friend, writer Leonora Hornblow, didn't like Lynne, calling her "vain and affected." Spiegel attributed this to Lynne's insecurity. Joan Axelrod, the interior decorator wife of playwright-screenwriter George Axelrod, thought Lynne "very dear in spirit, [with] a wonderful laugh and a great kind of abandon about her. There was something so heartrending about it."

In October 1949, columnist Wood Soanes wrote that Baggett was returning to the screen after being "invalided for a year after injury in a swimming pool accident." There was no mention of the type of injury she had sustained.

Film audiences got their first glimpse of a blonde Lynne Baggett when *D.O.A.* (1950) previewed in December '49. As a "grieving" widow who knows more than she initially tells about the supposed suicide of her husband and the poisoning of Frank Bigelow (Edmond

Lynne trying hard to prove screenwriter Peter Viertel wrong when he said she did not have a "come hither quality" (courtesy C. Robert Rotter/Glamour Girls of the Silver Screen).

O'Brien), she gave a skillfully emotive performance. This was followed by supporting roles in *The Flame and the Arrow* (1950) and *The Mob* (1951). These smallish parts were not as vivid as the one in *D.O.A.* but Baggett showed that she could be relied upon to be interesting on camera. On stage, she did *What Every Woman Knows* (1950) at Los Angeles' Circle Theater.

Baggett and Spiegel clashed over her desire to resume her career (such as it was). The tension between the couple was fierce. It was later revealed that Baggett had had an affair with writer Irwin Shaw while her husband was doing pre-production work on *The African Queen* (1951). She also had a brief fling with that film's director, John Huston.

Spiegel later alleged that she destroyed the contents of his home, including cutting up his suits and six Picasso paintings. Additionally, the spatting Spiegels charged each other with adultery. Yet no official divorce was in the works just yet because supposedly Spiegel couldn't afford a settlement.

Baggett became an Arthur Murray dance instructor. It's unclear why she did not resume acting now that she had shed Spiegel.

In November 1953, she went to court asking for $3685 a month in temporary alimony, stating that Spiegel had abandoned her two years earlier to go on location for *The African Queen*. Baggett insisted he was worth at least three million dollars. In January '54, the producer was ordered by the court to pay her $500 a month.

As downhill spirals go, Baggett's would be a doozy.

On the night of July 7, 1954, driving a car she had borrowed from actor George Tobias, she rear-ended another vehicle. Its passengers included five boys returning from day camp; nine-year-old Joel Watnick was killed instantly. A panicky Baggett fled the scene, later claiming she went to a movie to "calm her nerves." The police tracked her down two days later. "When I went back and saw the boy lying there, I knew he was dead," she explained. "I didn't know which way to turn. You don't know what something like that does to you. I haven't slept in 48 hours. I wish I'd been killed instead of the boy."

She professed that she had "blacked out" after the collision, but no one believed her story. Arrested and charged with manslaughter and hit and run, she was released on a $5000 bond put up by her estranged husband. Her ten-day trial in October '54 resulted in an acquittal for manslaughter but, found guilty of felony hit and run, she was sentenced to 60 days in jail and three years' probation. "I cannot accept her story of a blackout and the jury couldn't believe it, either," Superior Judge Mildred Lillie remarked. "She was extremely rational soon after the accident, and from then until she was arrested two days later she used every resource at her command to get her car repaired and to conceal her identity." Judge Lillie further stated that Baggett's actions showed that she "lacked a feeling of human kindness and was concerned only with herself." A bit harsh. Baggett's lawyer remarked that Lynne "would carry to her dying day the psychological scars of having killed a nine-year-old boy." (Baggett and Tobias paid more than $40,000 due to six civil suits filed against them.)

"I still don't feel I belong here, but in a way the judge did me a favor," Baggett told reporters from her jail cell on New Year's Eve. "This is the end of a cycle of bad luck for me.... I have been filled with anxiety because of my marital problems. When I get out, I will divorce Sam, try to re-establish my personal life and try to work again. I've been in another jail of sorts the past three years."

Granted a divorce from Spiegel in March '55, she was given a cash settlement of more than $46,000, plus $38,500 in court and attorney fees. Baggett was also to receive $50,000 from profits from Spiegel's production company.

A return to acting stalled due to her personal troubles; she suffered from depression, and it was reported that she was going through encephalographic tests on her brain.

Besides a drinking problem, she was doing cocaine (according to Leonora Hornblow) and was being treated for peripheral neuritis (weakness, numbness and pain in hands, feet and other areas of the body). Her mother, who had stood by her for so long, passed away in 1957.

On June 7, 1959, she took an overdose of sleeping pills at her home. But she had called the telephone operator for help before she passed out, and was saved in time. To get into her house, the police removed the hinges from the back door. In August, Baggett fell in her bedroom. She subsequently claimed that she had been trapped under her foldaway bed for six days; she went to the hospital delusional, mumbling inco-

Lynne showing off her legs for the Warner Bros. cameras (courtesy C. Robert Rotter/Glamour Girls of the Silver Screen).

Lynne had one of her best roles as a widow with secrets in *D.O.A.* (1950) with Edmond O'Brien (courtesy C. Robert Rotter/Glamour Girls of the Silver Screen).

Lynne with Bud Abbott on the set of *The Time of Their Lives* (1946) (courtesy John Antosiewicz).

herently, dehydrated, paralyzed from the knees down, and suffering from malnutrition. There was reason to believe her story was made up and she was only on the floor since the day before. A friend said she was perfectly fine before that. Baggett was sent to a psychiatric ward for observation.

By October '59, she was moved to a private sanitarium. "She is still unable to walk," wrote Louella Parsons, "but her doctors say she will surely recover in a few more weeks. Meanwhile, Sam [Spiegel] is completely financing her care and seeing to it that she has every comfort and luxury."

On March 22, 1960, just six weeks after being released, a 35-year-old Baggett was found dead in her Hollywood apartment by her nurse. She was stretched out on her bed; nearby were "some orange tablets and blue and white capsules." Her nurse told police that Baggett had requested that she be undisturbed until late in the day because "she wanted to get a lot of rest." Army Archerd wrote, "Friends of Lynne Baggett don't believe she was a suicide because of a happy note sent by her last week. She had no financial worries. Sam Spiegel had amply taken care of all her needs. And, she was on the road to recovery."

By this time, Spiegel had a new wife, Betty Benson (30 years his junior). Benson later told Natasha Fraser-Cavassoni that Spiegel initially refused to pay for Baggett's funeral: "Sam seemed to shrug it off and get on his merry way.... He didn't like things that were unpleasant or depressing— illness or hospitals—and he didn't like

Lynne." Eventually he sprang for the funeral but did not attend. Baggett is interred at Forest Lawn Memorial Park.

Lynne Baggett Filmography

1943: *Air Force* (uncredited), *Three Cheers for the Girls* (short, uncredited), *Murder on the Waterfront* (uncredited), *Thank Your Lucky Stars* (uncredited).
1944: *In Our Time* (uncredited), *Grandfather's Follies* (short), *The Adventures of Mark Twain* (uncredited), *Hollywood Canteen* (uncredited).
1945: *Roughly Speaking* (uncredited), *Pillow to Post* (uncredited), *Rhapsody in Blue* (uncredited), *Mildred Pierce* (uncredited), *Star in the Night* (short), *Confidential Agent* (uncredited).
1946: *Cinderella Jones* (uncredited), *One More Tomorrow* (uncredited), *Janie Gets Married* (uncredited), *Night and Day* (uncredited), *The Time of Their Lives*, *The Time, the Place and the Girl* (uncredited).
1950: *D.O.A., The Flame and the Arrow*.
1951: *The Mob*.

Suzan Ball

One of the most courageous stories in show business concerns Suzan Ball. A star in the making with leads at Universal, she seemed to have a bright future. She was 19 years old when an injury on a movie set put in motion events that would lead to her untimely death at 21. The way she handled her illness was an inspiration and every turn for the worse was met with a positive outlook.

Of French, English and Irish descent, the first of two children, she was born Susan Ann Ball in Buffalo, New York, on February 3, 1934. She was the second cousin of Lucille Ball. (According to a 1952 Earl Wilson column, Lucy denied any relation. Gary Morton's cousin, author Lee Tannen, said the family never talked about Suzan and he didn't think they were related. However, genealogy records, provided by researcher Melanie Young, prove Suzan and Lucy were indeed cousins.)

The family moved to Detroit, Miami and Buffalo before finally settling in North Hollywood. Her father owned a travel agency. In the 1940s, Susan's mother operated a charter airline service for Camp Cooke (later Vandenberg Air Force Base).

Striking portrait of Suzan Ball's cat eyes (courtesy C. Robert Rotter/Glamour Girls of the Silver Screen).

The teenager auditioned and won a spot on Richard Arlen's local television show *Hollywood Opportunity*. Suzan didn't win, but her singing came to the attention of bandleader Mel Baker, who hired her as a vocalist while his band was in Southern California.

In August 1951, Suzan was cast as a dancing girl in Monogram's *Aladdin and His Lamp*. Publicity wavered between two stories on how she was discovered—and both involved having her picture taken after baking a cake. But both versions were untrue. Ball had been living at the House of the Seven Garbos, a boarding house for young movie hopefuls, and was recommended for a screen test at

Jeff Chandler (*left*) and Scott Brady are prepared to protect Suzan Ball in *Yankee Buccaneer* (1952) (courtesy C. Robert Rotter/Glamour Girls of the Silver Screen).

Universal-International. In the test, she did scenes from *The Postman Always Rings Twice* and *Crossfire*.

The teenager was signed to a contract and columnist Edwin Schallert wrote that the studio planned a "spirited build-up." The dark-complexioned Ball was taller than most, 5'7"; the *Santa Maria Times* wrote, "Her dark brown hair and hazel eyes blend a sultry beauty reminiscent of Jane Russell and Linda Darnell."

Her first U-I role was a bit in *The World in His Arms* (1952), and she received "Introducing" billing in her next, *Untamed Frontier* (1952) with Joseph Cotten and Scott Brady. As the treacherous dance hall girl thrown over for Shelley Winters by bad boy Brady, Ball projected a cool worldliness—and bore more than a passing resemblance to Faith Domergue, then-wife of *Untamed Frontier* director Hugo Fregonese. She was promoted to leading lady for her next, *Yankee Buccaneer* (1952), in which stars Jeff Chandler and Scott Brady vied for Ball's Portuguese Countess Margarita La Raguna.

She was lucky right off the bat to get roles in the studio's Technicolor action pictures opposite seasoned leading men. Her dark beauty was ideal for color. She told John L. Scott, "Color does things for me…. I look like a different person in black and white." She was perfect for exotic roles, particularly Native Americans.

In another Technicolor actioner, *City Beneath the Sea* (1953), Ball played a saloon singer in love with Anthony Quinn. (Robert Ryan and Mala Powers were the main couple.)

Although she had hoped to get a chance to display her singing talents, she was dubbed on the song "Handle with Care."

On the set, a romance developed between her and the married Quinn, 28 years her senior. In his autobiography, he called Ball an "absolutely breathtaking young actress, one of the fabulous beauties of her day," adding that when they first made love, "She had never been with another man, and I received her like manna from heaven." Much of what Quinn writes about Ball, his "one true love," can be taken with a grain of salt. His timeline of events in her life is off; he almost completely ignores Suzan's future husband Richard Long and claims that he (Quinn) was with her throughout her subsequent illness. He also alleges to have built a house for her "with my own hands: I designed it; laid the foundation, the pipes for plumbing; everything. There was joy in the work, knowing that it was for Suzan." She never lived in it, he adds. He waxed poetic about her in a highly romanticized view of the love they shared. There was no denying that Suzan was in love with him—their affair even made Dorothy Kilgallen's column ("Screen starlet Suzan Ball is carrying a torch for an Actor Who Belongs to Somebody Else"). Quinn's version of events sounds like the dreams of a womanizer with a guilty conscience, relating what he *hoped* had happened. It is probably correct that she was "the great tragedy" of his life—and his greatest guilt.

The relationship continued on their next film, *East of Sumatra* (1953), in which they showed a strong romantic chemistry. In *Sumatra*, engineering supervisor Duke Mullane (Jeff Chandler) goes to Tungga to negotiate with the tribe's King Kiang (Quinn) to excavate tin from the area. The king's intended, sultry half-caste princess Minyora (Ball), becomes interested in Duke, much to the king's displeasure. While watching Ball and Quinn's intense final scene, as the king lies dying, one can't help but wonder if their real-life doomed association played a part in how they movingly acted the scene.

During the making of *Sumatra*, Ball suffered an injury to her right knee while rehearsing for her dance number. The studio doctor treated it and she went back to work.

At the beginning of '53, she was on tour in the East when she hurt the knee again in a car accident in the Berkshire Mountains; her vehicle was sideswiped by a truck and her knee banged the window winder. "I had some difficulty in walking after that and a doctor put me in bed for awhile," Suzan told Julian Hartt. "Then I took a train back to Hollywood to make *War Arrow* [1953]."

War Arrow starred Maureen O'Hara and Jeff Chandler, and Ball por-

Suzan Ball and Anthony Quinn had an affair while filming *East of Sumatra* (1953) (courtesy C. Robert Rotter/Glamour Girls of the Silver Screen).

trayed the headstrong, restless ("I'm not a savage!") daughter of an Indian chief (Henry Brandon). Her controlled performance belied what was going on behind the scenes: In the middle of production, she "suddenly became violently ill," but was unsure of the problem. "There wasn't any reason for it and I never thought of the leg, but I had to sit 20 minutes before I could get the strength to move." Finishing the picture, she said, was "torture," but after she did, she was again bedridden. (Editors later trimmed her *War Arrow* scenes to eliminate any noticeable limping.)

By now she had ended her affair with Quinn and began seeing a fellow Universal contract player, 26-year-old Richard Long, whom she'd met in the studio commissary. (Quinn claims after his and Ball's break-up, Suzan and Richard met and quickly married just before she died, but this isn't true.)

By this time, doctors had determined that Ball had developed in her knee what is now called Ewing's sarcoma, "a rare type of cancerous tumor that grows in your bones or the soft tissue around your bones, such as cartilage or the nerves" (WebMD). She had radiation treatments but her doctor wanted to amputate. Ball sought another opinion. Her new doctors were thinking of cutting out the cancerous bone and replacing it with plastic.

She was getting treatment every other day. According to the *Des Moines Register*, this included a special diet and "purifying her system by means of injections" (of what, they don't say). "Slowly, month after month, Suzan lost all her teeth," Anthony Quinn alleged. "She started taking all kinds of strange medications. One doctor had her on gunpowder pills mixed with gold, copper and iron. She tried everything, but nothing worked."

Universal kept her on salary and paid all her medical expenses—and would continue to do so. Ball was optimistic that she would be off crutches soon. "I am getting along fine," she told Bob Thomas. "The malignancy has stopped growing, and the doctor says I should be able to walk on both legs in a month."

She wanted to get back to work. "There's a script here called *The Black Lagoon* [*Creature from the Black Lagoon*] and a part in it for a girl who doesn't have to walk," she told Thomas. "I'm going to hound every executive in the studio until I get it." Although it was reported that U-I said she could be in the movie if she wanted, Ball was not up to filming and Julie Adams was cast.

While driving in Hollywood on October 17, 1953, Ball was in another car crash, mostly doing damage to her car and the one she rammed. The jinx continued: On November 28, she was in her kitchen making lunch when she slipped

"Hollywood's nicest romance": Richard Long and Suzan Ball (courtesy C. Robert Rotter/ *Glamour Girls of the Silver Screen*).

on some water from her dog's dish and fell. She broke her leg—the same leg she was having trouble with. The break was right through the tumored area. "After a year on crutches, I was all ready to go back to work. And now this happens. It makes you wonder."

At this time, she was sharing an apartment with her father Dale. (Suzan's parents had divorced. Her mom would remarry in 1954.) Richard Long, to whom she was now engaged, was a constant presence. Quinn alleged that he and Suzan were living in the apartment together and that he cared for her. ("[S]he blacked out in the bathroom of our apartment, and I cleaned up after her. I carried her to bed and washed her off and wept.... I nursed her as if she were my own child.")

A bone graft was performed, using a piece from her hip to replace the diseased bone. This operation was a failure; the badly deteriorated bone wouldn't knit; and a biopsy showed there was still a malignancy. She was again told her leg should be amputated. Ball wanted to delay this as long as possible, but "I kept needing more and more drugs to blot out the pain. I was going steadily down. I couldn't eat."

She couldn't hold it off any longer. On January 12, 1954, at Temple Hospital, Ball's right leg was amputated. Her father and her fiancé Long were at her side, the latter remarking, "We'll be married as soon as we can."

After a few weeks' recovery, Ball was to be outfitted with an artificial limb. She wanted to postpone her wedding to Long; she was determined to walk down the aisle without the aid of crutches.

Ball's courageous story was a hot topic and how she dealt with her hard luck captured the hearts of people across the country; she received flowers and thousands of letters. Ball spoke candidly in newspapers about her struggles, how she would adjust to the artificial leg and how she would continue to do normal everyday activities and continue to act. She got letters from returning servicemen who were also amputees. Suzan treated the subject as lightly as she could, even naming her "stump" Throckmorton—"Otherwise, people will be afraid to mention 'legs' or 'running' around me." She practiced walking with her artificial leg every day.

Ball found her courage, she told Aline Mosby, "by accepting what has to be." She added, "It's my one and only life, and I don't plan to ruin it with regrets. Self-pity is a waste of valuable time."

There was also Richard Long, "seeing me every day, spending the long nights at my bedside." Theirs was called "Hollywood's nicest romance" and their devotion touched many. Long told Mosby, "[Her leg] doesn't make any difference how I feel about her. When people have sincere feelings about one another, they prove it by their actions."

At the beginning of March '54, Ball was sued for $11,174 by Madeline Benavides, the woman whose car she hit that past October. Benavides claimed to have lost 19 weeks of work due to her head, chest, neck and back injuries. The case was settled out of court.

On April 11, 1954, at Santa Barbara's El Montecito Presbyterian Church, Ball and Long wed. Universal paid for the wedding and had costume designer Bill Thomas make her a $1000 bridal gown. She was wearing her artificial leg but was unsure if she could walk without the crutches—until the very last minute. There was an "audible gasp from the assemblage as Suzan entered the church without crutches," reported James Bacon. "She walked firmly down the aisle—with but a slight limp—on the arm of her father...." She also left the church without crutches with Long to greet the close-to-a-thousand people waiting to see the newly married couple.

On May 27, 1954, Ball made her first acting appearance in more than a year, a live episode of *Lux Video Theatre*, "I'll Never Love Again," where she played a wheelchair-bound girl suffering from shock after a car accident; Long was the doctor who helped her overcome her paralysis. Her big scene came at the conclusion when she got up and walked toward the camera. "I'm going to show the country I can walk," Ball told Walter Ames. "After at-

Suzan Ball's last film role came in *Chief Crazy Horse* (1955) with Victor Mature (courtesy C. Robert Rotter/Glamour Girls of the Silver Screen).

tendance at rehearsal," wrote Steven H. Scheuer, "I assure you there won't be a dry eye in the house." That extended to backstage when the cast and crew all applauded Suzan after the show. Cal Kuhl told Cecil Smith that in the five years he produced the program, it was his most satisfying episode. "This was her first professional appearance after her leg was amputated. I watched her from the control room. She seemed to walk a mile straight into those lights and cameras. Walking on that artificial leg like a queen. And I felt as if I took every step with her."

She was back before the cameras in June for Universal, playing Black Shawl, the wife of Victor Mature's title character, in *Chief Crazy Horse* (1955). The studio could have picked a less grueling assignment for her, but if we are to believe publicity, Suzan insisted on the movie. Shot partly on location in the Black Hills of South Dakota, it told—from the Native American's viewpoint—the story of the Indian people and the rise and fall of Chief Crazy Horse. In an effort to make Suzan comfortable, the studio limited her shooting schedule to a maximum of six hours a day and her nurse accompanied her on location.

Ball brought a quiet strength to Black Shawl and her scenes with Mature were heartfelt and handled expertly by the two actors. "I can't say enough good things about her," director George Sherman told Warren Morrell. "Not only has she tremendous courage herself but she has imbued everyone on the set with the same spirit. There are no complaints about sprained fingers and headaches. She has taught people a lesson. Suzan has great depth and feeling. Suzan always had a great feeling for acting. But since her amputation, she is even better. She has developed into a maturer woman."

She and her husband put together a song-and-dance act. A planned first appearance at the Chi Chi in Palm Springs was nixed when Ball had trouble with certain movements. A few months later, on December 17, 1954, they debuted in a two-week engagement at the Hotel Westward Ho's Concho Room in Phoenix. "Suzan Ball and Dick Long will lighten your heart and brighten your life with haunting tunes, original lyrics and gayest of comedy," promised the ads. The two nightly shows were difficult for her, and after gigs in Palm Springs and Buffalo the act was abandoned.

In April and again in June '55, Suzan was hospitalized for what was believed to be routine check-ups. By July she was at City of Hope Medical Center in serious condition. The cancer had spread to her lungs. "All they can do now is keep her comfortable with supportive treatments," said a hospital source quoted by Aline Mosby. "She is fed fluids and is under heavy sedation. Her chest has been drained. When she's breathing comfortably, she's fine. But she has a bad cough." Officially, a City of Hope spokesman said that Ball was occasionally being administered oxygen, was resting comfortably but she was still "in diagnostic stages."

More misfortune: While Suzan was in the hospital, the gift shop owned by her father Dale and cousin Doris burned to the ground. The $10,000 worth of stock was not insured.

For almost a year, Suzan's doctor and Richard Long knew that the cancer had returned but kept it from her. "When she did have some trouble, we managed to camouflage the symptoms as something else," Long told Bob Thomas. "The doctors thought it would be better that way, in order to keep up her mental attitude. She was in and out of Cedars of Lebanon. Finally, we could not keep the news from her."

At the end of July, she left City of Hope and was put in the care of her private physician. About a week later, on August 5, 1955, the 21-year-old Ball died at her Beverly Hills home. Long was at the Columbia Ranch finishing up *Fury at Gunsight Pass* when he was informed of her passing. The movie's female lead, Lisa Davis, told author Tom Weaver in 2008,

One night [Ball] was extremely ill, and Richard was in a terrible state the next day. And that was the day that another actor, Marshall Thompson [the husband of Long's twin sister Barbara], came to the set to tell Richard that she had passed away.

One of our sets there at the Columbia Ranch was a Western-style mortuary, with coffins, and on the day that she died, I held him while he was sobbing, crying, standing there on that set, surrounded by all those wooden coffins—it was very grim.

This conflicts with Kirk Crivello's book *Fallen Angels*, which claims that Long was at her deathbed when a semi-conscious Ball whispered her last word—a dramatic "Tony," referring to Anthony Quinn. "This unfortunate incident was to haunt him for many years," Crivello alleged.

Ball's funeral at the Church of the Recessional, paid for by Univer-

Suzan Ball, in *East of Sumatra* (1953), acts sultry for publicity cameras (courtesy C. Robert Rotter/ Glamour Girls of the Silver Screen).

sal, was attended by more than 1000 people, with those unable to get inside listening to the service outside via loudspeaker. There was an outpouring of love from fans and those who just followed her courageous story; they had filled the church with cards and flowers.

"Suzan Ball Long taught us all a lesson of patience in pain," said Dr. Louis C. Evans in his eulogy. "Here was a brave soul. She taught us to wear a body like a loose garment; it never constricted her nor strangled her spirit." She was interred, wearing her wedding dress, at Forest Lawn.

Suzan Ball Filmography

1952: *Aladdin and His Lamp* (uncredited), *The World in His Arms* (uncredited), *Untamed Frontier, Yankee Buccaneer.*
1953: *City Beneath the Sea, East of Sumatra, War Arrow.*
1955: *Chief Crazy Horse.*

Helen Burgess

Helen Burgess made only four movies, two of them released while she was alive. After her death at the age of 20, *Photoplay* lamented the actress they called one of the "loveliest and most promising of the year's discoveries...." She had had good fortune immediately in Hollywood when she made her film bow in Cecil B. DeMille's *The Plainsman* (1936), playing the wife of Buffalo Bill Cody (James Ellison). Paramount had plans for their new contractee and the possibilities seemed endless.

But, as fast as it had started, it ended even faster.

She was born Helen Margarite Burgess on April 26, 1916, in Portland, Oregon, the second of two daughters of an agent for Metropolitan Life Insurance. Shortly after her birth, she moved with her family to Tacoma, Washington. In 1926, they relocated again, to Los Angeles, where Burgess attended Hollywood High.

A movie fan, she decided to become an actress, and she and her sister Stella Mary enrolled at Edward Clark's Los Angeles dramatic school. Later publicity said Helen appeared in more than 60 plays with Clark's Academy Players, but there is evidence of only two, *Fadeaway Smith* and *Scarlet Fox* (both 1935). In her review of the former, the *Los Angeles Times*' Katherine T. Von Blon singled Helen out, calling her a "lovely girl, surrounded by a rich air of glamour," adding: "She also displayed intelligence and reserve in her acting."

In 1936, while the teenage Burgess was doing the play *The Seventh Year* at Los Angeles' Spotlight Theater, Paramount scout Jack Murton saw her and a screen test was arranged. Signed by Paramount in May, she expected that she would immediately get a part in a picture, or, as she said in a widely circulated self-penned article, "at least be called on to play atmosphere in

Helen Burgess exuded a girl-next-door wholesome beauty (courtesy C. Robert Rotter/Glamour Girls of the Silver Screen).

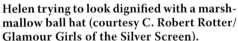

Helen trying to look dignified with a marshmallow ball hat (courtesy C. Robert Rotter/ Glamour Girls of the Silver Screen).

Cecil B. DeMille called ill-fated Helen Burgess "the greatest screen find in my career" and the "finest natural actress I have ever seen" (courtesy C. Robert Rotter/ Glamour Girls of the Silver Screen).

a film or two...." But nothing was done with her until the end of June, when DeMille noticed her in the commissary and thought she'd be perfect for the supporting role of Louisa Cody, wife of Buffalo Bill, in his big-budget western *The Plainsman*. After screen-testing her a couple of times, DeMille awarded her the part. He called her "the greatest screen find in my career" and the "finest natural actress I have ever seen." The director later told Eleanor Packer, "I broke a rule of 25 years' standing when I chose Miss Burgess for the part of Louisa Cody. It was the first time that I have cast a player without previous screen experience in an important role. But, as soon as I saw Miss Burgess, I realized that she had the making of a strong and appealing screen personality." Publicity went so far as to call the inexperienced Burgess a "second Helen Hayes"—which was a looooong stretch.

Before *The Plainsman* was released, Paramount's film cutters listed her as one of the five "most beautiful and accomplished newcomers" and the Hollywood Press Photographers' Association put her among actresses most likely to reach stardom.

Columnist Packer went even further:

> The surprising thing about Helen's sudden leap from obscurity into fame is the fact that she has no trace of the startling, dramatic beauty which the world associates with Hollywood actresses. She is almost what is called "plain," or "homely." She would pass unnoticed in a crowd of most typical Hollywood girls. Why then did DeMille pick her out? She has something greater than mere beauty. Something more important to the screen than a standardized prettiness. She possesses what cameramen call a "photogenic face," one capable of revealing "inner emotions" to the eye of the camera.

On January 27, 1937, the same month *The Plainsman* opened, Burgess eloped with her music teacher, Herbert Rutherford, to Yuma, Arizona; the marriage lasted all of three

hours. After the ceremony, she asked him where they were going to live, and Rutherford reportedly told her that "he intended to return to his own home and said that I should go back to my mother's. He told me he had no intention of establishing a home for me and had no means with which to support me." Less than a week later, she sought an annulment, alleging that Rutherford had married her to "spite another woman, but he wouldn't tell me who she was."

Paramount announced that Burgess would appear in *Souls at Sea* opposite Gary Cooper and George Raft, but instead co-starred her with pilot-turned-actor John Trent in the second feature *A Doc-*

Helen gets the glamour treatment (courtesy C. Robert Rotter/Glamour Girls of the Silver Screen).

Buffalo Bill Cody (James Ellison), his wife Louisa Cody (Helen Burgess) and Wild Bill Hickok (Gary Cooper) in Cecil B. DeMille's *The Plainsman* (1936).

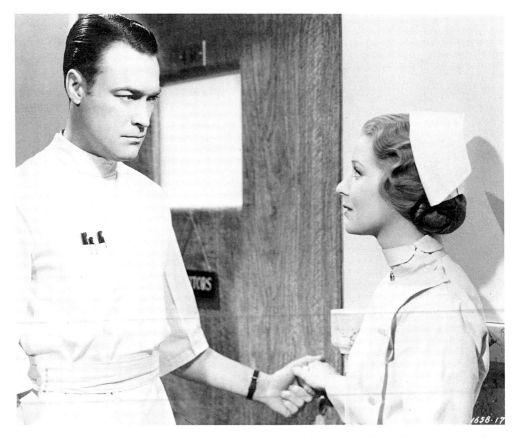

John Trent and Helen Burgess as doctor and nurse whose initial conflicts turn into love in *A Doctor's Diary* (1937).

tor's Diary, followed by a supporting part in the B *King of Gamblers*. If Paramount was planning on elevating Burgess to star status, they were first making her pay her dues in their B product.

In early April 1937, work was almost complete on the Philo Vance whodunit *Night of Mystery* when Burgess caught a cold and collapsed on the set. Days later, her condition worsened and she developed lobar pneumonia. Supposedly, she was too ill to be transferred to a hospital. A day after being placed in an oxygen tent, April 7, 1937, Burgess succumbed to her illness; she was 19 days away from her 21st birthday. (She had one day's work left on *Night of Mystery*. It was necessary for the ending to be hastily rewritten.)

Upon hearing of Helen's death, both her mother and sister collapsed and were put under a physician's care. (Her father had died in 1934.) Three days after her death, on April 10, last rites for Burgess were performed at a private service at the Little Church of the Flowers at Forest Lawn. John Trent, her *Doctor's Diary* co-star, was one of the pallbearers. At Paramount, work stopped for two minutes as everyone bowed their heads in silent tribute to Burgess.

"Shortly before pneumonia cut short her career," wrote Harrison Carroll two weeks later, "Helen Burgess played in a picture called *King of Gamblers* and enacted a death scene that brought tears to the eyes of players on the set. One of these, Fay Holden, remarked to the actress on the realism of her dissembling. 'I know death,' replied the young player. 'I have spent many uncomfortable hours in the past few weeks thinking of death.' Superstitious Hollywood will interpret this as premonition."

Both *King of Gamblers* and *Night of Mystery* were released posthumously. Cecil B. DeMille, perhaps as a gesture to his late discovery, cast Burgess' sister Stella Mary in a small part in 1942's *Reap the Wild Wind*.

Helen Burgess Filmography

1937: *The Plainsman, A Doctor's Diary, King of Gamblers, Night of Mystery*.

Susan Cabot

"I really felt that she was one of those people who should have had a major career," Roger Corman said of Susan Cabot, "and for whatever reason, a career did not take place."

Of Russian-Jewish heritage, Harriet Pearl Shapiro was born in Boston on July 9, 1927. (At least one source claimed she was delivered at St. Elizabeth's Hospital in Brighton, Massachusetts.)

In 1950, when she was just starting in Hollywood, the actress claimed to have been raised in the Bronx, attending school there with studies in ballet, art and music. "I always wanted to be an artist," she told Lucille Mabbott, "but I was sidetracked." Some of this might be true, but "sidetracked" was an understatement: It was more like a detour through Hell. After her father abandoned them, her mother Muriel was institutionalized; neither of her two aunts wanted to take care of her, so young Harriet was raised in several differ-

ent foster homes. After Cabot's death, psychiatrist Carl Faber testified in court that while in foster care, she was "emotionally and sexually abused," causing her to suffer from post-traumatic stress syndrome. Faber explained, "She had extreme irrational terror, as abused children and war veterans do, about these experiences, and was in and out of psychotherapy her whole adult life."

The "official" story goes that a 17-year-old Harriet joined the Harvell Players at East Sebago Lake, Maine, making her debut in *Guest in the House*. "We went to East Sebago because we got the best theater for the little money we could afford," she told Marjory Adams. "We wrote our own plays—couldn't afford royalties for playwrights. We couldn't afford to advertise them and we stood on street corners and acted out scenes so people would come to the theater to see the rest of

Tomboyish Susan Cabot in a portrait from the western *Gunsmoke* (1953) (courtesy Tom Weaver).

24

the play." Her assertion that they didn't have enough money to advertise makes it difficult to determine if this story is true or not.

What we do know: On July 30, 1944, in Washington, D.C., as a way to get out of foster care, the teenager married a childhood friend, painter–interior decorator Marten Eden Sacker. (His first name has been given as Martin and Mark, his surname as Szeka, Szekarkiewicz and variations of that.) Her first press notice came in 1946 when, with a name change to Susan Cabot, she sang at Manhattan's Village Barn. Supposedly, she also illustrated children's books.

Susan's film debut was as an extra in the noir classic *Kiss of Death* (1947), partly filmed in New York. In a nightclub scene, she's seen from the side sitting at a table, easily identifiable by her Morticia Addams–length hair. Susan made additional money by doing early television commercials and designing jewelry. She was trying to save enough money to study opera in Italy.

According to what source you believe, she was spotted in 1949 by either casting director Max Arnow or producer Wallace MacDonald on an episode of TV's *Hollywood Screen Test* or in a commercial. This resulted in her getting the lead as a native girl opposite Jon Hall in MacDonald's *On the Isle of Samoa* (1950). "You should see the hairstyle I wore in *Samoa*," she exaggerated to Lucille Mabbott. "It was awful! I had a thing down over my eyes and nose which made you want to push it aside and ask who's there."

Universal-International cast Susan as an Indian girl in the Van Heflin starrer *Tomahawk* (1951), which had location shooting in Rapid City, Michigan. She was taught Sioux by John War Eagle (who played Red Cloud in the film). "Learning to speak lines in Sioux was not difficult," she said, "for I have had to have a nodding acquaintance with several languages while studying opera."

Near the end of filming *Tomahawk*, she and the cast entertained Rapid City locals in a "Pow Wow party" at the Alex Johnson Hotel. Newspapers were particularly impressed by Cabot's "melodious voice" which "labeled her as an outstanding singer as well as an up-and-coming actress" (*Rapid City Journal*).

At Warner Bros., Susan had an uncredited part as murder victim Nina Lombardo in *The Enforcer* (1951). Although press reports claimed she would be Humphrey Bogart's "leading lady," her character was talked about much more than she was shown.

Meanwhile, U-I, impressed by her *Tomahawk* performance, signed her to a

Jon Hall is a thief wrongly accused of murder who meets and falls in love with native girl Susan Cabot in *On the Isle of Samoa* (1950) (courtesy Tom Weaver).

contract. In October '50, about a month after the announcement of her signing, Susan and Sacker separated for the first time.

"Bill Goetz signed Susan Cabot for an acting part in *Tomahawk*, then discovered that she sings—but beautifully," wrote Hedda Hopper. "He may dust off one of Deanna Durbin's old pictures and remake it with her."

He didn't. U-I reasoned that Susan was so good at playing a Native American in *Tomahawk*, why not repeat? It was the start of a series of films where she portrayed "dark, exotic little things": In *Flame of Araby* (1951) she was a fiery Corsican dancer who didn't do much of anything but "[m]ostly wiggled her hips and shoulders in a half-savage dance" (Ben Cook). She was Cochise's (Jeff Chandler) pregnant wife in *The Battle at Apache Pass* (1952) and a Persian bow-and-arrow–wielding friend of the title character in *Son of Ali Baba* (1952). "I'm either in jungles or gypsy wagons," Susan complained to Erskine Johnson. "I don't know why. My coloring is exactly like Elizabeth Taylor's. Do they put her in a sarong? No." Her small stature (five-foot, 96 pounds) was blamed for her casting difficulties.

At the beginning of 1952, columnist Jack Garver remarked, "The studio has brought her along gradually but now the pressure is on to make her a big name in short order. Her chief desire is to get into a picture in which she won't have to play an Indian or western girl."

Universal basically saw Cabot as either an exotic or a tomboy; the remaining pictures on her contract, her only lead roles at U-I, were of the latter variety: *The Duel at Silver Creek* (1952), *Gunsmoke* (1953) and *Ride Clear of Diablo* (1954). In all three she was Audie Murphy's love interest; the combination worked extremely well.

She and Sacker finally parted company in late '53 and she made the dating rounds with Marlon Brando, Hugh O'Brian, Arthur Loew, Jr., and others.

In 1954 Cabot opted to leave Universal; some sources say because they wouldn't give her a pay raise, others because she just didn't like her roles. Some years later, she told a *Press and Sun Bulletin* reporter that one reason she left movies was "I never got a chance to sing."

Moving to New York, Cabot got serious, studying with Sanford Meisner at the Neighborhood Playhouse and taking singing lessons. Off-Broadway, she did *A Stone for Danny Fisher* (1954–55) at the Downtown National Theater. (In 1958, Hollywood turned *Danny Fisher* into the Elvis Presley vehicle *King Creole*.)

From there, in 1955, Cabot did *Much Ado About Nothing* at the Brattle Theatre Shakespeare Festival in Cambridge, Massachusetts, and *The Two Gentlemen of Verona* at the Neighborhood Playhouse.

Cabot signed on to do *Shangri-La* (1956), a headed-for-Broadway musical adaptation of James Hilton's novel *Lost Horizon*. It had some good talent attached to it: music by Harry Warren with book and lyrics by Hilton, Robert E. Lee and Jerome Lawrence and a cast headed by Lew Ayres, Jack Cassidy, Carol Lawrence and Alice Ghostley. Susan was tapped to play Lo-Tsen, who longs to leave the Valley of the Blue Moon in the Tibetan paradise (a role played in the 1937 movie *Lost Horizon* by Margo). On April 15, 1956, while *Shangri-La* was still playing out-of-town tryouts, NBC-TV's *Wide Wide World* devoted a 15-minute segment to the show's rehearsals; Ayres and Cabot did a scene for the cameras.

Shangri-La opened in Boston on May 1, 1956, and was beset with problems. Although Cabot went on, it was announced she was leaving the cast and would be replaced in the next performance by Shirley Yamaguchi. Lew Ayres also left the show. The production continued to struggle; when it reached Broadway in June, it closed after 21 performances.

Cabot went into stock: *Champagne Complex, Knickerbocker Holiday* and *Kismet.* "Susan Cabot … lends dignity and a promising voice to the role of the heroine," the *Asbury Park Press'* Carl Goldstein said of her in the latter.

A return to Hollywood the following year brought a recurring spot on TV's *Pantomime Quiz,* a role on *Kraft Television Theatre* ("The First and the Last" with Edward Mulhare) and her first film for low-budget indie producer-director Roger Corman, *Carnival Rock.* The overwrought drama, laced with musical acts (notably The Platters), gave Cabot an opportunity to sing ("There's No Place Without You" and "Ou-Shoo-Bla-D"), dance, catfight with Iris Adrian and drive a love-obsessed carnival owner-turned-baggy pants clown to arson.

Previous movie roles gave Cabot little to work with, but Corman's exploitation films were another story. The budgets may have been scanty and the shooting schedules short, but most of them gave an intense Cabot an acting showcase. It's no wonder she is now best known for these films. Cabot told film historian Tom Weaver that Corman "gave me a lot of freedom, and also a chance to play parts that Universal would never have given me. Oddball, wacko parts, like the very disturbed girl in *Sorority Girl* [1957] and things like that. I had a chance to do moments and scenes that I didn't get before."

In *Sorority Girl,* a troubled, neurotic Cabot is an heiress with mother issues who attends a Southern California university and torments her fellow students. Unfortunately, it was probably a movie that hit close to home: By this time, her mother Muriel had reappeared in Susan's life and was living with her. Their relationship would remain strained and cause Cabot increasing mental anguish. Weaver, who knew Cabot in the 1980s, brought a VHS tape of *Sorority Girl* to Cabot's home to show her and her grown son Timothy; Tim was so upset by his mother's performance as the sadistic, emotionally disturbed Sabra that he fled from the room.

Susan holding her own with Viking leader Richard Devon in *The Saga of the Viking Women and Their Voyage to the Waters of the Great Sea Serpent* (1957) (courtesy Tom Weaver).

Set in ancient times, *The Saga of the Viking Women and*

Their Voyage to the Waters of the Great Sea Serpent (1957) is considered campy but it gave Cabot one of her best roles as Enger, a dark priestess who wants Desir's (Abby Dalton) man. Of all the Viking women, the duplicitous and devious Enger is the most ruthless, confident in her power over men even after the Viking women are abducted by the men of a primitive tribe.

About the villainous parts she was given in Corman's films, Cabot remarked to Weaver, "I loved it from the standpoint of their being a challenge, but it was very hard for me to play an unfeeling character—to do or say something cruel to another person, not feeling it in my bones or in my heart, and know that that other person is suffering. I've been victimized by people like that, and it hurts."

After a slight detour away from Corman (another Indian girl in *Fort Massacre* and an episode of *Have Gun—Will Travel*), she did two Cormans back to back, *War of the Satellites* and *Machine-Gun Kelly* (both 1958). The latter was the better of the two as she played Flo Becker (modeled after the real-life Kathryn Thorne) to Charles Bronson's title character. Cabot projected a cool, sardonic presence, handling Bronson with a sure and steady hand, the only person not afraid of this gangland legend, until it becomes clear that she is really the one in charge. Her sudden burst of anger at the conclusion when Bronson turns yellow is extremely effective and some of the best acting she had done on screen.

Filmed in the Philippines in March and April 1958, *Surrender—Hell!* (1959) starred Keith Andes as real-life World War II hero Col. Donald D. Blackburn, who fights the Japanese in the jungles with his guerrilla forces. Second-billed Susan helps him at the beginning of the movie. It was not a happy experience for Cabot. The shoot was marked with many discomforts, including the heat and leeches, and she was down to 83 pounds. The small size of her role in the finished film was, according to Marjory Adams, because of a "serious disagreement over contractual relations." Cabot left the production early. "The unplayed portion of her role," continued Adams, "was rewritten and a pretty native actress given the part." In the scenes with Cabot that were shot, her dialogue was spoken by another actress in post-production.

In July 1958, when Corman had trouble with leading lady Lita Milan not showing up for the filming of *I Mobster*, Cabot stepped in to replace her and even shot some scenes, before Milan returned.

At the end of '58, Cabot got the role that would cement her screen fame: Janice Starlin, head of a cosmetics company, who reverses the aging process with a serum made from the royal jelly of queen wasps in *The Wasp Woman* (1959). The mixture works but has murderous side effects. Campy as it was, it was still a good showcase for Cabot and she was able to make her character sympathetic.

She did some TV (*Ellery Queen* and more *Pantomime Quiz* episodes) and several films were offered her, such as *Tarzan, the Ape Man* (1959).

In April 1959, Cabot got a lot of newspaper attention from her dates with King Hussein of Jordan, who was then visiting Los Angeles. Both downplayed their relationship. In January 2018, declassified documents revealed that the CIA wanted Hussein to have "female companionship" while in the U.S. Cabot initially turned thumbs-down on their request, but once she met him, things happened naturally.

Louella Parsons: "Hollywood is talking about: The purely political reason why King Hussein was so ungallant as to deny he had met Susan Cabot after he was seen so frequently with her on his recent trip to Hollywood. (His Highness apparently discovered

Ad for *The Wasp Woman* (1959).

her real name is Shapiro, and just as Liz Taylor's movie has been banned in Jordan since she embraced Judaism, so went Hussein's 'enchantment' with Susan.)" The two got along so well they continued to see each other secretly for a few years.

"Susan Cabot confided she is giving up Hollywood for the second time," wrote Harrison Carroll. "She's heading for New York." She complained to columnist Don Royal that she had made "[p]icture after picture that I wasn't particularly proud of making. But I have tried in every film to get some kind of meaning out of my part. So the time wasn't entirely wasted. And I did earn some money." It was now time to look for parts she "should have tried for years ago." She continued:

> I've reached the stage where I understand myself a little bit. Now I want to fulfill myself. I know I haven't realized my potential at all. I've got this little apartment now that's a mess, but it's wonderful for me. I'm sculpting, and painting and getting reacquainted with New York. I'm not bitter about Hollywood, but it's time for me to get a move on. Life is very exciting if you work at it.

To Tom Weaver in 1985, she said, "I felt that I had more within me to explore, as a music and art major and as a person. And the way my film career was headed, I didn't feel that that was going to offer me a way to develop any more, except on a very superficial level. I mean, how many *Wasp Woman*s can you do? I wanted to get back to New York—the Museum of Modern Art—my art studies. I began to study music again. I just went back to the things I really loved. I also traveled, and toured with a lot of musicals."

Cabot did stock (*The Seven Year Itch*, *Paint Your Wagon*, *The Voice of the Turtle*); off–Broadway (*Intimate Relations*); a *Have Gun—Will Travel* episode in which she accused the producers of overdubbing all her dialogue (they didn't); she was replaced in Philadelphia by Suzanne Pleshette in the Broadway-bound *Golden Fleecing* (1959); had a recurring role in the daytime soap *Brighter Day* (1960); and performed in nightclubs.

In 1962 and '63, she had some health issues. During a performance of *Intimate Relations*, she suffered a burst appendix and peritonitis and was rushed to the hospital. In January '63, she underwent another operation, reasons unspecified. "She refused to sign the necessary waiver, permitting the surgery—unless she had a chance to phone her psychoanalyst, for permission," wrote Leonard Lyons. "Her analyst, of course, consented ... 'Phoning your analyst on this,' said her surgeon, 'is like calling a surgeon to cut out an anxiety problem.'"

For the rest of '64, Cabot remained out of sight, presumably moving to England. When she reappeared in 1966, she now had a son, Scott (aka Timothy) Wingate, born in Washington, D.C., where she was staying with an aunt, on January 27, 1964. She claimed that her marriage to a British diplomat was "on the rocks," but refused to say anything further about the union. (She told others that Timothy's father was either an FBI or CIA agent who went on a mission—and never returned.) Timothy was born prematurely, an emergency cesarean section after surgery for a twisted intestine. "I'm glad just to be alive," Susan said to Dorothy Manners. "I couldn't walk for eight months following the birth of Scott. Both the baby and I barely made it. The poor little fellow spent his first four months in an oxygen tent. But we are thriving and so, so glad to be back in California." What she didn't say was her son had some brain damage, had periodic seizures and suffered from acute hypoglycemia.

"Susan Cabot may not earn an Oscar for her next role," wrote columnist Charles McHenry, "but she should pick up a lot of residuals. She'll star in a potato chip commercial." Acting work was obviously becoming harder to come by.

In June 1968 in Las Vegas, Cabot married Michael Roman, 15 years her junior. At the time he was an aspiring actor; the two met in an acting workshop. "I went in, there were a lot of professionals there, and Susan was one of them," Roman told Tom Weaver. He continued:

> These working pros would take over when the head guy or gal wasn't there. This night I went in and Susan was in charge of the class, and ... bang, bang, all the bells went off. I was uptight and nervous, so she worked with me, and then we started working together every day.... I think the first night was a Tuesday, all the way through Saturday. Friday night, I asked her to marry me.

Susan and son Timothy in the 1980s (courtesy Tom Weaver).

Besides the undeniable chemistry, they shared much more: "We'd known each other only a few weeks," Cabot told Harrison Carroll, "but it's beautiful, a real spiritual union. On our first dates we talked about different religious faiths and philosophies. I know it's unusual for Hollywood, but it made us very happy." Roman adopted Susan's son.

In the late 1960s and early '70s, Cabot tried to get back into acting via the small screen: *Bracken's World*, *The Man and the City*, *Owen Marshall, Counselor at Law*, *The Unknown*, etc. She also did some summer stock and sold her own paintings. The main reason she didn't act as often was worries over her son and his care which she didn't trust to anyone else.

Susan's mother Muriel was living with her, Michael and Timothy, and she would drive Susan crazy. Michael Roman explained to Weaver:

> In a sense, it was like having another kid. [Susan's mother] was a very good-hearted, loving person. You could see where she was "off" now and then, she'd go babble and blab about things, nobody was listening to her, you'd be out of the room and hear her talking. But she was good with Tim, she *lllloved* Tim. But she'd go off the deep end, bless her heart. [She and Susan had] a love-hate relationship.... Susan loved her 'cause it's her mom, [but] she was pissed at her because she [Susan] (a) was now a parent to her mom, and (b) she must have had resentment from having had to fend for herself when she was a kid. Her mom would allllways reminisce about things in the past, and it was like: "All right, let it *go* already, there's nothing you can *do* about it." So that's what drove [Susan] crazy.

Along with his other problems, Timothy had been diagnosed with dwarfism. Starting in 1970, Cabot injected him with an experimental growth hormone taken from the pituitary glands of cadavers. He was just one of 10,000 kids participating in a nationwide program by the National Institutes of Health. While it's been reported that Cabot gave him shots three times a day for 15 years, Michael Roman says that it was actually once a day or once every other day for "about six months, nine months" (a big difference). Physically, the treatments worked: He grew to 5'4" and 150 pounds. But mentally he was on a tightrope. He suffered from grand mal seizures, an epilepsy that caused loss of consciousness. The National Institutes of Health had discontinued the program because "certain batches" were infected with a virus that caused Creutzfeldt-Jakob Disease, a rare degenerative brain disorder. Some patients suffered from other neurological problems.

Cabot and Roman divorced in 1981. "We spent five years in individual and conjoint therapy before we broke up, so it just didn't happen overnight," Roman says. "Susan was an extremely, *extremely* intelligent individual. No common sense, but bright and intellectual. Photographic memory. But sometimes a blithering idiot. And at one point [in her very early life], she was gonna chuck it all away and become a nun. But they kicked her out of there, they said, 'This isn't for you!' [*Laughs*] *She* told me this story—*I* don't know!"

One of the main problems was that Cabot wouldn't allow Roman to be a real father to Tim. Roman explained to Weaver:

> After a certain point, and very quickly, she would never trust me alone with him, because I treated him *normal*. Tim would say, "I want to do *this*." I'd say, "No, we're gonna do *this*." Tim: "But I want to do *this*." "Well, no, *we* are going to do something else." And the minute she heard him raise his voice, boom, she was *on* me: "You let him do what he wants to do!" [*Roman to himself:*] "Holy shit, man, this is not gonna work...."
>
> To give you a prime example, it got to the point where we sent Tim to cotillion, to learn manners and ballroom dancing and stuff. He was just a little kid, seven, eight. At the Beverly Wilshire Hotel, he had his cotillion party. And we'd teach him table manners, and the thing was, "Keep your elbows off the table." Of course, he's a kid, his elbows would end up on the table, and she'd say, "Tim. Elbows!" "Oh! Okay!" This went on a couple times, and then she went out to the

kitchen, and I said, "Tim. Elbows!" "Okay." We were having dinner. She'd come back in; she'd go out again. Again: "Tim. Elbows!" And she just couldn't take it. She came into the dining room and she just ripped into me and screamed, and just would not stop. "Leave him *alone!*" and just on and on! She sent him to his room. When she was done screaming at me, screams like you can't believe, she goes into his room and she starts screaming at *him*. And the first words out of her mouth: "What's *wrong* with you? You know your father was *right!*" And I thought, "Holy shit…!" You talk about giving a little guy mixed signals! And this went on in just about everything.

We were seeing psychiatrists *and* psychologists. [Therapist] Mike Topp was the kind of a guy who'd force you into a corner. Mike was a straight shooter, and he kept pushing and pushing and pushing me. I was just scared to death to say, "Susan, I don't want to *live* with you anymore." I would say that to *him* when it was one on one, and he said, "You have to say it to *her*." And I literally stuttered when I said it: "I love you, but I, I, I, I, I, I can't *live* with you!" *That* was the beginning. When *that* came out of me, I realized, "Whew. I survived. I'm not dead!" That's just basically what did it for me. It broke my heart like you can't believe. To this day, even. I look back, I mean, it's over and done with, 35 years or whatever it's been, but it was just *so* sad, so so so sad.

Timothy was an art student at Pierce College in Woodland Hills. He was into weight-lifting and martial arts and the walls of his room were covered with Bruce Lee posters. He had a particular fascination with swords. His medications included steroids, Synthroid, hydrocortisone and testosterone. Not surprisingly, Cabot was overprotective of him. A neighbor said they were "very, very close…. She never went any place without him. He was very dependent on her." Michael Roman told Weaver:

> Here you had an extremely creative individual [Susan], and the greatest thing that a woman can create is another life, that literally comes out of her. And this artistic person creates this life … and the life is flawed. Can you imagine? The anger, the desperation, the fear, the anxiety, the mixed feelings? "The greatest thing I could create is a life, and this life is flawed! There's something wrong with it!" So what she was trying to do was just protect this precious creation that she created, came out of her, and that's where she was so protective of him.

December 10, 1986, 11:30 p.m. The police received a call from 22-year-old Tim, who said intruders broke into the house and attacked him and stole about $70,000. He said he was unsure about his mother.

When the police arrived, they first had to contend with three vicious Akita dogs. "They impeded our investigation for a while," Detective Joe Diglio said. "It took us a long time to get animal regulation out so we could conduct our investigation." For six hours before animal control arrived, the cops "stood as far away as we could from them. They were big. They weren't leashed. They had command of a good portion of the house."

They finally found a nightgown-clad Cabot, 59, on her bed, the back of her skull completely crushed; she had been struck repeatedly while lying there face down. A "calm and cool" Tim said a "curly-haired Latino," dressed as a ninja, broke into the house and killed her. He claimed he had tried to fight him off—to prove it, he showed the cops a tiny bruise on his head and a small cut on his arm. (Deputy District Attorney Bradford E. Stone: "That's hardly the degree of injury one would expect from a death-defying battle with a Ninja warrior.")

The detectives were immediately suspicious because there was no sign of a struggle and Timothy was making contradictory statements. He was arrested and held without bail. The detective in charge said there was a "long-running feud" between mother and son and they had argued prior to Susan's murder.

Under questioning, Tim broke down and admitted to bludgeoning Cabot to death. The murder weapon was a weight-lifting bar, which he hid in a box of detergent in a clothes hamper. Timothy's lawyer Chester Leo Smith said that because of various medical problems, Timothy's "social and emotional development" were stunted.

According to the *Los Angeles Times*, "[By] focusing on Roman's mother's fragile mental condition, her unkempt home and her authorization of controversial drugs for her son, the defense intends to show that she may have contributed to her own death." Smith said Timothy was an "emotional wreck as a result of an overprotective mother and a severe growth deficiency that has made him dependent on strong medications with dangerous side effects." He added, "Mr. Roman is probably, really, an experiment of the human race." Timothy was still taking medications, ones that caused mood swings; Cabot sometimes tried to regulate the dosage herself, without success. His high school math teacher told police that when Tim did not take his meds, "he was virtually unable to add two-digit numbers."

Cabot was described in court records and in newspapers as a faded, alcoholic, reclusive movie actress, obsessed with her looks, who experienced "recurrent mental breakdowns" and paranoia, and lived in a hilltop house in Encino surrounded by "massive filth and decay." It was even asserted that Cabot took Timothy's hormone drugs herself because it was purported to slow the aging process and remove weight without exercise. This yarn has been presented as fact, perhaps because it so closely resembled the storyline of her most famous movie, *The Wasp Woman*. Michael Roman told Tom Weaver:

> She *never*, ever took any of those shots. Like her mom, Susan was just blessed with clear skin, clear complexion, no wrinkles. Her mom never had a wrinkle on her face, even when she was in her 60s and 70s, when I knew her, or 80s. Not a one. Susan had a beautiful complexion. The only downside is, she would overdo her makeup. And the reason she did that is, she was afraid, she was bashful, and this was a security blanket, she put all these layers or—*my* word—*masks*, that she was hiding behind! She didn't *need* 'em. Did not need 'em at *all*. It broke my heart to see that happen, but there was nothing I could do to [convince] her, "You don't *need* this shit!"

Cabot was blamed for exacerbating Timothy's disturbed and immature mental state with her dramatic and overprotective nature. The press had a field day referencing *The Wasp Woman* and likening Cabot to Norma Desmond from *Sunset Blvd.* (1950). In short: the victim became the accused.

In 1989, Tim's attorney sought to transfer him from the Los Angeles County Hall of Justice to a Van Nuys jail. By this time, it was "revealed" that Cabot had been receiving $1500 a month from the Keeper of the King's Purse, i.e., from King Hussein. "There is written indication in the handwriting of Susan Roman," Chester Leo Smith said, "this money is from a trust.... For better or worse, it looks like child support." Being half–Jewish and half–Arab, "a direct descendant ... of the Prophet [Mohammed]," could be dangerous for the incarcerated Timothy because "religious Arabs would not look favorably upon a descendant that was half–Jewish, and might try to kill him." Smith's motion was denied.

This, like a lot of stories about Cabot, was not true. Michael Roman told Weaver that King Hussein didn't send a "monthly stipend" as reported:

> No no no no no. Now and then, whenever she needed something, she'd call, and he would send some cash for her. After our divorce, there's no question in my mind that Sam [Hussein's nickname] must have really helped her. He was just a very generous person. He'd call on her birthday, on her mom's birthday, and they'd chat like friends. It was almost like a brother-sister relationship, they really hit it off, aside from the romance that they had many years before. They just had a good friendship.

Susan had never said one way or the other who the father of her son was. Actor Christopher Jones (1941–2014) believed with certainty that Timothy was his. "I had only seen [Tim] once in my life," Jones told Pamela Des Barres. Jones said that Susan told Timothy that "his father was an Englishman … and that I was dead." When asked why Cabot would do this, Jones replied, "We'd only been together three weeks, then I just sort of disappeared." Like Susan's mother, Jones' mom had been institutionalized.

Michael Roman was never told by Susan who the father was, but he is sure it was Jones: "When I talked to the lawyer that was in on the case, he said, 'Mike, this guy Christopher Jones came to see Tim, and if ever a father and son looked alike, they did in this instance.' Jones never got to see Tim, but he *was* Tim's biological father." Jones had fathered seven other children (with multiple women) and, as Roman points out, some of them allegedly had physical problems. "Just like Tim," Roman told Weaver. "All things point to the fact that it came from the father's side of the family, the physical problems."

In May 1989, the judge ordered a mistrial because Timothy's lawyer Smith had become ill. Timothy's family was going to dismiss him anyway; Michael Roman was appalled by how "unfocused and unprepared" Smith was. The lawyer had allowed a 90-minute tape recording of detectives interviewing Timothy because he wanted jurors to know they had "leaned on him pretty hard." Instead, they heard Timothy shouting back at his interrogators "and never seemed close to breaking down," which "appeared to undercut the expressed defense goal of showing Roman to be mentally fragile" (*Los Angeles Times*). Smith also cross-examined a police officer who said Timothy had confessed to slaying his mother after an argument. Deputy District Attorney Bradford E. Stone said he would not have been able to introduce the confession in court because it was made after Timothy asked to speak to an attorney. Timothy's family couldn't understand why Smith had even brought it up in court.

In September 1989, with two new lawyers, Timothy changed his plea of not guilty by reason of insanity to not guilty. They sought to prove that he was incapable of forming the intent to kill required of a murder conviction. His lawyers also waived his right to a jury trial.

Cabot's psychologist of seven years, Carl Faber, testified that on the day of her death, she told him she would kill herself if not for her son. "She said her reason for living was her son. I heard a tone in her voice that I'd never heard before. She told me, 'Carl, I'm tired. I want to go and if it wasn't for Timothy, I would.'" He said she suffered "tremendous despair" and was "capable of irrational action." Faber sympathized with Tim because he surmised that "Cabot brought those fears to Timothy for hundreds of hours."

The new attorneys' approach was that, yes, Timothy killed his mother but he did so under the influence of mood-altering medications and after being provoked by Susan's "aggressive, irrational behavior." Videotape of the inside of Cabot's dilapidated house was shown and was shocking: "It was beyond my imagination that a person of such success and notoriety at one time could live in such indescribable conditions," Van Nuys Superior Court Judge Darlene E. Schempp remarked.

When an emotional Timothy took the stand, it all became about self-defense. He said his mother was in bed after two days of asthma attacks and that night she seemed to be having a nervous breakdown—an "extreme psychotic episode" was how it was described in court. "She was screaming … calling for her mother … talking to herself. I thought I'd better get help.... Then she started saying, 'Who are you?'" When he tried to call paramedics to help her, Timothy testified, Cabot attacked him with a scalpel (which she had used for gardening) and a weight-lifting bar (which she had in her room to help her get in shape). "I was trying to push her away ... just to get out of that room." The next thing he realized, she was dead.

On October 10, 1989, Timothy Roman was convicted of involuntary manslaughter, sentenced to three years' probation and ordered to seek psychiatric counseling. He was given credit for the two and a half years he already served in jail awaiting trial. Judge Schempp said there was no evidence that Roman premeditated his mother's murder. "There is no question that the defendant loved his mother very much," she added. The murder was "not the result of a criminal mind," she remarked.

Michael Roman and his mother Elizabeth were "just overjoyed" with the verdict. "Oh, what we have gone through. Timothy and I are just drained," said Mrs. Roman. "It's time to start a whole new life. We are taking him away from this area, this town." Michael sympathized with his adopted son and stood by him. "It was a very, very trying life living with Susan. Extremely trying. And that was on the best of days."

Timothy said in 1991, "I'm trying to get away from the past and start a new life." He dropped from sight, living with Elizabeth Roman in Pasadena, although he did appear (filmed in shadows) on a 2000 *Mysteries & Scandals* episode devoted to his mother. Michael told Weaver:

> My mom and Tim were together from let's say '88, '89, when we moved out of the house, 'til the day he died in 2003. And they were like two kids. My mom had a miserable life. We come from Europe, and she had just a tumultuous life. So the two of 'em hit it off. They were living their lives together as two kids. They were both taking art classes and going on trips, everywhere together. They really liked each other. And my mom was very protective.

Tim's health was said to have improved after his medication dosage was lessened. But the growth hormone injections of his distant past caught up with him. Michael Roman:

> What they didn't tell us was, because of the way they got the pituitary glands [from human corpses], there were no safeguards. The diseases that some people had were just passed on. And the most insidious disease was this Creutzfeldt-Jakob Disease. And the way that bloody thing works is, once it's in your system, it can come to life immediately, to up to 40, 50 years later. It can incubate in your system for up to ... who knows? They didn't know how long.

Charles Bronson menaces Susan in *Machine-Gun Kelly* (1958).

But once it comes to life, you're dead within 90 days, 60 days, okay? And that's what happened with Tim.

He was at my mom's and I was talkin' to him, I'd call a couple times during the week and we'd talk, we'd chat and so forth. And this one night, I'm talkin' to him and … the phone's gone. I had to call back. The line's busy. So finally, I got through again, I said, "Mother! What's goin' on?" And my mother—with a Hungarian accent: "Michael.... I deed not want to tell you...."

"What? What?"

My worst fear: "Tim eez acting very straaange." I knew it was coming to life. I said, "Mom, get him to the emergency room *now*. The disease is coming to life." I was by his bedside the next day, and we talked, and he was still okay, and he talked to my wife Barbara. The next day, he was just gone … unconscious. He lingered there for a day or two, and then we put him in, like, a nursing home, in the Azusa area near my mom. That's where he passed away [on January 22, 2003].

Cabot, too, suffered much in her life and in death also lost her good name, with many wild rumors circulating about her final years, not helped by the aforementioned *Mysteries & Scandals* which treated her shabbily and mocked her memory.

She was buried in an unmarked grave at Culver City's Hillside Memorial Park. That changed in April 2012 after a petition went through to have her gravesite marked by a plaque. At last, she got some sort of dignity back.

Susan Cabot Filmography

1947: *Kiss of Death* (uncredited).
1950: *On the Isle of Samoa.*
1951: *The Enforcer* (uncredited), *Tomahawk, The Prince Who Was a Thief* (uncredited), *Flame of Araby.*
1952: *The Battle at Apache Pass, The Duel at Silver Creek, Son of Ali Baba.*
1953: *The Bond Between Us* (short), *Gunsmoke.*
1954: *Ride Clear of Diablo.*
1957: *Sorority Girl, The Saga of the Viking Women and Their Voyage to the Waters of the Great Sea Serpent, Carnival Rock.*
1958: *Fort Massacre, War of the Satellites, Machine-Gun Kelly.*
1959: *Surrender—Hell!, The Wasp Woman.*

Mary Castle

"I want to be an actress on my own—not a plaster cast of anyone else," Mary Castle told columnist Maralyn Marsh in 1950. But she resembled one of the world's most famous actresses and beauties, Rita Hayworth, so that was easier said than done.

Under the Hollywood studio system, movie moguls had an imaginative way of keeping temperamental stars in line: They would sign lookalike actors, whose presence on the lot served to remind said stars that they could be replaced at any minute by a carbon copy. (For example, MGM had James Craig as their junior Clark Gable.) Of course, this wasn't fair to the lookalikes, who rarely got a decent break and could never quite measure up to their charisma-packed star counterparts.

It was Mary Castle's misfortune to be the mirror image of Rita Hayworth. She was more of a lookalike than most "threats" and that was ultimately her downfall. Castle had the face first (Hayworth had help from plastic surgeons to look the way she did) but Rita was first to make that face famous. Castle had a lot of talent, but alas, her appearance worked against her.

Of Irish and Quapaw Indian descent, Mary Ann Noblett was born on January 22, 1931, on a ranch in Pampa, Texas, "in the Panhandle where it can get cold and dusty," she told columnist Barbara L. Wilson. Mary's third cousin once removed was *Beverly Hillbillies* star Irene Ryan, who was born Irene Noblitt.

Older brother Erby taught the four-year-old Mary trick riding. The Nobletts subsequently moved to Fort Worth and Phillips, Texas (the latter now a ghost town). For two years, Mary had tuberculosis and missed school. "They had me all ready to be sent away

Mary Castle "looking more like Rita Hayworth than Rita Hayworth does" (courtesy C. Robert Rotter/Glamour Girls of the Silver Screen).

to a TB home," she told Earl Wilson, "but my mother couldn't stand to see it. So I stayed home. Plenty of rest and sleep cured me." When she recovered, she took up swimming. Art was another early interest, and one of her paintings went on display at Phillips Junior High School.

In 1943, the family settled in Long Beach, California. Mary told several columnists she graduated high school when she was 15. She also said she was married and divorced at that age, to account for the presence of her daughter Judith, who was born December 10, 1946. But in fact, Mary did not marry the father of her child. "The father, a Navy man stationed in Long Beach, never took responsibility for Mom," Judith's daughter Cynthia said. "Grandma had a burgeoning career, so she left her parents to raise [Judith]."

At age 19, the 5'6", gray-green–eyed redhead was modeling for bathing suit ads. She now called herself Mary *Castle*, which was a family name. Warner Bros. signed her but all she did was play bit parts. Work also came via producer Jerry Fairbanks' commercial films.

A Columbia talent scout saw her photo in a magazine, brought her to the studio's attention, and she was signed. The reason was not based on any perceived talent or even her beauty: It was because she bore a marked resemblance to the studio's biggest star, Rita Hayworth.

In 1949, Hayworth married Prince Aly Khan. Columbia had a lot of money tied up in their association with the Love Goddess but she was being difficult and refused to make any movies. Castle seemed the perfect weapon against Hayworth's fragile ego. Called the lady "who looks more like Hayworth than Rita does," Castle was 13 years younger and eager for success.

Columbia publicity played up Castle as Hayworth's successor and claimed she was going to be "groomed for some of the roles originally intended for Rita" (Jimmie Fidler). But while Castle did indeed bear a likeness to Hayworth, the comparisons ended there and the studio had no intention of starring Castle in any major movies.

Columnists began taunting Hayworth about Castle, as if Rita would be scared by the "young, terrific and talented" (Harvey in Hollywood) newcomer. Residing in Europe, Hayworth probably couldn't have cared less that she would be replaced.

Columbia immediately set about getting their money's worth: In July 1950 alone, Castle filmed three quickies: *The Tougher They Come* (with Wayne Morris), *Prairie Roundup* (Charles Starrett) and *Texans Never Cry* (Gene Autry).

Introduced in the first few minutes of *The Tougher They Come*, she is sitting at a bar, blankly staring ahead, her resemblance to Hayworth startling. Her line readings are deliberately slow and sultry to mimic her famous counterpart. It wasn't much of a role, it was simply planted there as a sort of stunt casting—Columbia showing off their mini–Rita.

Her best chance at Columbia was in the SuperCinecolor western *When the Redskins Rode* (1951) as Elizabeth Leeds, "Williamsburg's most famous beauty," part Shawnee Indian and all French spy, who is trying to seduce a Delaware Indian prince (Jon Hall) to persuade his people to fight with the French against the British. As a low-watt femme fatale, Castle plays it a little too self-consciously. She is at her best in her final scene when she has been found out and being led away to the pokey. Composing herself and smoothing out her hair, she coolly remarks, "Well, gentlemen, shall we call on the governor?"

Her follow-up was a smallish part in *Criminal Lawyer* (1951) starring Pat O'Brien and Jane Wyatt. Castle's brief scenes with Marvin Kaplan gave evidence of some untapped comic ability.

Being a pawn in Columbia's battle with Hayworth did Castle no good. Amid talks that a newly separated Rita would return to the studio, Castle's contract was allowed to lapse on March 7, 1951—or as Edith Gwynn remarked, "She was let go when Rita tied the can to Khan in Cannes."

"I never minded that I looked like Rita," Castle told James Padgitt. "I thought it would be a help. But now that she might be coming back to Hollywood, I've got my doubts." She admitted to Erskine Johnson that she was "very unhappy" about the focus on Hayworth: "Finally the studio stopped arranging interviews with the press. Newspaper people would ask me how it feels to look like Rita and I'd snap at them." She knew that if she had been able to stay at Columbia, she would work in "just westerns or sit around and draw salary for doing nothing. That's no good."

Castle related to the *Daily News'* Jess Stearn her one and only meeting with Hayworth: "I was under a dryer one day at the hairdressers, when Miss Hayworth came in with a friend. She didn't say a word to me, except 'How do you do,' and then, after staring hard, she said to her friend, 'My nose is straight, hers turns up. She doesn't look a bit like me.'"

As a freelancer, she did television (*Fireside Theatre, Racket Squad*), as there was "no lookalike taboo in TV," wrote Erskine Johnson. But when *Variety* reviewed her *Fireside Theatre* episode "Treasure of the Heart," they wrote, "Some of the camera shots by Ben Kline would be the envy of Rita Hayworth, whom she resembles."

Uncredited, she had a non-speaking part (in two brief scenes) as a member of Bing Crosby's USO troupe in *Just for You* (1952); it was meant as a Technicolor test for a possible Paramount contract. Although she looked stunning, the studio passed on her.

Her role in Columbia's war movie *Eight Iron Men* (1952), produced by Stanley Kramer and directed by Edward Dmytryk, was as "Girl" in several dream sequences. Castle's image dominated the advertising and made it seem the whole film was about her ("She's the girl who walks in their sleep!") instead of soldiers trapped behind enemy lines. (She was also featured in scenes specially shot for the trailer.) Columbia again played up Castle's likeness to Hayworth.

During 1952 and '53, she was voted "Number 1 Dream Girl" by the correspondents of the First Marine Air Wing in Korea; "Miss Curve-X" by the sponsors of Better Posture Week, and "Miss Cactus" ("be-

Mary as saloon singer Cora Dufrayne in *Gunsmoke* (1953) (courtesy C. Robert Rotter/Glamour Girls of the Silver Screen).

cause she has the most leafless limbs in the movies") by the Southwest Cactus Breeders' Association. She was also "Miss Crime Prevention" of 11 Western states, an ironic title given events in her later life.

In 1952, Universal-International gave her supporting parts in two back-to-back westerns. In *The Lawless Breed*, she played gambler-gunfighter John Wesley Hardin's (Rock Hudson) doomed bride-to-be; it was her best role and acting to date. Unencumbered by any stylized Hayworth mannerisms, she was natural and sincere. In the Audie Murphy starrer *Gunsmoke*, she had a flashier but smaller part as tough cookie saloon singer Cora Dufrayne.

By May 1953, Castle was on her way to England to co-star with Scott Brady in *3 Steps to the Gallows*, which was released in the U.S. as *White Fire*. She again played a nightclub singer, this time helping Brady clear his brother of murder charges and prevent his execution. Louella Parsons claimed Mary was "front paged" on her arrival and got a "reception seldom accorded any star less than a Lana Turner or an Ava Gardner." Newspaper reports centered on her status as Hayworth's double. Although publicity items about Castle claimed she was trying to downplay her Ritasemblance by changing her hair and makeup, this was not the case; nothing was altered and they could still pass for twins.

She turned down the lead opposite Dennis O'Keefe in the British-made thriller *The Diamond Wizard* (1954) to co-star on a TV series; "There's nobody on TV I look like," she told Erskine Johnson. At the end of '53, she was contracted to the Republic TV western *Stories of the Century*, which started airing in syndication in January 1954. Every week,

Mary Castle, Scott Brady and Conrad Phillips (*right*) in the British-made *3 Steps to the Gallows* (1953).

railroad detectives Matt Clark (Jim Davis) and Frankie Adams (Castle) got involved with notorious and infamous characters of the Old West.

While her character was subordinate to Davis', Castle got in her licks and proved to be a good-natured, plucky asset to the series. Lighter moments include her frisking Jean Parker ("Cattle Kate") and trying to make Jim Davis jealous with a love letter ("Sam Bass"). She had numerous undercover assignments ("I've been everything from a schoolteacher to a circus performer," she says in "The Doolin Gang"). Castle played up to some of the outlaws, throwing her curves at Sam Bass, John Wesley Hardin, Joaquin Murrieta and Ben Thompson.

She also got into the action, having catfights with Marie Windsor ("Belle Starr") and Joan Shawlee ("The Doolin Gang"); cold-cocking Gloria Winters with a right cross ("Little Britches"); pistol-whipping Bruce Bennett ("Quantrill and His Raiders") and Slim Pickens ("The Wild Bunch of Wyoming"); and making a lunge for a bad guy's gun ("Doc Holliday"). Decades before *Marathon Man*, "Doc Holliday" features a scene where the title character (Kim Spalding) tries to get information out of Frankie by using his dentistry tools for some tooth-pulling persuasion.

In an episode about Black Bart, Bart (Arthur Space) is trying to run away as a stage driver (Frank Sully) shoots at him and misses. Castle grabs his rifle ("Gimme that!") and wings Bart with her first shot. "And golly, can that lady shoot!" says an onlooker.

Castle's character came in for her share of wounds, such as an arrow in her arm ("Geronimo"). The worst was saved for her last episode ("Clay Allison") when she got knocked out by the butt of a gun and then, as she struggled to her feet to shoot a fleeing robber, got plugged herself and left for dead.

All of Castle's 26 episodes were directed by Republic stalwart William Witney. His adept handling gave the series its verve. "I know if Dad were alive today, he would praise Mary Castle," his son Jay Dee Witney says. "I remember meeting her, she was always really nice on set and I never heard Dad say anything to the contrary. I even think she came over to the house a few times."

Stories of the Century won an Emmy for Best Western or Adventure Series. At the start of '55, Castle was replaced by Kristine Miller (as Margaret "Jonesy" Jones). Miller told Boyd Magers that she had been the original choice for the series but had to bow out due to pregnancy. "So Mary did the first ones. They decided they needed a change, so they called me, and at that time, my baby was six months old so I did the final 13." While Miller was an adequate replacement, she simply couldn't match Castle's strength, humor and chemistry with Jim Davis. With Miller saddled up beside Davis, the show now had a different energy. Director Witney also left after doing four episodes with Miller. Author Mike Nevins, who was friends with Witney, told author Wesley Hyatt, "I think he told me he got bored," but Nevins felt it might also have been because of Castle's absence. "I don't think Kristine Miller was in Mary Castle's league," Nevins remarked.

Castle dated writer Sy Bartlett and actor Fernando Lamas. The latter relationship was stormy. In April 1954, Harrison Carroll reported that the two had a "spat" in Palm Springs and "later, Mary's car was sideswiped and overturned. She suffered a black eye and other painful injuries." The next day, Lamas sent flowers to her bedside and "apparently the disagreement was patched up." Sheilah Graham wasn't buying the car crash story. "Fernando Lamas knows all about Mary Castle's black eye. It was not a [car] door."

She was absent from movie and TV screens for most of 1955. In August of that year,

Castle underwent an unspecified operation and spent two weeks at Cedars of Lebanon. After her release, she was cast in *Good Morning, Miss Dove* starring Jennifer Jones and Robert Stack. On her first day of filming, she collapsed on the set. "Actress' doctor says that her condition is not serious," wrote *Variety*, "but that she will be unable to work for at least a week." She was replaced by Peggy Knudsen. At the end of September, a month after that column ran, Castle had a supporting part in *Lux Video Theatre*'s adaptation of "The Enchanted Cottage."

When she turned blonde for the Bowery Boys comedy *Crashing Las Vegas* (1956), columnist John Bustin wrote, "Mary Castle, a perennial starlet who's had difficulties getting rolling because of her remarkable resemblance to Rita Hayworth, is looking a lot less like Rita with her new blonde hair." Also in 1956, she had the lead as a saloon singer with Rod Cameron in the low-budget western *Yaqui Drums* and did two episodes of *The Bob Cummings Show* and a *Chevron Hall of Stars*.

Screen work was sporadic, but she stayed in the news by doing publicity and attending openings and premieres. In January 1957, she was seen on *Cheyenne*, *The O. Henry Playhouse* and two different *Adventures of Ozzie and Harriet* episodes. In one, she used a convincing Cockney accent.

She shared another similarity with Hayworth: picking the wrong men. In April 1957, Castle eloped to Las Vegas with William France Minchen, a wannabe actor (under the name William Grant) born into a wealthy Texas oil family. He was dependent on his mother, who kept him on a tight leash financially. Their honeymoon was cut short when she was called back to Hollywood to reunite with Jim Davis for a western reminiscent of *Stories of the Century*: *Last Stagecoach West* (1957), made by Joseph Kane and Rudy Ralston's indie company Ventura Productions for Republic release. It was about railroad detective Bill Cameron (Davis) and the daughter (Castle) of a mail stagecoach operator turned cattle rustler (Victor Jory). Castle's character is more of a conventional leading lady than in *Stories of the Century*, but her chemistry with Davis was still potent. It was directed by Kane, but had little action.

She also did episodes of *Dragnet* and *Perry Mason*.

On Christmas Eve, 1957, Castle and Minchen had an argument at a Sunset Strip intersection as their car blocked traffic and "she took time out to pummel [her husband]" (*Los Angeles Times*). After two deputy sheriffs escorted the couple back to their home, an intoxicated Castle was arrested for reportedly biting and kick-

A blonde Mary vamps Huntz Hall to obtain his secret gambling skill in *Crashing Las Vegas* (1956).

Mary had one of her best early roles as Rock Hudson's doomed bride-to-be in *The Lawless Breed* (1953).

ing them. Wrote the *Pasadena Independent*, "The actress called the deputies 'punks' and threatened to have them fired."

On January 16, 1958, Castle responded to Minchen's divorce suit by countersuing for separate maintenance, asking for $635 a month. In February, he was ordered to pay $350 a month in temporary support. Minchen said he was unemployed, and that if it were not for the $700-a-month allowance his mother gave him, he would "starve to death." His lawyer remarked, "The mother should not be required to support Miss Castle," to which the judge retorted, "The mother should not be required to support a man of his age either."

Castle's only screen role in 1958 was an episode of Frank Lovejoy's series *Meet McGraw*. Minchen failed to come through with alimony. His mother had since died (on August 15, 1958) and he inherited her estate, but he still would not pay Castle. In December, she went to court seeking to have a bench warrant issued for his arrest. Castle's friend William Witney came through with two episodes of *Frontier Doctor* in the first half of 1959. (Witney also had Minchen in an episode.)

In September 1959, she went to Houston to finally divorce Minchen. When she returned to California that same month, there was more trouble: On the 14th, she was found unconscious on a Malibu beach, clad only in bra and panties. It was revealed that she went for a midnight swim with friend Carol Erickson and almost drowned when a wave knocked her down. A bartender from a local hotel claimed he "pulled her from the surf when he thought she was drowning, and when he returned after calling officers, he found her back in the water." Castle mistakenly thought Carol was still in the water and went to save her, but instead was felled by another big breaker. After being revived by artificial respiration, she was taken to Malibu Emergency Hospital. She filmed two low-budget movies not long afterwards, *The Threat* and *The Jailbreakers* (both released in 1960).

On October 28, 1959, she was arrested for public drunkenness when she and a young male companion created an early morning disturbance. About two weeks later, a drunk Castle was found in her automobile and responded to police intervention by biting, kicking, hitting and swearing at them. In her jail cell, she tried to hang herself by twisting her dress into a noose, attaching one end to a cell door and putting the other end around her neck. Found slumped in a semi-conscious state, she was revived and released on $105 bail. She was later fined $26.25. Although she admitted she was despondent over her recent divorce, she denied that she had attempted suicide.

In December, she was taken to court by Harry LaChance, Inc., for $4,500 spent decorating her apartment two years earlier. Castle explained that she was temporarily out of funds, and it was reported that she owned "nothing of value in California and whatever she does have is tied up in litigation in Houston, where her final divorce decree is due to be entered soon." In February 1960, she filed for bankruptcy, listing $13,678 debts and her assets as $300 worth of clothing. "Chums say she told them her millionaire Texan groom (now in Acapulco) left her with $20,000 in unpaid bills," wrote Walter Winchell.

On April 22, 1960, she was arrested again. Found sprawled out in her car in a Sunset Strip bar parking lot, she was "sullen and uncooperative" when approached by police officers. Castle denied she was drunk, claiming that she simply dropped her car keys and was lying on the seat trying to find them. "If I have to," she said, "I can tell a story about this that will take the top right off City Hall." Nothing more was said about this strange comment. "I am not guilty of anything and this is a deliberate attempt to ruin my career," Castle said, not realizing that at this point there was no career to ruin. (Her last screen job was an appearance on TV's *Tightrope* in March '60.) While in jail, she was also served a debt warrant from Harry LaChance, Inc., which still wanted its money. She was released after agreeing to turn over her 1956 Cadillac to satisfy the judgment.

Less than a week after her release, she pleaded guilty to failing to appear in court on a 1958 traffic violation, running a red light and not having her license, and was ordered to pay a $50 fine.

In June '60 it was announced that Castle had become a press agent for New Orleans Kitchen gourmet specialties. Her April drunk charge was dismissed in July. On September 6, she married insurance broker Wayne Cote. "All her friends hope there's nothing but happiness ahead for this girl who at one time was called 'Rita Hayworth's double,'" wrote Louella Parsons. By August 1961, she was seeking an annulment. They divorced the following year.

An acting comeback was planned, but it started and ended with the small role of an unnamed saloon girl in a 1962 *Gunsmoke* episode. At the beginning of 1963, Castle was working as a hostess at the Garden Room restaurant in the Hollywood Roosevelt Hotel. The *Los Angeles Times'* Art Ryon made space in his column for her:

> Miss Castle says she has practically given up pictures and television. "Unless someone offered me a series, and then I'd be a fool to turn it down." Sometimes described as looking more like Rita Hayworth than Rita Hayworth does, Miss Castle said: "I'm learning a new trade. Mr. Buswow, the maître d'; the chef, and everyone at the hotel have been wonderful to me." Asked if she might be planning a restaurant of her own, she parried, "Well, people always eat, even if they don't go to the

movies." Miss Castle said that some diners recognize her instantly, others give her a lot of puzzled double-takes. She seems happy.

On May 7, 1971, she married musician Erwin Angelo Frezza, but that union ended in July 1972. "Erwin was the love of her life," Mary's granddaughter Cynthia said. "My mom, sister and I were in the wedding. Unfortunately, Grandma's undiagnosed bipolar disorder played a huge role in ending that (and other) marriage(s) and her career (alcohol and erratic/manic behavior)."

Cynthia said of Castle's later years,

She lived in Beverly Hills for a time, while she was "hostessing" and working social events. She was receiving invites to western movie events in the '70s, and would always take Mom, me and my sister. The one I remember the most vividly is the First Annual Western Film Festival in 1976 at the Biltmore Hotel in Los Angeles. She was honored by Gene Autry with a Silver Plate.

Unfortunately, until she was diagnosed [as bipolar], her behavior was disruptive and upsetting to her family. Her mother had passed in 1969, but her father was getting older and his health was failing; he was in the care of her brother and his wife. Mary often came asking for handouts while she was finding her way after her acting career ended, and [in 1983] the unilateral decision was made to "disown" her, though she and I had a special bond and we did our best to remain in contact despite the family's wishes. (I was 14 at the time and she would visit me in secret at my school, unbeknownst to the adults.)

My sister is bipolar ... so I understand, but as a child, I could not [understand Mary]. Grandma put her family through hell, and it hurt Mom terribly. Deeply. I understand now, but telling a child that, "If you talk to your grandma, we will disown you too," is terrifying. I alienated myself from that side of the family for a very long time. Many of them died without me ever speaking to them again because I sided with Mary because I was sheltered from the truth for so long. Then when I was old enough, Mom explained that [Mary] suffered the same illness as my sister ... whom I grew up with. So basically, I could have understood it all along, had they tried to explain it....

She was still very manic in the '70s, which made her fun as a grandma, but also meant she was flighty. She would rush in and out of our lives. So Erwin was introduced and we were whisked into a wedding and then they disappeared. I didn't know him well except that whenever she spoke of him, it was with regret and great heartache.

Mary Castle in her later years (courtesy Cynthia Lee)

She was very social and warm. She had a wonderful sense of humor and loved to entertain (life of the party, singing, etc.) and paint. She had a loyal following, especially in South America and Asia, and she had pen pal admirers who fed her ego.

She was eventually diagnosed as bipolar and received the right dose of medication and was able to live a much more stable life. She lived in Joshua Tree, where she had a little ranch with horses, Lodi, and Palm Springs. She lived a very quiet life at this point—she had little option.

Grandma and I talked about her career a lot because I asked. She could recite her entire filmography and TV appearances by memory. [Although she was not bitter], there was regret and sadness because she truly loved performing. Grandma never boasted, but as her baby granddaughter, and little shadow, I asked her to tell me everything. So she would name drop just to satisfy me. She particularly adored Rock Hudson because he was very sweet to her. Jim Davis and Gene Autry were as well. She told me about all her leading men and friends and gigs. She would sing to me. Peggy Lee's "Black Coffee" was a favorite and was beautiful with her deep voice.

The '80s and '90s were very quiet and she really just spent her time enjoying her retirement at her little condo in Palm Springs. Well, fighting lung cancer took its toll. It was a gruesome end. She was feisty and neither she nor her hospice doctors saw the need for her regular medication at this point.

I was working and living in London at the time and flew in to say goodbye and help Mom take care of her belongings.

The 67-year-old Castle died in Palm Springs on April 29, 1998. Her daughter Judith passed away from idiopathic lung disease in 2017.

Mary Castle Filmography

1948: *Mexican Hayride* (uncredited).
1949: *Always Leave Them Laughing* (uncredited).
1950: *The Tougher They Come.*
1951: *Prairie Roundup, Texans Never Cry, Fun on the Run* (short), *When the Redskins Rode, Criminal Lawyer.*
1952: *Just for You* (uncredited), *Eight Iron Men.*
1953: *The Lawless Breed, 3 Steps to the Gallows, Gunsmoke.*
1956: *Come on Seven* (short), *Crashing Las Vegas, Yaqui Drums.*
1957: *Last Stagecoach West.*
1960: *The Threat, The Jailbreakers.*

Mae Clarke

James Curtis, who interviewed Mae Clarke and helped her with her autobiography, called her story "one of bad luck and missed opportunities, of mental illness and a life never lived as happily as it should have been. It's also a story of survival in a business where longevity counts for everything and talent is something one trades upon only when all else fails."

It was not an easy life: Clarke never seemed to get the breaks. Every time she would get going, something would happen, starting first with a nervous breakdown followed by an accident and further mental problems. All this resulted in the one time star becoming an extra just to survive. Through it all, the grapefruit is what people remember.

The oldest of three children, she was born Violet Mary Klotz on August 16, 1910, in Philadelphia and grew up in Atlantic City. Her father Walter, a movie theater organist, eventually composed more than 200 hymns.

A 1931 portrait of Mae Clarke when she was one of Universal's most promising stars.

She ended her education after the eighth grade, never making it to high school. The restless teenager attended Dawson's Dancing School and was considered a pretty good dancer. She hoofed it up at Atlantic City's Steeplechase Pier and in vaudeville and clubs where she was discovered by producer Earl Lindsay.

In New York City, she appeared in shows at the Strand Roof and the Vanity Club before going to Broadway for *Gay Paree* (1925–26) and *The Noose* (1926–27). She was joined in most of her stage endeavors by her friend, fellow dancer and roommate Ruby Stevens (aka Barbara Stanwyck). By this time, Violet had changed her name to Mae Clarke. "I only changed it because they laughed at Klotz," she wrote in her memoir.

Writer Anita Loos revealed to Earl Wilson that her real-life inspiration for the character of Lorelei Lee in her 1925 novel *Gentlemen Prefer Blondes: The Intimate Diary of a Professional Lady* was Clarke: "I was on a train going to California and I noticed a certain blonde on the train getting away with murder because she was a blonde."

In 1927, Clarke got a role in Broadway's *Manhattan Mary* dancing the "Five Step" with Harlan Dixon. During this show's run, the 17-year-old was swept off her feet by 34-year-old Lew Brice, the vaudevillian-gambler brother of Fanny. On February 6, 1928, two days after she left the *Midnight Mary* cast, they married in Chicago. As a wedding gift, Fanny got her boyfriend Billy Rose to co-write (with Ballard MacDonald) a stage act called "What's the Odds?" for the newlyweds. Sometimes they were billed as Mr. and Mrs. Lew Brice "of the distinguished Fanny Brice family."

With Fanny's help, Clarke made her film debut in 1929's *Big Time*. The transfer from stage to screen was smooth for her. The *Los Angeles Times*' Norbert Lusk praised her performance: "Simple, sincere, her acting is devoid of calculation as her appearance is of spectacular values." (Clarke later attributed her naturalness and underplaying to Fanny's way of approaching a song.)

This lead role resulted in a Fox contract and another lead in *Nix on Dames* (1929). By this time, she was supporting her parents and two younger siblings (with the advent of talkies, her father had lost his job as an organist for silent films).

On stage, Lew Brice had always been billed over his wife. But now that she was in Hollywood and getting more attention, his drinking and gambling increased. For years he was simply Fanny's brother, now he had to take a backseat to his wife. Clarke told Richard Lamparski in the early 1970s, "He hated being known as Mr. Mae Clarke, poor guy. But what man wouldn't?"

In January 1930, she filed for divorce because of Brice's "infatuation with cards," testifying: "After he started gambling, he told me that any queen in the deck was better than I."

Nine months later, while still wed to Brice, she was sporting an engagement ring from producer John McCormick, who was in the process of divorcing actress Colleen Moore. When news of the Clarke-McCormick romance hit the papers, something else was hit: Clarke's nose. The *Los Angeles Times* wrote she was in a "private hospital following an operation on her nose." Clarke explained in her autobiography that Brice broke it.

Clarke immediately took to screen acting and was often praised for her thoughtful performances. *Variety*, later reviewing *The Good Bad Girl* (1931), called her "an economical emoter. She never slops over nor does she follow the latest fashion of restrained acting by appearing to be on the first lap of a long and greatly needed rest."

Fox didn't know what to do with Clarke, loaning her out to RKO for *The Fall Guy* (1930) and giving her a supporting part and a lead (in 1930's *The Dancers* and *Men on Call*, respectively).

Let go by Fox, she freelanced. Nineteen thirty-one would be her breakout year with roles in the classics *The Front Page*, *Frankenstein* (as the title character's fiancée, Elizabeth), *The Public Enemy* and *Waterloo Bridge*.

She would never live down having a grapefruit smashed into her face by James Cagney in *The Public Enemy*; like it or not, it would follow her for the rest of her life. "This thing that took ten seconds to do has taken notoriety over my whole career. I might as well never have lived," Mae Clarke told *People* in 1987 about one of the most famous moments in Hollywood history.

That simple bit of business overshadowed all of the good acting work Clarke did before and after, including *Waterloo Bridge*. Some view the *Public Enemy* scene as comic; however, it's a nasty, sad scene of two unhappy people, and Clarke's sobbing at the fade-out is heartbreaking. She later claimed the grapefruit was an on-set script addition, but she didn't think it would make the final cut. One person who did like it: her ex, Lew Brice. According to Cagney, "He saw the film repeatedly just to see that scene, and was often shushed by angry patrons when his delighted laughter got too loud."

She was more impressive in director James Whale's *Waterloo Bridge*, playing a tragic prostitute in love with a soldier. Clarke always considered it the highpoint of her career, the best acting she had ever done—and few would argue with her. (For many years, her version of *Waterloo Bridge* was unavailable because of MGM's 1940 and 1956 remakes; it reemerged in the late 1990s.) To the end of her life, Clarke kept a letter sent by the author of the source play, Robert E. Sherwood: "I was moved and thrilled and overcome by your marvelous performance in *Waterloo Bridge*, for which I wish I could thank you adequately." For Mae, his expression of thanks was more than adequate and the letter remained a cherished possession.

Her performance resulted in Universal briefly sharing her contract with Columbia. Most of her roles were in Bs, which prompted columnist Edward E. Gloss to call her "an actress capable of better than her studio will give her...." Still, it was just a matter of time before Clarke achieved real stardom.

But it all came crashing down.

In June '31, there was some inkling of trouble when she told interviewer Dan Thomas about her need to write poetry: "Most of my poems so far have been written when I was angry. They are an outlet for my emotions and are about the only things that keep me from actually blowing up at times."

When her nervous breakdown came in March 1932, she had to bow out of the Universal B *Radio Patrol*. She was sent by her family to a sanitarium for a rest, but the "rest" turned out to be a horror: Clarke was doped up most of the time and locked up in what she later described as torture devices. For over two months she had to endure electroshock therapy. "Without sedation," Clarke wrote in her

Mae Clarke, seen here with Kent Douglass, considered her role in the original *Waterloo Bridge* (1931) her best (courtesy Greg Mank).

autobiography. "I was almost murdered and I survived. In fact, I even smelled death coming out of my pores."

In her autobiography she insisted she was physically, not mentally, ill and a victim of overwork. "I needed intravenous feeding and blood and rest. I didn't need half-nelsons and big men sitting on my stomach. That's what happened."

In July, still not well enough to go before the camera, she needed a rest from her "rest cure." Universal terminated her contract using what columnist John Blaker called their "illness clause."

"Since I was ill," Clarke told Robbin Coons, "I've had a terrible time convincing some producers I really was well enough to work." She downplayed her ill health at the time saying it was "greatly exaggerated" in the press; if anything, they couldn't report her full, horrendous ordeal. To hear Clarke tell of her illness at the time, it was a minor inconvenience that resolved itself and would never return. If only that had been true.

In September '32 the freelancer went back to work with good roles in the indie *Breach of Promise* and RKO's *Penguin Pool Murder*. After months of fever and medicines, Clarke found that her hair had become brittle and lifeless (it's obvious in *Breach of Promise*) and finally she decided to take drastic action and cut it short, a style not typical of Hollywood's leading ladies back then. ("Mae Clarke's boy bob, in a day when the very short cut is distinctly out, manages to give her a 'flair' that has helped put over her new individuality"— Alice L. Tildesley.)

In November 1932, she underwent an appendix operation.

At the beginning of '33, Clarke got one of her better parts in Columbia's *Parole Girl* where she seeks revenge from the man who put her in jail. "[H]er acting—always sincere and intuitive—has taken a new depth and sheen," wrote the *Chicago Tribune*'s Mae Tinee. "Miss Clarke's performance is apparently effortless, and yet she makes every word, glance, and intonation count."

It looked as if her career was getting back on track, especially when she was signed by MGM and played opposite John Gilbert in director Tod Browning's *Fast Workers* (1933); a possible movie with Clark Gable was in the offing.

On March 1, 1933, she and actor Phillips Holmes were driving home from a party when Holmes, unable to see clearly in the fog, swerved to dodge an oncoming car and struck a parked car. According to Clarke, "My jaw went straight forward onto the dash. Broke [my jaw] right in half, hanging down this way, spitting out teeth." She also sustained facial cuts. She had been in the early days of filming a lead role with Robert Montgomery in *Made on Broadway*, and had to be replaced by Sally Eilers.

The talk around town was that Clarke had a dark cloud over her—a jinx. "I've had three bits of health trouble," she told Grace Kingsley, "first that nervous breakdown … then the appendicitis operation, and lastly the automobile accident just before going into an MGM film. I think I'm through with bad luck, that way anyway. But I'm rapping on wood just the same."

Her first movie after the accident was RKO's *Flaming Gold* (1933) with Bill Boyd and Pat O'Brien. Unlike Universal, MGM waited for her to get well and started to give her parts, mostly leads in their B product.

Just after finishing *Penthouse* in the summer of 1933, Clarke sued Phillips Holmes for $21,500, charging him with negligence and intoxication, asserting that her injuries left her with impaired speech and a face "drawn into unattractive, unbecoming and unnatural lines when speaking," which "impaired her work in pictures, thereby damaging her career and earning capacity." (Perhaps to counteract her remarks about her looks, MGM circulated an item from "Studio Beauty Experts" who felt her broken jaw "changed the contour of her face and enhanced her beauty.") While this suit was going on, Clarke and Holmes were in the process of shooting the Goldwyn movie *Nana* (1934).

At Warners, Clarke reunited with Cagney for *Lady Killer* (1933) and in one scene he dragged her by her hair, caveman-style! Back at Metro, she filmed some scenes for the Marion Davies starrer *Operator 13* (1934) but was taken off the production and replaced because, the studio said, she was "too pretty." In her autobiography, Clarke explained, "Marion Davies got what she wanted. And if she didn't want somebody in a scene with her, then she didn't have to have them."

A warning sign that things were not going well came in a March '34 Harrison Carroll column: "Mae Clarke phoned the MGM studio not to expect her on March 2, as she intended to spend the day lying in bed in a dark room with all the doors and windows locked." This behavior was attributed to her jinx and how things just seemed to happen to her around or on that date. "I'm not taking any more chances," Clarke supposedly said.

That same month, her case against Holmes was dismissed when he agreed to pay her hospital bills. (They remained friendly, and both later appeared in *The House of a Thousand Candles*.)

In April she finished up a supporting part in WB's *The Man with Two Faces* (1934). Between then and June, she didn't make any movies. Her idleness was interrupted by a stay at Cedars of Lebanon for "a room, a bed, and five days' rest" (Walter Winchell). Her "rest cure" was thought to be nothing serious and she had a Columbia film coming up. That didn't happen, nor did a role in MGM's *Straight Is the Way* (1934), where she was replaced by Gladys George. That was because, as Harrison Carroll pointed out, her "rest in the hospital is much nearer a nervous breakdown than they'd have you believe."

Louella Parsons called it a "serious breakdown," and this statement was borne out by George Shaffer's comment: "Fanny Brice visits her nearly every day but some of the days her friend is so tired or sick she doesn't recognize Fanny." By this time, she had been moved to a private sanitarium, where she was given electroshock; she would soon finish her rest at home with her family. RKO wanted her for *Murder on a Honeymoon*, but Clarke wasn't up to it. Near the end of '34, she was an extended guest of her friends, the Ralph Bellamys.

Again, her illness was put down to overwork. An absurd syndicated piece by Dan Thomas blamed all her personal difficulties on playing siren roles: "So it will be a younger, merrier, and more charming Mae you will see on the screen in the future," he wrote. "From now on she's going in for light comedy and romantic loves. And she's confident that, as a result, her own life will be made much brighter and happier—minus the tough breaks which made her known as Hollywood's original hard luck girl."

If only life were that simple.

By now the original five days' rest had become ten months. Clarke later said she was devastated when Universal cast Valerie Hobson as Elizabeth in the *Frankenstein* follow-up *Bride of Frankenstein* when it started filming in January '35, but she was still recovering. The following month, she returned to the soundstages in Fox's *The Daring Young Man* with James Dunn.

After each personal issue, Clarke had to start over in Hollywood and by the mid–30s it

The Monster (Boris Karloff) meets Dr. Frankenstein's bride Elizabeth (Clarke) in the classic horror film *Frankenstein* (1931).

had taken its toll. MGM had let her go and she gradually became a prisoner of the B-movie mills, the sun having set on any hopes she had of becoming a major star. Still a highly capable actress, she might not have liked the Bs but she shone in her outings with such actors as Lew Ayres, Ralph Bellamy, James Ellison, John Payne and Jack Holt. Mae heard that dancer Margaret Price, who had taken Mae under her wing on stage ten years earlier, was ailing and had to stop dancing, and she arranged for Price to work as her stand-in.

At Grand National, she teamed for the last time with Cagney in the hit comedy *Great Guy* (1936). She had a multi-picture contract at Republic, where she had the lead in former co-star Lew Ayres' only foray as feature director, *Hearts in Bondage* (1936).

"When you have an illness in pictures, producers never get over the idea that it's chronic," she told Robbin Coons at the end of '36. "I learned that this idea was keeping me out of some parts, so I proved I could take it. I did pictures for independent companies, where the hours were long and hard. If work like that couldn't break me, and it didn't, nothing can." In 1938, Coons remarked that the majors didn't employ Clarke after a while because "producers doubted she could finish a picture if they gave it to her."

Clarke had been engaged at separate times to actor Sidney Blackmer and to Dr. Frank G. Nolan, but it was Pan-American Airways pilot Stevens George Bancroft who became her second husband on September 15, 1937, in Agua Caliente, Mexico. Clarke later described him to Mildred Schroeder as the "kind of fellow who jumped in the nightclub pool at the Fairmont and flew under the Golden Gate Bridge."

Her mother was quoted in newspapers as saying Mae would retire from the screen and settle down to the "strict duties of a housewife." After the "I dos," the couple moved to Rio de Janeiro, where Bancroft was stationed.

Traveling with her husband, Clarke learned to fly, but she was getting restless and mentioned that she was thinking of returning to acting as early as '38. The couple moved that year to Coral Gables, Florida. In an interview with local columnist Helen Muir, Clarke said she missed Hollywood and her friends out there. She mentioned that when Bancroft was away, she had a "Siamese cat and the Coral Gables police for company. The officers of the law stop by two and three times in an evening as they make their rounds to make sure Mrs. Bancroft remains unmolested." Her interests were reading, sailing, fishing and gardening. Recalling her movie days, she named Spencer Tracy her favorite actor and *Turn Back the Clock* (1933) as the favorite of her films and stated that she missed her golf games with Wynne Gibson ("She calls me the Iron Queen").

In August 1938, while visiting her mother in Hollywood, she was asked if she would return to acting. "No, indeed," Clarke replied. "Marriage is far too important a career in my life to be interested in another one. We are happy and contented and from now on I'm plain Mrs. Stevens Bancroft, housewife."

Marital bliss ended in January 1940 when she filed for divorce and moved back to Hollywood to write a book and a couple of plays. Nothing materialized writing-wise.

Jean Harlow and Mae Clarke as models looking for love (and rich husbands) in *Three Wise Girls* (1932).

She did return to the screen with a contract at Republic ("Mae Clarke works at Republic, says she needs the money"—Sheilah Graham). It was announced that she would get the lead with John Wayne in Republic's *Lady for a Night* (1942), but she lost the part to Joan Blondell. In another Wayne vehicle, *Flying Tigers* (1942), she had a small, well-played role as the wife of an outcast flier who is later killed. The *Los Angeles Times*' Edwin Schallert wrote of her performance, "Mae Clarke, in a few scenes, impresses."

Also, during the war, she was a member of the North Hollywood unit of the Women's Ambulance and Defense Corps.

A contract at Paramount wasn't as good. About her inconsequential role as a receptionist in *And Now Tomorrow* (1944), Drew Pearson wrote rather ominously, "We reckon she, too, wonders about her 'tomorrow.'" That same year she was working at Lockheed as a junior clerk.

In February 1946, she married realtor Herbert Langdon, who had been a radio singer and pianist before the war. Again, matrimony resulted in retirement from the screen—but not for long. This union also encountered turbulence and crash-landed in September '47 and she headed for Reno. The childless Clarke never remarried after this last stumble down the aisle.

Republic briefly came back into her life and Clarke was given her best latter-day roles with the studio as leading lady of *Daredevils of the Clouds* (1948), *Streets of San Francisco* (1949) and the serial *King of the Rocket Men* (1949). She always gave Republic president

Grant Withers watches as Mae Clarke takes charge in Republic's *Daredevils of the Clouds* (1948).

Herbert J. Yates credit for helping her when she needed it, having faith in her abilities, and being a good friend.

In 1949, MGM signed her as a dress extra. It was a comedown from her heyday, but at least she was getting a steady paycheck at a time when her health was precarious. Nineteen fifty started with another nervous breakdown. She had just come back from a trip to Colorado where a Catholic girls college presented two songs Clarke and her father had written for the school's production of *Babes in Toyland*. "My daughter has never lost her ambition and her ability," her mother told Eliza Schallert. "Both she and I have great faith in her talent and we know that this is only a temporary setback."

Mae Clarke and Tristram Coffin ready for action in the Republic serial *King of the Rocket Men* (1949) (courtesy Bob Burns).

She was off screen until June 1950 and then resumed work at MGM. Not everyone was sympathetic. Columnist Mike Connolly mentioned her appearance at Danny Beck's Masquers show and the emcee's introduction of Clarke: "Hi, Mae, didja bring your grapefruit? And I hear you just got three days' work at Monogram." Connolly thought it in bad taste, adding, "But she handled him like a real trouper." She couldn't support herself as an actress and in between screen jobs she drew unemployment checks and worked as a receptionist and a nurses' aide at a local hospital.

In 1952, Clarke co-wrote with her father the song "Just a Little More Waiting," which was recorded by Jimmy Wakely on Capitol. She and Wakely had appeared together in Monogram's *Gun Runner* (1949), a rare chance to see Clarke as a real baddie.

In 1953, she was in the news when she was put on probation for neglecting to declare $43 (or $39, sources differ) in earnings. It was revealed that the one-time star was living in a "something less than modest apartment." She told Bob Thomas, "Sure, things aren't going so well for me now. I've had my share of heartbreaks. But I've had a lot of satisfaction, too.... I still have faith in my abilities as an actress. I know I can do the job. When I can no longer get jobs, I'll quit and do something else. But not until then."

Still, finding work was tough. "Lotsa pals have helped Mae Clarke land several film and video jobs," wrote Army Archerd. "More are needed." She played party guests, ship passengers, nurses, telephone operators; most of her film characters were nameless. She called these her "subsistence parts" because they helped pay the rent and buy the groceries. You really had to look sharply—and quickly—to see her in these films. Being reduced to an extra must have been a trying and humiliating experience but she held her head high and did her job the best she could. "You go through hell to be in this business, because you love it," Clarke later told *Premiere* magazine's Jesse Green. She related in her memoir that Bette Davis was more than gracious to her on the set of *The Catered Affair* (1956), even though years before Davis had lost the coveted lead in *Waterloo Bridge* to Clarke. Not so nice: Henry Fonda (*A Big Hand for the Little Lady*) and Julie Andrews (*Thoroughly Modern Millie*).

Clarke was in and out of sanitariums and she continued to face legal problems, which added stress to her lonely, borderline poverty life. Television brought her some work: *Cowboy G-Men, Waterfront, Dragnet, Four Star Playhouse, The Lineup, The Public Defender, Jane Wyman Presents the Fireside Theatre, Crossroads, Lux Video Theatre, Broken Arrow, The Loretta Young Show, The Life and Legend of Wyatt Earp, The Deputy, Perry Mason, F Troop, Batman*, etc.

In 1955, she got some attention for a then-daring episode of *Medic* ("When I Was Young") which dealt with menopause. "It's the best role I've ever had," Clarke told Emily Belser. "I've had longer roles in my life, but never one as good as this." After filming of one key emotional scene, the crew applauded her.

In addition to health setbacks and her bipolar disorder, Clarke was also hampered by a serious drinking problem throughout her life, which probably didn't help her mental issues.

In October 1957, Clarke sued Paramount Television and KTLA-TV horror hostess Ottola Nesmith. The latter had dressed and acted like a crazy old hag during a televising of *Frankenstein* and claimed to actually *be* Mae Clarke. Clarke did not enjoy the depiction of herself as a "demented, has-been actress" or that the pseudo–Clarke uttered, "What does it matter if I can't pay my bills? It doesn't matter about my present-day poverty … today's actresses … they can't act."

Clarke told the press that she felt she was being boycotted by the industry because of her lawsuit and wanted a quick resolution to it so she could resume working. Clarke lost the suit but Paramount Television, facing a retrial, settled with her for an undisclosed sum.

In 1963, she had a recurring role on *General Hospital*. The year was tough, though. "The work has been slow," she remarked to Bob Thomas, "but something good might come up. You never know—it might happen tomorrow."

She directed children's plays, had displays of her art work, and took a theater arts class at Berkeley. Her father passed away in April 1964. About five months later, Mae was named actors' repertory director of the Stinson Beach Arts Foundation and was active in trying to develop the Atheneum Center. "Offering aid to the young artist will be one of our major aims," Clarke told Mildred Schroeder. "Our immediate project is fund-raising for the Atheneum, which will be a complex of art buildings and facilities." After the initial fundraising, nothing else happened on the project.

Her acting career came to a close in the late 1960s. Even though she was available for jobs throughout the 1970s, she got nothing. She was cast in *Watermelon Man* (1970), but stated that they forgot to call her in to shoot her bit; she did, however, pose for publicity shots with the film's star, Godfrey Cambridge, who held a grapefruit in front of her.

In 1974, Clarke presented her old co-star with a grapefruit tree on *AFI Life Achievement Award: A Tribute to James Cagney*. The rest of the decade was devoted to more health issues but her spare time was spent painting, writing children's books, recording books for the blind, and teaching acting to children.

Clarke told Judith Michaelson she was living in a North Hollywood apartment "under very reduced circumstances." She was alone and depressed, especially after her mother's death in 1979; "after awhile, the only person I saw was the mailman." That changed when she was forced to move when her building was set to be demolished to make way for a condominium. In 1980, Clarke entered the Motion Picture & Television Country House in Woodland Hills.

This move brightened Clarke's life considerably. "I've had more notice since I've come here," she told Michaelson. "Here I can walk outside and not be alone. I can talk to people. I can go up to the office. Or walk through the beautiful gardens." While she was there, other residents included Mary Astor, Regis Toomey, Stepin Fetchit, Ellen Corby, Rose Hobart and Viola Dana.

She remained feisty. When Robert Wagner came to film at the facility, Clarke wasn't impressed. Sipping her coffee at lunch, she remarked, "He should come and ask me for *my* autograph."

She was still battling some demons, and told the *Los Angeles Times*' Patricia Ward Biederman that before she got up in the morning, she repeated the words, "Happy, happy, happy, happy, happy!," explaining that "it makes me laugh at myself." Another resident, writer DeWitt Bodeen, told author Greg Mank, "Mae has days when she's not all here, not even back somewhere in the past, but just seething and roiling with misery."

An 81-year-old Clarke was suffering from cancer (which she had successfully beaten years before) when she died at the Motion Picture Hospital on April 29, 1992. ("Hard luck" right to the end: Her passing got less attention than it might have in the media, as that was the first day of the Rodney King riots.) She is interred next to her parents at North Hollywood's Pierce Brothers Valhalla Memorial Park.

Just before her death, Clarke was asked how she wanted to be remembered. She referenced something James Cagney had said about her: "Mae Clarke was a very professional actress who knew what was required of her and did her job excellently." And then she added, "I think I'll leave it at that."

Mae Clarke Filmography

1929: *Big Time, Nix on Dames.*
1930: *The Fall Guy, The Dancers, Men on Call.*
1931: *The Front Page, The Public Enemy, The Good Bad Girl, Waterloo Bridge, Reckless Living, Frankenstein.*
1932: *Three Wise Girls, The Final Edition, The Impatient Maiden, Night World, Breach of Promise, Penguin Pool Murder.*
1933: *Parole Girl, Fast Workers, Turn Back the Clock, As the Devil Commands, Penthouse, Flaming Gold, Lady Killer.*
1934: *Nana, This Side of Heaven, Let's Talk It Over, The Man with Two Faces.*
1935: *Silk Hat Kid, The Daring Young Man, Hitch Hike Lady.*
1936: *The House of a Thousand Candles, Hearts in Bondage, Wild Brian Kent, Hats Off, Great Guy.*
1937: *Trouble in Morocco, Outlaws of the Orient.*
1940: *Women in War.*
1941: *Sailors on Leave.*
1942: *Flying Tigers, Lady from Chungking.*
1944: *And Now Tomorrow* (uncredited), *Here Come the Waves* (uncredited).
1945: *Kitty.*
1948: *Reaching from Heaven, Daredevils of the Clouds.*
1949: *Gun Runner, Streets of San Francisco, King of the Rocket Men.*
1950: *The Yellow Cab Man* (uncredited), *The Reformer and the Redhead* (uncredited), *Annie Get Your Gun* (uncredited), *The Skipper Surprised His Wife* (uncredited), *Duchess of Idaho* (uncredited), *Mrs. O'Malley and Mr. Malone* (uncredited).

1951: *Three Guys Named Mike* (uncredited), *Inside Straight* (uncredited), *Mr. Imperium* (uncredited), *Royal Wedding* (uncredited), *The Great Caruso* (uncredited), *The People Against O'Hara* (uncredited), *Callaway Went Thataway* (uncredited), *The Unknown Man* (uncredited).

1952: *Love Is Better Than Ever* (uncredited), *Singin' in the Rain* (uncredited), *Skirts Ahoy!* (uncredited), *Pat and Mike* (uncredited), *Holiday for Sinners* (uncredited), *Fearless Fagan* (uncredited), *The Miracle of Our Lady of Fatima* (uncredited), *Horizons West*, *Thunderbirds*, *Because of You*.

1953: *Confidentially Connie* (uncredited).

1954: *Magnificent Obsession*.

1955: *Women's Prison*, *Not as a Stranger*, *I Died a Thousand Times* (uncredited).

1956: *Come Next Spring* (uncredited), *Mohawk*, *The Catered Affair* (uncredited), *The Desperadoes Are in Town*.

1958: *Voice in the Mirror*.

1959: *Ask Any Girl* (uncredited).

1966: *A Big Hand for the Little Lady*.

1967: *Thoroughly Modern Millie* (uncredited).

Dorothy Comingore

In 1940, when she was cast as Charles Foster Kane's second wife in Orson Welles' *Citizen Kane* (1941), Linda Winters was a decidedly small-time actress, having appeared in 16 films. That output consisted of leads in Bs and small, uncredited parts in bigger productions. If she was known for anything, it was not acting, but rather being outspoken and a bit difficult.

With *Citizen Kane* and a name change to Dorothy Comingore came instant recognition and possible stardom. Her strong, almost self-destructive personality, however, wasn't having any of it. A series of poor choices, bad luck and the Blacklist quickly tanked her career.

Of German descent, she was born Margaret Louise Comingore on August 24, 1913, in Los Angeles, the daughter of an electrotyper and labor activist. Her great-uncle, prominent surgeon John A. Comingore, was one of the first professors of the Indiana Medical College. When Margaret was nine, she and her family moved to Oakland. Her sister Lucille later owned a San Francisco nightclub called Honey Lou's.

At the University of California at Berkeley, Margaret studied religious philosophy. After about a year, she dropped out and moved to Taos, New Mexico, where she was an artists' model and worked in a museum. Around 1936, Comingore married writer Robert Meltzer, who was reportedly involved with Communist causes.

In Carmel, California, she continued modeling and began acting in little theater productions using the first name of Dorothy. In one, *The Cradle Song*, she was spotted by Charlie Chaplin. They had tea together to talk over her budding career.

There was extensive publicity about Chaplin's intentions toward the auburn-haired green-eyed Comingore. Did he want to put Comingore under personal

An RKO portrait of Dorothy Comingore from the early 1940s.

contract for a possible movie together? Were they romantically involved? Meltzer was supposedly unhappy about the situation, but Comingore and Chaplin both denied anything was going on or that she even wanted to be in movies. "There is no contract," Chaplin remarked, "and there is no contract under consideration." But he added, "If she comes to Hollywood, entirely on her own initiative, I will do what I can to secure a screen test for her."

Comingore insisted that she didn't actually know Chaplin, nor want or need his help. Through her own stage connections, she contacted an agent who got her a screen test at Warner Brothers. "All I hope now," she told Frederick C. Othman, "is that nobody will think I'm trading on the notoriety I received in connection with Mr. Chaplin."

After being signed at Warners, her name was changed from Dorothy Comingore to Kay Winters and it was announced that her first picture would be *Three Girls on Broadway* (later called *Broadway Musketeers*), as the third wheel to Ann Sheridan and Margaret Lindsay. This didn't happen, and Comingore was used in bits and for bathing suit publicity. ("I want to be an actress and not another cutie," she told the front office.) From Kay Winters she became Linda Winters, but nothing much changed. Robbin Coons reported that when Comingore visited the set of *Angels with Dirty Faces*, James Cagney reassured the restless contractee, "Don't worry. They have to 'discover' you about a dozen times before it takes." He didn't know just how prophetic those words would be.

Her Warner Bros. stay lasted about three months and then her option was not taken up. "I could understand a studio letting me go if it knew whether I was any good or not," she told Milton Harker, "but no one knows whether I am an actress or not." Allegedly, she told off one of the producers there before she left the lot.

As a freelancer, she had the lead in the indie *Prison Train* (1938). Despite its low budget and short supply of box office "names" (Fred Keating, Comingore, Alexander Leftwich, James Blakeley), it was well-regarded as an original and exciting thriller of a gangster (Keating), his naïve sister (Comingore), frame-ups, and the gang war that brings the action to the title locomotive.

Columnist Milton Harker claimed that during this period, Comingore was in such dire straits "that sometimes she had to steal food from her pets and sometimes they had to steal food from her." *Modern Screen*'s James Carson later wrote that the reason Comingore had trouble getting parts at the beginning of her career was "very crooked teeth, noticeable especially when she laughs." Or, maybe, as some implied, her strong personality was a turnoff.

After a failed test at Hal Roach for *The Housekeeper's Daughter*, she inked a Columbia contract. Al-

Dorothy in 1940 posing outside for RKO publicity cameras.

though she lost a good role (to Rita Hayworth) in Howard Hawks' *Only Angels Have Wings* (1939), she would get more opportunities at Columbia than she did at Warners.

Now divorced from Meltzer, she wed screenwriter Richard A. Collins in Los Angeles on May 18, 1939. (Meltzer worked as assistant director and uncredited writer on Charlie Chaplin's *The Great Dictator* [1940]; wrote for radio; and was one of the screenwriters of Orson Welles' *It's All True* [1943].)

Comingore's post–*Citizen Kane* publicity would claim she was nothing but a bit player at Columbia, but this is untrue. She had the top female roles in *North of the Yukon* (1939) and *Pioneers of the Frontier* (1940) and also acted in the studio's Three Stooges and Charley Chase two-reelers. In between, however, there were lots of uncredited bits. "Everybody told me I was a bum actress," she remarked to Frederick C. Othman. "They said I'd never learn. I was terribly discouraged."

Finally, she claimed, she quit Columbia in disgust because of the large percentage of bits she had been doing. "No one can say I haven't learned the hard way," Comingore laughed to *Hollywood* magazine's Thomas Vaughn. She also reportedly called Columbia head honcho Harry Cohn a schmuck to his face.

Through press agent Herbert Drake, Comingore met with Orson Welles, who was looking for an actress to play Susan Alexander, the mistress and then second wife of pub-

Charles Foster Kane (Orson Welles) watches as his bored wife Susan Alexander (Dorothy Comingore) works on a puzzle in *Citizen Kane* (1941).

lisher Charles Foster Kane, in his first Hollywood film as director, *Citizen Kane* (1941). "So he had me read some of the lines," she told Othman, "and he told me I did it very intelligently. This was about the first kind word anybody had said to me in Hollywood. It gave me a tremendous lift." Welles also admired her spirit when he heard that Chaplin had offered her a bit in *The Great Dictator* and she turned it down.

After some tests, Comingore got the role—but then had to tell Welles that she was pregnant. "Fine," he said, "that'll prove that I'm really going to finish this movie once you start working on it." Welles had been in Hollywood a year with a lot of ideas but had yet to actually make a movie. (A week after filming wrapped, she gave birth to her daughter Judith.)

Controversy dogged *Citizen Kane* from the beginning,

as it was thought to be an attack on newspaper tycoon William Randolph Hearst; Susan Alexander was allegedly based on his mistress, actress Marion Davies. It is widely believed that in real life, Hearst tried to make Davies into a dramatic actress when her real forte was comedy; in *Citizen Kane*, Kane pushes the untalented Alexander into becoming an opera singer. (Comingore's singing was dubbed by Jean Forward.) Welles denied that he was doing a veiled biography but Hearst, using his connections, tried to sabotage the production.

When *Citizen Kane* opened, it was heralded as one of the greatest films ever made. Comingore's multi-layered performance got its fair share of the kudos, and it was predicted that her career would soar.

An example of her feisty, outspoken nature: After Comingore's performance garnered laurels from critics, director Frank Capra was asked what he thought of it. "Fine," he said. "You know, she's been in a number of my pictures." According to Harold Heffernan, an angry Comingore wired Capra, "You mean I was in *one* of your pictures [*Mr. Smith Goes to Washington*] a number of times!"

RKO signed her to a contract, and then wanted to change her name back to Linda Winters; the actress raised Cain and got to stick with Dorothy Comingore. And she had her own ideas about how she wanted her career to progress: "I don't want to be rushed into anything, so I'm asking the studio to be careful about my next picture," the Associated Press quoted her as saying. "I know my capabilities, and if this first big role is good, I want to live up to it. I've seen lots of 'One-Picture Girls.'"

RKO planned a star buildup but, she told Othman, "they immediately offered me parts in a couple of little pictures. They seemed like such bad little pictures that I didn't want to play in them." Some of the movies she turned down were *Unexpected Uncle*, *Highways by Night*, *Valley of the Sun*, *Weekend for Three* and *The Big Street*. Loanouts to other studios, such as Paramount for the Other Woman part in *The Major and the Minor*, fell through. She sought dramatic parts with substance, not fluff. Welles wanted her for his production of *Sister Carrie*, and she would have done it, but it was never made.

During a personal appearance tour in the summer of '41, Comingore became so annoyed while doing a radio interview in San Francisco that she left. "I got up at seven o'clock in the morning and arrived at the radio station an hour early to go over the interview with the radio interviewer," she explained. "She got there two minutes before the broadcast and showed no interest in finding out my name or my history. So when she called me Miss Comingoo and my picture *Citizen King*, I wouldn't stay there another minute."

While it's been alleged that Hearst had a vendetta against her for portraying what he thought was a savage reflection of Davies in *Citizen Kane*, Comingore was partly at fault for ruining her own career during this period. *Kane* may have been a masterpiece of filmmaking but it was not a box office success, and Comingore should have concentrated on trying to keep busy by acting in a variety of projects and building up her name. Instead she turned down one movie after another and became known as a suspension queen.

> I'm sorry Dorothy Comingore, who showed such promise in *Citizen Kane*, is hindering her career by finding fault with every screen role the studio proposes.—Jimmie Fidler

Finally, in 1942, without making another movie, she and her difficult attitude were dropped by RKO. She insisted to Othman that there was a "great deal of prejudice against anyone who had worked in *Citizen Kane*. I don't know why, but there was." But, in fact,

Dorothy Comingore movingly enacts Susan Alexander's alcoholic decline in *Citizen Kane* (1941).

since that picture's release, some of its stars, including Joseph Cotten and Ruth Warrick, seemed to have no problems. In Comingore's case, she turned down every opportunity given her. She chose to remember that she lost out on the lead in *The Impostor* (1944) and, therefore, no one wanted her.

Freelancer Comingore finally followed up *Citizen Kane* with a supporting role in the 1944 indie *The Hairy Ape*. Brushing aside her mangled career, she joked to Robbin Coons about her absence: "My last picture? Well, there were five or six of them—all of which might be titled 'Suspension.'" Regarding *The Hairy Ape*, she told Coons, "I took this role without even reading the script. After all, one can't go wrong on Eugene O'Neill and this play."

Well, yes, you can. Robert D. Andrews and Decla Dunning's stagy, updated adaptation of O'Neill's tale of class conflict just didn't work for 1940s audience sensibilities. Susan Hayward, as a spoiled, manipulative socialite inciting a burly ship stoker (William Bendix), had the best, meatiest role, with Comingore supporting as a goodie goodie with no color or nuance. Critics were harsh, calling her performance amateurish. The *Dayton Daily News*' Audrey Stanfield said Comingore was "largely handicapped by a curious unfamiliarity with the profession to which she aspires—acting." Ouch.

After all the accolades she received from *Citizen Kane*, this was a comedown—a poor choice for a follow-up.

"Maybe I'll stay in pictures this time—though I'm retiring again for awhile after it, to have another baby," she told Coons. After the birth of her son Michael, no more movies were offered.

In France, on August 21, 1944, her first husband Robert Meltzer was killed in action. Three years after his death, the Writers Guild of America West created the Robert Meltzer Award, which, according to their website, "Honors one act of bravery by remembering another, recognizing an artist's singular act of courage in defense of freedom of expression and the rights of writers everywhere." In 1952, after the late Meltzer was posthumously named as a Communist before the House Un-American Activities Committee, his name was taken off the award. It would be reinstated in 1991.

By 1945, she and husband Collins had separated. That year she expressed some regret to columnist John L. Scott: "Certainly I want to act. Do you know anyone who wants to discover me again? I'm lots smarter than I was four years ago. I used to shoot off my mouth to certain big shots in movies. I'm still able to 'speak my piece' on occasion, but judiciously, my boy, judiciously." Her main interest was politics, and she told Scott, "I'll be glad to lecture you on politics, unions, strikes, [union leader] Harry Bridges...."

Throughout the 1940s, Comingore raised money for medical aid for our then-ally Russia; lectured about the need and value of Soviet-American relations and Russian culture; took part in a joint anti–Fascist refugee dinner; and spoke on how to remedy poor housing.

According to documents from the Federal Bureau of Investigation, wrote the *Los Angeles Review of Books'* Kathleen Sharp,

> Dorothy had landed on a government watch list for the crime of "distributing Communist literature to Negroes." It's true that Dorothy had canvassed Watts, stumping door to door for actor Albert Dekker, a state Assembly candidate. (He won.) And yes, she had worked with musician Lead Belly and singer Paul Robeson to try and desegregate whites-only USO clubs. (They succeeded.) And she had indeed urged voters, soldiers and Baptist teetotalers to support "union solidarity" whenever possible. At a time when Hollywood workers were organizing themselves, she became a marked woman.

All this would later come back to haunt her.

John Loder and Dorothy Comingore in a glamour shot from *The Hairy Ape* (1944).

From October 27 to November 17, 1945, she appeared in the Broadway flop *Beggars Are Coming to Town* with Paul Kelly and Luther Adler. (In 1947, it fared better as a movie, *I'll Walk Alone*.)

In 1946, she and Collins divorced and the following year she married writer Theodore Strauss. Her career was at a standstill, with the gossips insisting that Hearst was blocking her from working. More likely is that Comingore had alienated herself from Hollywood.

In 1949, she had a small

part in MGM's *Any Number Can Play* and began doing a little television work (*Fireside Theatre*, *Rebound* and *The Doctor*). In April 1951, her ex-husband Collins went before the House Un-American Activities Committee, said he had been a Communist, and named names. His act upset Dorothy very much. "I suddenly realized I was married to an informer," she told director Joseph Losey. "I felt like a collaborator after the liberation, and so I went out and had my hair shaved off." She had to wear a wig for her role in Losey's indie *The Big Night* (1951).

Her excellent performance in that film might have led to more screen opportunities, but during this period, her whole life came crashing down. In 1952, she divorced Strauss five months after giving birth to their son Peter. The year was about to get much worse. In October, Comingore had to fight two battles: She was called to testify before HUAC and she was taken to court by her ex Collins, who was attempting to wrest custody of their children from her; the kids had been living with him for the past two years but he wanted to make it official and restrict their exposure to Comingore.

Due in part to her actions in helping those less fortunate and for her lectures on Soviet relations, she was branded a Communist—and was named one by a friendly witness. Comingore's request to face her accuser was denied.

She was asked by HUAC committee Chief Counsel Frank Tavenner, "Were you a member of the Communist party?" Comingore replied, "I am counting to ten. I do that occasionally when I am angry."

She refused to say whether she was ever a Communist, but said that her father always taught her to fight for the Bill of Rights and then charged the committee with "making an organized effort toward another world war" and that they were "on the side of organized insanity and are conspiring to destroy my country and my people and my people's rights."

Again, she was asked if she was ever a member of the Communist party. "Don't you ever get bored with that question?" she asked.

Again: "Are you now a member of the Communist party?"

She responded, "You are cute."

Her alternately combative and flippant attitude did not go over well.

Collins brought up her HUAC issues at the custody trial, no doubt an attempt to cover up his failure to pay her thousands of dollars in alimony and child support. He accused her of a "long history of drinking," of threatening suicide, and of allowing the children to "associate with persons of doubtful loyalty."

Comingore's own loyalty to America was questioned and became the focal point of the custody trial. When Collins' lawyer asked, "Are you a member of the Communist party?," Comingore's attorney countered, "I feel this is so far outside the issues of this case that I am called upon to instruct her not to answer and I so instruct her." His protestations were overruled, and Comingore simply stated,

> My people have been in this country, they have helped settle this country—they helped to found New Amsterdam and to settle Kentucky. There has been a Comingore in every war since the beginning of this country. I believe and they believe in loyalty to this country in everyday life. I've lived a loyal life notwithstanding your presumptuous questions.

Near the end of the trial, she was asked if she had once said that HUAC had "entered into an organized conspiracy to destroy my country and my people and my people's rights." Comingore responded, "I said that." She then added that she loved America and resented anyone trying to impugn her honor as a loyal American. (*Guilty by Suspicion*, a 1991 movie about the Blacklist era, featured the Comingore-inspired character of a troubled actress hounded by the committee, and ultimately committing suicide.)

She then directed her words to her self-righteous ex: "I supported Mr. Collins. I bore Judith just two weeks after I finished work in a picture and was expecting Michael while I worked on another picture. Mr. Collins was pretty well ensconced on a couch himself—he was a hypochondriac who took extremely good care of himself." In the end, she lost custody of the children, but was able to get some of the back alimony owed her.

All the stress caused by HUAC, her custody battle, her inability to get acting jobs because of the Blacklist, and her drinking led to a nervous breakdown.

On March 19, 1953, while sitting in a Santa Monica bar, Comingore was arrested on a vice charge. The undercover vice officers claimed that the 40-year-old tried to "barter

Billed as Linda Winters, Comingore made her film debut in the indie *Prison Train* (1938).

her affection for $10" (*Los Angeles Times*) because she said she was a "little short of money right now." Comingore declared she was framed: According to her, they offered her a ride home, "then they stuck a marked $10 bill in my pocket and drove me downtown to the County Jail."

More than a week later, she was confined to the psychopathic ward of County General Hospital awaiting a hearing brought on by her ex, Theodore Strauss. He wanted her sent to a state hospital for her chronic alcoholism.

In May 1953, Strauss signed the commitment papers for her to enter Camarillo State Mental Hospital because of her physical and mental breakdowns and her drinking, which was done "often in a solitary fashion and frequently in the morning." Dr. Robert Litman said, "Life outside a hospital has become too complicated for her right now. With proper treatment, she may recover." The prostitution charges were dismissed at the end of June.

In the late 1950s, she was traveling by car with a boyfriend, enroute from Cape Cod to New York, when a snowstorm forced them to stop in Stonington Borough, Connecticut. At a bar, they met postal worker John Crowe. He didn't like the way Comingore was being treated by her companion, so Crowe asked the two to stay with him nearby, and then proceeded to get rid of the boyfriend. On May 7, 1962, Comingore married Crowe and lived the rest of her life with him in Stonington Borough.

Crowe was protective of Comingore because she had a lot of physical problems in her later years (from, reportedly, a broken back). However, she seemed to have found a peaceful haven with Crowe.

A 58-year-old Comingore died on December 30, 1971, of pulmonary disease at Lawrence Memorial Hospital in New London, Connecticut. She had also been suffering from cancer.

In 1991, her high school friend Millicent Niesen said of her, "She was a real victim. It was terrible what she went through. She lost custody of her children. She was an 'unfriendly' witness. But Dorothy was no phony. If she said something was so, it was so. She was the only person I knew in Hollywood. She had absolute integrity. That was the beautiful shining thing about her."

Dorothy Comingore Filmography

1938: *Campus Cinderella* (short, uncredited), *Prison Train, Comet Over Broadway, Trade Winds.*

1939: *Blondie Meets the Boss, North of the Yukon, Outside These Walls* (uncredited), *Good Girls Go to Paris* (uncredited), *Coast Guard* (uncredited), *Five Little Peppers and How They Grew* (uncredited), *Golden Boy* (uncredited), *Oily to Bed, Oily to Rise* (short, uncredited), *Scandal Sheet, Mr. Smith Goes to Washington* (uncredited), *The Awful Goof* (short).

1940: *Cafe Hostess, Convicted Woman* (uncredited), *Pioneers of the Frontier, The Heckler* (short, uncredited), *Rockin' Thru the Rockies* (short).

1941: *Citizen Kane.*

1944: *The Hairy Ape.*

1949: *Any Number Can Play.*

1951: *The Big Night.*

Patricia Dane

Many a pretty actress can quickly find their lives and careers derailed in Hollywood, whether by marriage to a celebrity, hard living, lack of ambition, or personal issues. Taking no chances, Patricia Dane guaranteed herself neverlasting stardom by hitting all four.

She was born Thelma Pearl Pippen in Blountstown, Florida, on August 4, 1918; her father died just after her birth, and she resided with her grandparents for a while. She was raised in Jacksonville, Florida, and Birmingham, Alabama. When her mother wed an insurance man, Thelma modified his surname of Burns and thereafter went by the name Thelma Byrnes and then Patricia Byrnes.

The 18-year-old was shopping in a Birmingham store when she was asked by salespeople if she had ever modeled. This started her on a modest modeling career. She studied dress design at the University of Alabama, but got restless and dropped out to go to New York. During this time, she claimed she was married to a Julian Lang of Rochester, New York, but there seems to be no record of this union; if it did happen, it was quickly dissolved.

The fun-loving, hard-drinking party girl made a splash with all the eligible males passing through New York City, including Errol Flynn, Bruce Cabot, James Stewart and Rudy Vallee. She also dated Franklin Delano Roosevelt, Jr., until she found out he was married. In October 1939, she changed her name to Patricia Dane on the advice of her "sponsor" Howard Hughes.

20th Century–Fox scout Ivan Kahn screen-tested her but, wrote Jimmie Fidler, Kahn would only give her a contract "if her one handicap can be overcome. Miss Dane looks

Patricia Dane, looking very Hedy Lamarr-ish, in one of her first MGM portrait sittings.

too much like Hedy Lamarr." Some handicap! Wrote Louella Parsons, "Everybody at the Bali thought Pat Dane, Rudy Vallee's girlfriend, looked just like Hedy Lamarr until Hedy herself walked in with Gene Markey."

In 1940, she was briefly with Warners without getting any screen time. "Somebody should tell pretty Patricia Dane, a stock girl at Warners, that her chances might be better if she would change her name to something that doesn't sound so much like Priscilla Lane," wrote Harold W. Cohen. It didn't matter since she didn't stay long under contract.

In late 1940, the dark-eyed beauty was cast in MGM's *Ziegfeld Girl*, starring Lana Turner, Hedy Lamarr and Judy Garland. Along with Myrna Dell and Jean Wallace, Dane was an uncredited showgirl. Because Lamarr was in the cast, Dane had to change her hairstyle: "The old part-in-the-middle-and-long-bob

Patricia Dane had her first substantial screen role as an "older woman" who practices her wiles on Mickey Rooney in *Life Begins for Andy Hardy* (1941).

coiffure was too much like Hedy Lamarr's," wrote Harrison Carroll.

Hedda Hopper reported that during the *Ziegfeld Girl* production, Dane was fired because she didn't come to the set on time; Harrison Carroll simply wrote there was "some kind of argument" and she was taken out of the "Minnie from Trinidad" number (and replaced by Claire James).

Then Metro turned around and gave her a term contract. Early on, it was implied that MGM was using Dane as a way to get a difficult Hedy Lamarr to behave; but it was doubtful Dane was "in line for some of her roles" as Sheilah Graham mentioned.

At first, the studio wanted to change her name to Sandra Sherwood, but this didn't happen. According to Louella Parsons, Louis B. Mayer said that with proper grooming, Dane could be a brunette Jean Harlow, although she fit more closely to the Lamarr mold. The studio gave her the (mercifully) short-lived tag "The Yoo-Hoo Girl."

Her first big role was *Life Begins for Andy Hardy* (1941); the series was considered a way to showcase MGM's up-and-coming actresses. Dane seemed to be more difficult (and habitually late) than the actress she was hired to keep in line. Sheilah Graham penned a rather unflattering account of Dane's attitude during the shoot, relating a problem she had with director George B. Seitz on how to play a scene until star Mickey Rooney intervened to sweet-talk Dane into it. Graham wrote, "I don't think Miss Dane is going to be an easy female for direction. She is the temperamental kind. For instance, she holds up shooting for 20 minutes because she insists on re-making up her face herself—something that a professional could have done in a few minutes." Graham concluded that to achieve success, Dane would "have to lose the self-satisfied expression that currently mars her pretty face."

The studio also felt she had to lose some pounds. "She and Hedy Lamarr are known as Metro's cream puff twins," wrote John Truesdell. "Both gals are pushovers for bonbons and pastries and consequently spend many unhappy hours together in the studio steam cabinets shucking off the pounds." In 1943, Dane was hospitalized as the "result of too many reducing pills" (Dorothy Kilgallen). Hugh Dixon went so far as to write that her reliance on dieting pills almost cost Dane her life.

Still, things were looking good and she made an impression vamping Rooney with her "uncouth Oomph," wrote Truesdell. "Pat is magnificent! She's big—she's voluptuous. She's sensuous and she's sweet." One problem he could foresee, acting-wise: "For some unaccountable reason this Southern belle picked up a strong Brooklyn accent, and that's one of the headaches her studio now faces. They're trying to strain the Brooklynese out of her sexy voice." (Her speech lessons are obvious in *Somewhere I'll Find You*, but Dane was never able to completely rid herself of her accent.)

She followed the Hardy movie with a small but nice part as Robert Taylor's moll in *Johnny Eager* (1941) and a sultry supporting one vamping for the Nazis in Abbott and Costello's 1942 updating of the musical *Rio Rita*. One of the highlights during this time: her second-billed part in the B *Grand Central Murder* (1942) as a nasty, temperamental actress who becomes a murder victim. She was given her only leading lady assignment in *Northwest Rangers* (1942), a remake of the studio's earlier *Manhattan Melodrama* (1934).

Dane was well-liked at MGM for her ribald sense of humor, tough but sweet demeanor, and I-don't-care approach to her life and career. Reportedly, MGM producer Harry Rapf got on her case one day when she was late to the set. "Do you know that your absence has cost this company at least $20,000?" To which Dane retorted, "And your being here on time has cost this company twice that amount." Hedda Hopper, who reported this incident, added, "That's tellin' 'em."

Dane was seen out with a

Dane reclining in a chair.

variety of men and was supposedly engaged to art director Cedric Gibbons and director Anatole Litvak. Just after finishing a supporting part in Red Skelton's *I Dood It*, Dane visited the set of *Girl Crazy* (1943) and met bandleader Tommy Dorsey, who had a role in the movie. Weeks later, on April 8, 1943, Dane, 24, married the 37-year-old Dorsey. He did not want his new bride to work and she did not.

She was still under contract to MGM and projects were announced for her, including *Between Two Women* (1945), but she did not go against Dorsey's edict. The Dorsey-Dane union was tempestuous from the start. Both were big drinkers with terrible tempers and they often fought, most times in public. Dane laughingly referred to herself and Tommy as "the new Battling Bogarts."

They also shared a wild side. Dorsey reveled in Dane's exhibitionism and encouraged it. He loved that she would flash her breasts to his band members, his friends, or to whomever was passing by—Dorsey was proud of what he called "the greatest tits in town." Spectators were also treated to the sight of the panties-less Dane exposing herself at her husband's urging; she had shaved Dorsey's initials into her pubic hair.

Years before, she had dated Tommy's bandleader brother Jimmy, so there was some

drama there. On one occasion at the Indianapolis Theater, Jimmy was presenting a birthday cake to Tommy when Jimmy suddenly shoved the cake into Dane's face. What resulted was one of the brothers' famous fistfights.

But that was nothing compared to what went down on August 5, 1944. Dane was at the center of a "battle royal" at a party at the Dorseys' apartment. It all started when actor Jon Hall danced with her and then "jokingly" put his arms around her shoulders. (Or, as one report put it, "he began admiring Miss Dane's contours Braille style.") Giving new meaning to his nickname of the Sentimental Gentleman of Swing, Dorsey delivered an uppercut to Hall's jaw.

The ensuing alcohol-fueled melee left Hall with part of his nose missing, a

Patricia Dane had her one and only leading lady assignment in *Northwest Rangers* (1942) with William Lundigan.

concussion, a head wound requiring 32 stitches, and a stab wound under his chin. Hall wanted to "forgive and forget," but D.A. Fred N. Howser brought the case to the grand jury; Dorsey, Dane and their friend, gambler Allen Smiley, were charged with felonious assault against Hall. Panamanian actor-sailor Antonio Icaza got into the act and claimed that his ear had been cut with a bottle, and he brought a $40,000 suit against Dorsey.

The eight-day trial was one of hazy, differing recollections of that night. It was claimed that Dorsey and Smiley took turns beating up Hall. Dane reportedly did the most damage: Icaza alleged that she came at Hall with a kitchen knife "and smacked his nose with it."

It was also reported that another partygoer, actor Edward Norris, was kicked in the face by Dane as he was lying on the floor. Norris' date, Jane Churchill (reportedly the third cousin of Winston Churchill), was also involved in a mini-scuffle with Dane: The women ripped each other's dresses off and Churchill claimed that Pat "pulled three patches of hair out of my head the size of quarters."

On December 7, 1944, the charges against Dorsey, Dane and Smiley were dismissed, bringing to an end what reporters called "the screwiest hodgepodge of jurisprudence this city has ever seen." The trial featured wildly conflicting testimonies, the stories varying as much as "the shades of purple and green surrounding the eyes of most of the participants" (United Press). The question of who cut off Hall's nose was never answered satisfactorily. Icaza turned out to be the biggest loser: He was jailed on suspicion of perjury and later deported. The judge called him a "fabulous, masterful fabricator of falsehoods, a perjurer

Patricia Dane as gangster Robert Taylor's moll in *Johnny Eager* (1941).

pure and simple, demonstrated innumerable times out of his own mouth.... He told so many stories that even the prosecution tossed in the sponge."

The Dorsey marriage bumped along, with reports here and there of an impending separation. Finally, on August 26, 1947, Dane filed for divorce, citing Dorsey's constant traveling with his band as the main factor. She said she was tired of sitting in dressing rooms. Their parting was extremely friendly; Pat refused alimony, so Tommy gave her a new Cadillac and a settlement of a quarter of a million dollars.

"From now on, it's going to be a film career for me," she told John Todd. "I interrupted my career once—but now I'm going to concentrate on it. I can't guess, of course, what the future holds for me. But I've learned the fun of living is not knowing what tomorrow will bring." What came through for her were two siren supporting parts in *Joe Palooka in Fighting Mad* and *Are You with It?* (both 1948).

Patricia Dane with her then-husband, bandleader Tommy Dorsey (in costume for *Broadway Rhythm*), on the MGM lot in August 1943.

For months it was understood that Dane and Dorsey were headed for a reconciliation, but on March 27, 1948, Dorsey wed 24-year-old nightclub dancer Jane New. Dane told the press, "Tommy's mother called me with the news. It is a big shock. I have been talking to Tommy almost every night. He was supposed to fly out here Monday. I'm hurt that he didn't let me in on the secret, but I suppose it's just one of those things." (She and Dorsey would continue to see each other for years.)

On the night of October 22, 1948, Dane met actor Robert Walker at a private party and they later went to a bar to have a few drinks. Dane was at the wheel of Walker's 1949 Cadillac, "driving erratically" and on the wrong side of the road, when police officers closed in. The cops chased them for three blocks before forcing Dane to stop. Police claimed the two were "drunk, noisy, loud and boisterous." Walker, who resisted arrest and had to be forcibly subdued, reportedly told one of the officers, "I've been drunk for 25 years, but this lady [Dane] is certainly not drunk. Heck no; she could drink this whole jail full of liquor and never get drunk." Dane pled guilty to a drunk-driving charge and was fined $150. Her "escapade" with Walker resulted in a broken engagement with wealthy Carl Larson.

In 1950, with acting work hard to come by, Dane appeared in burlesque. Lana Turner, a friend from her MGM days, requested that Dane be cast in *A Life of Her Own* (1950), but Pat foolishly turned it down as being too small a part. A comeback in a major supporting role in Hope and Crosby's *Road to Bali* (1952) turned out to be an uncredited one as a handmaiden. She also acted on local Los Angeles television and nationally on *Fireside Theatre* and *The Lone Wolf*.

In the early '50s, she was involved with writer Bill Morrow, who was associated with Bing Crosby on television. It was frequently reported that he and Dane were either on the verge or secretly wed. In March 1951, Dane underwent unspecified major surgery. It was the start of a period of illness for the struggling actress.

In *The Harder They Fall* (1956), Dane was seen fleetingly as a party girl Rod Steiger tries to introduce to Humphrey Bogart. When Bogie doesn't want her, Steiger starts making out with her. This uncredited, no-dialogue part was Dane's last on film.

On November 26, 1956, a month after Tommy Dorsey's wife Jane filed for divorce, the bandleader died suddenly after choking in his sleep. To Dane's surprise, Dorsey had left her a $26,000 insurance policy. "It's a sad way to get money," Dane said, "but I admit it will be a great help to me." Two days before his death, he had canceled a $100,000 policy meant for his estranged wife.

Three years later, Dorsey's widow brought a judgment against Dane in the amount of $6347, her share of the estate's inheritance tax. At that time, Dane testified in court that she was broke and had spent most of the money Dorsey had left her. She claimed she had suffered foot and leg injuries in a 1956 boating accident that left her unable to work.

In the early 1970s, Dane moved to Blountstown, Florida, to be near her recently widowed mother. She spent the rest of her life working as a librarian at the Calhoun County Public Library and at the local courthouse. Her mother died in 1976.

In 1988, the *Tallahassee Democrat Sun*'s Andy Lindstrom interviewed Dane, who was living in her late mother's house and spending "her evenings alone, reading Taylor Caldwell novels…. She wears bifocals now. But her hair is still 'electric brunette,' as a Hollywood gossip columnist once described it. Her throaty voice and feisty ways still turn heads." She still wore a ring Dorsey had given her, a 25-carat diamond with the initials

T.D. on it. "I was something back then," she chuckled, looking at a photo of herself in her heyday. "But I was stubborn, too. That's why I don't own the world."

A 76-year-old Dane died on June 5, 1995, of lung cancer in Blountstown. At the local Pine Memorial Cemetery, her headstone reads: "Thelma Pippen Byrnes (Mrs. Tommy Dorsey)."

Asked by Lindstrom if she had any regrets, Dane responded, "Sure, a few. But you try to think of all the good times, right? And I had a lot of those."

Patricia Dane Filmography

1941: *Ziegfeld Girl* (uncredited), *I'll Wait for You* (uncredited), *Life Begins for Andy Hardy*, *Johnny Eager*.
1942: *Rio Rita, Grand Central Murder, Somewhere I'll Find You, Northwest Rangers, Personalities* (short, uncredited).
1943: *I Dood It.*
1948: *Joe Palooka in Fighting Mad, Are You with It?*
1952: *Road to Bali* (uncredited).
1956: *The Harder They Fall* (uncredited).

Dorothy Dell

In 1934, Dorothy Dell was an up-and-comer, one of Hollywood's most promising rookies. She had been a hit on Broadway and was now taking the movies by storm with her natural screen presence and lovely contralto voice. Paramount gave her leads right off the bat and had bigger plans for the 20-year-old. Her story was one of the saddest what-might-have-beens in show business.

Born Dorothy Dell Goff on January 30, 1914, in Hattiesburg, Mississippi, she was the first of two daughters to a lumber man. She was about a year old when she won her first beauty contest. (Her sister Helen was born in 1915, the year often attributed to Dorothy.) In 1925, the family moved to New Orleans and she began acting in school productions. Her mother later told Robbin Coons,

"She has something emotionally moving in her countenance and is handicapped at present by what producers consider a resemblance to Mae West," wrote Mollie Merrick about Dorothy Dell (courtesy C. Robert Rotter/Glamour Girls of the Silver Screen).

> Since Dorothy was a little baby, she's had her heart set on being an actress. If it had been something else she wanted to do, I'd have encouraged her in that, too. I knew she wanted to be an actress. She was just a tiny tyke when I found her one day "acting" in front of a mirror. After she saw Valentino in *The Sheik*, she and [her sister] Helen enacted it at home. Dorothy, with a sheet wound around her head, played the sheik, and abducted Helen, who was Agnes Ayres.

Organist Wesley Lord got her an engagement at the Saenger Theatre, where she sang his composition "Louisiana Moon." This resulted in her singing over the radio.

Her mother said, "I had hoped Dorothy would go through college, and possibly teach, or to follow her early inclination to study to be a trained nurse."

Instead, in 1930, titled Miss New Orleans and Miss United States of America (there was no Miss America that year), Dorothy was sponsored by the American Legion to compete at the International Pageant of Pulchritude in Galveston, Texas. She was named Beauty Queen of the Universe, aka Miss Universe (not the same-name pageant that started in the '50s). "Of course, I have a career in mind," she told reporters. "I am going to be a real, honest-to-goodness actress like Marie Dressler." Such ambitions, however, had to wait.

She turned down offers from Florenz Ziegfeld, Earl Carroll and George White because they would not take her sister Helen and best friend Dorothy Slaton (aka Lamour). Fanchon and Marco signed all three and they were featured in the revue *American Beauty*. (Helen later acted on the stage and was a band vocalist with Gus Arnheim.)

Dorothy then went into the headed-for-Broadway musical *Making Mary* (1931). Karl Krug wrote that she "strolls in and out of the proceedings without accomplishing much in the way of anything except an alluring exhibit of her own personal charms. They are, as you may have suspected, considerable." The show never reached New York.

Warner Brothers signed her, but instead of giving her roles, they had her make personal appearances (billed as Dorothy Dell Goff). Then they let her go. Cast in *Ziegfeld Follies of 1931*, which opened on July 1, 1931, she dropped Goff from her name. Writer Alice Denhoff praised Ziegfeld's choice of the "plumply pleasing" Dorothy and his desire to move away from the "disingenuously gaunt figures of 1929 or 1930. Instead, we see a refresh-ing roundness, a softness of con-tour, a peaches-and-cream, satiny smoothness and softness." There were those who dismissed Doro-thy as just another beauty contest winner. Then, wrote Shreveport, Louisiana, society columnist Mrs. Benjamin Gray, Dorothy "stood up on the night the Follies opened and, to a tune, inquired, 'Was I drunk?' ... [Her naysayers] re-canted. A beauty prize winner [had] made good." Everyone talked about Dorothy's big number, Chick Endor and Charles Farrell's now-classic "Was I Drunk?" During the *Follies* run, Dorothy's idol, sing-ing star Ruth Etting, became sick so Dorothy filled in for her in addition to playing her own part.

At this time, Dorothy began dating crooner Russ Columbo. In November 1931, Louis Sobol re-ported that one night the twosome started to elope "but changed their minds when Columbo's car

A fashion portrait of Dorothy (courtesy C. Robert Rotter/Glamour Girls of the Silver Screen).

stalled." Also stalling was their romance, cut short by Columbo's disapproving manager Con Conrad.

After the *Follies* closed on Broadway on November 21, the troupe began a five-month road tour. After this, Dorothy sang on radio with Rudy Vallee, helped film newcomer Dick Powell with his screen test at Brooklyn's Vitaphone Studios, and sang in nightclubs.

Her screen bow came in the filmed-in-New York Warner Bros. Vitaphone short *Passing the Buck* (1932). She had a broken arm (presumably from a June '32 car accident) and, before she went before the cameras, she "removed her plaster cast, which was tied to her arm with bandages, and went through her number in grand style" (*The Film Daily*).

In September '32, Walter Winchell dropped a bit of odd news: "Dorothy Dell denies that she is secretly sealed to M. Durso. Of course!!! ... The story as told by her to intimates says it happened June 10 at Greenwich under her real tag, Goff.... They parted after the ceremony, it appears." The "Is You Is or Is You Ain't" groom was bandleader-trumpet player Mike Durso. There were denials all around and soon Durso was engaged to a Broadway showgirl.

Dorothy was heard over the airwaves and was in the short-lived (June 1933) Frank Fay revue *Tattle Tales*. Not long after this, she was signed to a Paramount contract. Some called her "the second coming of Mae West," whom she slightly resembled. "Almost

"I didn't think I had a chance, because I'm a little too plumpish. Due to the [Mae] West influence, thank goodness, a few 'curves' don't make any difference anymore." Dorothy at the beach (courtesy C. Robert Rotter/Glamour Girls of the Silver Screen).

every girl in the world, including myself, dreams about getting into the movies," Dorothy told Hubbard Keavy. "I didn't think I had a chance, because I'm a little too plumpish. Due to the West influence, thank goodness, a few 'curves' don't make any difference anymore."

The consensus on *Wharf Angel* (1934), her Paramount debut, was that it was fairly routine, but critics were bowled over by its leading lady. She plays a waterfront tart with a heart of gold, fought over by two guys (Preston Foster and Victor McLaglen). Dell showed remarkable ease and a worldliness beyond her years. Her one song was Robin and Rainger's "Down Home." Mollie Merrick found Dorothy to be

[s]omewhat different in type from the conventional over-slenderized movie girl.... [She] is not the conventional beauty either. She has something emotionally moving in her countenance and is handicapped at present by what producers consider a resemblance to Mae West. The costumes of the picture emphasized this in the early part of the film but the girl developed her own personality as the story moved on and threw an emotional

verve into it which bodes well for her future career.

Paramount knew they had something special and cast her in *Little Miss Marker* (1934) as the slightly rough-edged but warm Bangles Carson (great name), who sings Robin and Rainger's "I'm a Black Sheep Who's Blue," "Low Down Lullaby" and "Laugh You Son of a Gun," the latter with star Shirley Temple. Temple later remembered that a scene was interrupted by Dorothy's "unrehearsed giggles…. We held hands, enjoying the sense of impromptu gaiety…. Time and again during the film she turned out to be a splendid foil for my

Dorothy gazes at the camera in this glamour shot (courtesy C. Robert Rotter/Glamour Girls of the Silver Screen).

energy and exuberance. My special affection for her was based on this positive attitude, one which made me feel inches taller than I was."

Dorothy and Jack Oakie starred in *Shoot the Works* (1934), notable for her singing of Harry Revel and Mack Gordon's "With My Eyes Wide Open I'm Dreaming." The studio had her penciled in for leads in *The Lemon Drop Kid* and *College Rhythm.*

After *Shoot the Works* wrapped, Dell went to two funerals: Lilyan Tashman and *Shoot the Works* cast member Lew Cody. She was later heard to remark, "I wonder who'll be next?" referring to the superstition that Hollywood deaths come in threes.

At the time, she was engaged to artist Nat Carson and planning to travel to London for a six-month honeymoon. On the night of June 7, 1934, she and family friend Dr. Carl Wagner went dancing at the Marcell Inn in Altadena. Sometime after one a.m., as Wagner was driving her home, they were attempting a tricky curve at Lincoln Avenue in Pasadena. The speeding car's tires hit the curb and they skidded off the road. According to one news report, the vehicle took "one of the most remarkable freak arcs ever recorded in an accident": It struck a boulder, from there bouncing into two light poles and a palm tree before overturning. The car became "an unrecognizable mess of twisted steel—a sickening, ghastly wreck" (*Salt Lake Tribune*). Twenty-year-old Dorothy was killed instantly. Thrown out of the car, Wagner smashed his head against the asphalt paving; six hours later he died at a nearby hospital without regaining full consciousness.

Six-year-old Shirley Temple was working on *Now and Forever* when news came to her about Dorothy's death and she became hysterical. She recalled later that the director took advantage of this by shooting a crying scene. Temple was praised for her "performance," but she remarked, "Only I knew it was more fun to shed fake tears than real ones."

At Dorothy's Hollywood memorial service, friend Ruth Etting sang "The Rosary." The funeral was attended mostly by friends, with only Etting and co-star Jack Oakie representing Hollywood. Hundreds of onlookers waited outside the church.

Dell's body was flown to New Orleans, where thousands lined the streets to get a look at her casket. Her remains were escorted by the American Legion and police to Metairie Cemetery where she was interred. *Shoot the Works* premiered at the end of June.

In 1936, AP ran a story called "Stars Avoid Disaster Hall As Unlucky Movie Omen":

Dressing Room No. 101, the "Disaster Hall" in makeup row at Paramount Studios, is still untenanted today.

No. 101 is the most sumptuous of all the dressing rooms in the row, but neither Gladys Swarthout nor Irene Dunne, to whom it was offered recently, would move into it.

It has a bad history and they know it.

No. 101 was built, some years ago, for Pola Negri and furnished to her taste. It is richly appointed and larger than any other cubicles where the stars make up. But shortly after Miss Negri moved in, she was stricken with a serious illness and eventually left the studio. Clara Bow was the next occupant of 101. Her retirement came soon after she moved in, along with illness and a plethora of lawsuits.

Sylvia Sidney, who followed her, escaped serious trouble, but did have a few minor difficulties during her occupancy.

The last person in 101 was the beautiful Dorothy Dell, who ... lost her life in an automobile accident several years ago.

So Miss Swarthout and Miss Dunne separately declined, with thanks, when offered "Disaster Hall."

In 1940, Dorothy Lamour, who always credited Dorothy Dell with helping her get her big break in the early 1930s, tried to repay the favor: She took Dell's sister Helen as her protégée and sought to get her into movies. The younger Dell never made it, and she retired from show biz for marriage. Tragedy revisited the family in 1942 when Helen's

Preston Foster and Victor McLaglen (*right*) fight for Dorothy's affections in *Wharf Angel* (1934).

Bangles Carson (Dorothy Dell) and Sorrowful Jones (Adolphe Menjou) look on in concern as Martha Jane (Shirley Temple) has met with an accident in *Little Miss Marker* (1934).

five-day-old daughter, to be christened Dorothy, died. Helen died at age 54 in 1970; one of the contributing factors was, according to her death certificate, "probable cirrhosis."

Dorothy Dell Filmography

1932: *Passing the Buck* (short).
1934: *Wharf Angel, Little Miss Marker, Shoot the Works.*

Sidney Fox

In Bette Davis biographies, Sidney Fox seems to be portrayed as someone thwarting Davis' early career. Although Bette eventually nabbed two Oscars and achieved the type of stardom which would elude Fox, she still had bitter feelings in Whitney Stine's 1974 biography *Mother Goddam*: "Pretty obvious, the relationship between studio head and actress [was the] real reason I did not get *Strictly Dishonorable* [1931]. Miss Fox was *not* right for the part."

Davis' (and others') assumption about Fox and Universal production chief Carl Laemmle, Jr., has tainted Sidney's reputation among film historians, who have added that she was *maybe* also carrying on with Carl Sr. Nothing of the sort has been proven. Universal producer Stanley Bergerman told author Rick Atkins that rumors of romantic involvement between Sidney and Carl Jr. were "far from the truth. The only thing that she and Junior had between them was kindness and talent."

Whatever the true nature of the Fox-Laemmle relationship, it has successfully obscured her career achievements. In 1931, she and Bette Davis were at the same point in their acting careers and it almost looked as if Sidney would pull ahead. But personal troubles and health issues contributed to Sidney's undoing.

Of Russian-Jewish descent, she was born Sarah Sidney Leifer on December 10, 1907, in (according to census records) Austria; she used the nickname Sadie during her early years. She was about four years old when the family immigrated to New York. Her parents divorced not long afterwards. In 1917, the ex–Mrs. Leifer married a man named Joseph Fox, and Sidney took her stepfather's surname. The family lived in New York and then New Jersey.

According to Sidney's publicity, "An untoward event in her family [Mr. Fox los-

A winsome 1932 portrait of Sidney Fox (courtesy John Antosiewicz).

ing all his money] made it necessary for Sidney, at the age of 13, to earn her own living." The teenager worked as a stenographer, wrote a fashion and/or advice to the lovelorn column, modeled clothes, and supposedly studied law for one semester of night classes at Columbia University.

The acting bug bit and she look drama lessons from Louise Gifford (who also coached Sylvia Sidney, Bette Davis, Marguerite Churchill and Martha Sleeper). This led to her briefly finding a place in John Martin's Johnstown, Pennsylvania, stock company, appearing in the plays *The Big Pond*, *Wedding Bells* and *The Ghost Train*.

Sidney made her Broadway bow in *It Never Rains* (1929), which had a six-month run. This was followed by the comedy *Lost Sheep* (1930). "The first night audience liked, rather

Behind the scenes of *Murders in the Rue Morgue* (1932) with (*standing, left to right*) director Robert Florey, Bela Lugosi, Noble Johnson and (*in foreground*) Sidney Fox and cinematographer Karl Freund (courtesy John Antosiewicz).

better than the play, the work of Sidney Fox," wrote Deming Seymour. "In *Lost Sheep* she achieved for the first time what might be termed a triumph … and she was quite overcome by it. She wept a little as she kept answering curtain calls, and the audience found itself feeling a little sorry that such a sweet child should be the victim of such a sordid misunderstanding as the playwright created around her." The *New York Times* praised her "frail, girlish beauty and her pert spirit. Nothing could be more tenderly disarming than the freshness of her acting."

After Carl Laemmle, Jr., saw a performance, the *Los Angeles Times* reported in June 1930 that Fox was not only signed to a Universal contract, but assigned the lead in director Rupert Julian's *The Cat Creeps*. Julian was quoted by the *Times* as saying that Sidney was "another Mary Pickford, with a glow of humor and mischief, but with large emotional powers also." But the cat crept without her: Fox had a run-of-the-play contract with *Lost Sheep* and continued to act in it on Broadway and then in Chicago.

By November 1930, the official word was that Fox was a Universal contract player. "We expect to star or co-star Miss Fox in a number of important productions," Carl Jr. said. She film-debuted in the title role in *The Bad Sister* (1931), a film notable for being Bette Davis' first movie. Sidney was loaned out to Fox to co-star with Spencer Tracy in *6 Cylinder Love* (1931). "Sidney Fox continues to get unfavorable casting breaks in pictures," wrote *Variety*'s Ruth Morris. "She made her debut as the horrible little wretch in *Bad Sister*, but may now be seen as the selfish, whining silly of *6 Cylinder Love*. She plays the part excellently, too well to make audiences remember that, as a baby-talking social climber, she is merely meeting the demands of direction and script."

Many fans feel that Fox had her best role as a naïve Southern girl who falls in love with a womanizing opera singer (Paul Lukas) in *Strictly Dishonorable* (1931). "Perhaps Miss Sidney Fox's dress belies the ingenuousness of the nature of Isabelle Parry, the character she interprets," wrote the *New York Times*' Mordaunt Hall. "But that is but a minor shortcoming considering the sincerity Miss Fox delivers to her part. Her pleasing Southern drawl and her tenderness are charming." Bette Davis wanted the part but the simple character better suited Fox.

In 1931, Fox was named one of the WAMPAS Baby Stars. Others in the impressive group: Joan Blondell, Frances Dee, Constance Cummings, Frances Dade, Rochelle Hudson, Anita Louise, Joan Marsh, Marian Marsh, Karen Morley, Marion Shilling, Barbara Weeks and Judith Wood.

Davis was up for another part that

Fox in a fashion portrait.

went to Fox: Mlle. Camille L'Espanaye in the Universal Horror *Murders in the Rue Morgue* (1932). It's Fox's best-known movie, but in it she gives what many consider her worst performance. In 1932, better roles came in the less well-known *The Mouthpiece* (made on loan to WB), *Once in a Lifetime* and *Afraid to Talk*.

On May 10, 1932, Sidney was backing her car out of her garage when she lost control. She rolled off a 40-foot embankment and "after a somersault in the air, landed in a tree." Pulled from the wrecked car by a milk truck driver, she suffered cuts, bruises and shock.

Universal loaned her to European producers for G.W. Pabst's *Don Quixote* and the Emil Jannings vehicle *Die Abenteuer des Königs Pausole*. In November '32, she was back in the U.S., but out at Universal: Her contract was allowed to lapse.

On December 14, 1932, Sidney eloped to Harrison, New York, with Universal's New York story editor Charles Beahan. She and her husband spent most of their time in New York. It was here that she made her first movie since leaving Universal, the indie *Midnight* (1934)—ultimately released by Universal. *Variety*'s Cecelia Ager thought the role brought a "new sincerity and now and then a touch of heartbreak…. Sidney Fox comes back in *Midnight* a better, sweeter, even tolerable little girl Her tendency to precociousness deftly reined by direction, she gives a straightforward performance…."

While some felt she had improved as an actress, Fox asserted that she was in retirement due to her marriage. Her husband had joined Columbia as a producer and the

Sidney Fox and Jack Oakie co-starred in the comedy *Once in a Lifetime* (1932).

studio waved a contract in front of Fox as well, with the possibility of them working together. She turned them down. "I'd rather he used some other leading lady for his first picture," she told Grace Kingsley. "I have other offers; only I want to select the role. I got tired of playing parts I didn't like under contract." Yet she made no movies at this time. Other sources claim she nixed the Columbia offer because she was set to star in Beahan's play *Dearly Beloved*—but that project was delayed.

On their one-year anniversary, the Beahans remarried in a church wedding. Columnist Rian James alleged the act wasn't "nearly so much a matter of sentiment as it was of stilling a flood of persistent rumors to the effect that their romance was on the rocks." James also asserted that Beahan "nearly socked a local scribe in the eye" for suggesting marital trouble.

A few days after the marriage

(*Left to right*): **Sidney Fox, Lew Ayres, Boris Karloff and Genevieve Tobin in** *The Cohens and Kellys in Hollywood* **(1932) (courtesy Greg Mank).**

ceremony, Louella Parsons reported that Fox was "recovering from a serious illness." This would become a regular occurrence, although no details were ever given. Columbia wanted her for their picturization of Jane Austen's *Pride and Prejudice*, to be produced by her husband, but this project fell by the wayside.

On New Year's Eve, 1933, the couple had a fight at a party; Fox ended up going home with Ann Dvorak and her husband Leslie Fenton. Days later, she announced she was filing for divorce. The Beahans reconciled on February 4, 1934.

That month, Sidney talked to Alma Whitaker about her career, saying she "was not happy when she first came to Universal," and that she had been "afraid of pictures and afraid of expert competition. [After studying acting with Frances Robinson-Duff], I came back better equipped for my work in every way and I mean to be a first-class actress. I want to be as good as Hepburn in *Morning Glory*, which I have seen four times." She had just been signed to appear in RKO's *Down to Their Last Yacht* (1934), which she bragged had been written specially for her. "I had many offers last year, but Charles made me turn them all down because they were not good enough."

Before she started filming *Yacht*, there were more marital dust-ups. Fox alleged that Beahan "celebrated the reconciliation by beating her" and she responded by again filing for divorce. According to Fox, he drank excessively, and choked, struck and cursed her; married life was "one abuse after another." (Making this even more disturbing: Sidney was 4'11" and 94 pounds; her husband tipped the scales at 250.) By the end of February '34,

Sidney had withdrawn her divorce, but she picked it up again the following month. She added to her list of complaints that he stopped her from "following her profession."

Most of 1934 was taken up by matrimonial break-ups and make-ups and lawsuits filed against them ($150 doctor bill, $176.67 hotel bill, $67 flower bill). She was awarded a divorce in April '34 after stating, "He had a most terrible temper. I was afraid to go near him most of the time. He would insult me and call me horrible names." By May, all was forgiven. "It's permanent, for the time being," she remarked. The couple did not get good press with their marriage-go-round adventures. In Ed Sullivan's June '34 column, he made the odd remark, "[They] didn't reconcile until she pledged to stay away from roulette tables."

It didn't take a genius to figure out that Fox's movie promise had ended with her marriage. *Down to Their Last Yacht* (RKO's biggest flop up to that time) and *School for Girls* (filmed in June '34, released '35) were her last motion pictures. (In 1941, the *Elmira Star-Gazette* wrote that *Yacht* "should never be mentioned in her presence.")

In 1935, Fox played a week-long stage engagement in Long Beach in the play *The Pursuit of Happiness* and was featured in a vaudeville sketch at the Orpheum Theatre in New York. In July '35 it was reported that she would co-star with Frank Parker in the musical *Sweet Surrender*, which Beahan had adapted for the screen. In August, she was out of the picture due to illness and was replaced by Tamara. Walter Winchell claimed that Fox told him she wasn't sick at all but had been fired.

Sidney Fox is a jury foreman's daughter who confesses to the murder of her lover, gangster Humphrey Bogart, in *Midnight* (1934).

Nineteen thirty-six started promisingly with the announcement that she was a serious contender for the role of Lotus in MGM's *The Good Earth* (1937), but this was not to be. She had a major operation and spent four months in bed, during which time she insisted she had grown three quarters of an inch in height. "I suppose the growth is now at an end," Jimmie Fidler wrote, in all seriousness, "but I could not fail to see the half-bewildered, half-frightened light in Sidney's eyes as she told me her story."

On December 2, 1936, her 58-year-old father Jacob died alone as a charity patient at City Hospital in Buffalo, New York. His death was a result of stomach ulcers (and complications which developed) while he was laboring with a Works Progress Administration gang. Sidney had last seen him ten years previous, but occasionally had sent him money as he had fallen on hard times. "He was rather inclined to be proud," his friend Nicky told the *New York Daily News*. "He didn't want his daughter to know he was in need. In fact, if he could have gotten along without it, I don't think he'd accept aid from her." Fox paid for his burial.

In 1937, she was back on Broadway in *The Masque of Kings* (replacing Margo) and *Having Wonderful Time* (taking over for Katherine Locke). The *Harrisburg Telegraph*, reviewing the latter, said she "reminds of Janet Gaynor, but is much prettier." She was unable to appear in her husband's long-awaited play *Dearly Beloved* when it was finally staged at Maine's Ogunquit Playhouse. Fox ultimately had to leave *Having Wonderful Time* because of illness.

She spent the summer of 1938 doing *Yes, My Darling Daughter* in Matunuck, Rhode Island, and *Coquette* in Great Neck, Long Island, New York. The following year, she tested unsuccessfully at two studios for contracts. There was some radio and tests for the movies, but "delicate and high-strung" (Gladys Glad) Fox was sick with an unspecified illness and didn't resume her movie career.

In October 1940, she told reporters she would be "filing a new suit for divorce right away. This time the decree will become final. At last I know we can't make a go of it." But yet again, she and Beahan made up.

A year later, she visited relatives in Elmira, New York. She told an *Elmira Star-Gazette* reporter that she was headed for New York City to talk to play producers. She was "superstitious" about revealing her plans but revealed that the Shuberts "had promised to produce a play with herself as one of the stars if she'd get her husband to write it." Stressing that she wanted to work, Fox remarked, "Right now I've a terrific yearning to do a play and, believe me, if I don't find one, we'll write one." No plays were forthcoming.

Tests for parts in the movies *That Uncertain Feeling* (1941) and *Street of Chance* (1942) were unsuccessful.

On November 14, 1942, the couple had friends over to their Beverly Hills home. After they left, Sidney suggested to her husband that they go out dancing, but due to her declining health, he persuaded her to go to sleep. She and Beahan retired to their respective bedrooms, and the following morning, he found his 34-year-old spouse dead in bed with an empty prescription bottle nearby. The coroner was unable to determine if her death was a suicide or if her ingestion of sleeping pills had been accidental. Beahan said that Fox had been in "good spirits," although her health was poor.

Fox is buried in Mt. Lebanon Cemetery, in Queens, New York. Her grave marker, in English and Hebrew, reads "Our Beloved Daughter."

Sidney Fox Filmography

1931: *The Bad Sister, 6 Cylinder Love, Nice Women, Strictly Dishonorable.*
1932: *Murders in the Rue Morgue, The Cohens and Kellys in Hollywood, The Mouthpiece, Once in a Lifetime, Afraid to Talk.*
1933: *Don Quixote, The Merry Monarch, Die Abenteuer des Königs Pausole.*
1934: *Midnight, Down to Their Last Yacht.*
1935: *School for Girls.*

Charlotte Henry

"Charlotte to me doesn't seem to be acting at all, but to be what she's supposed to be—an imaginative child delightfully bewildered in her dream," the *Pittsburgh Press*' Kaspar Monahan wrote about Charlotte Henry's performance in *Alice in Wonderland* (1933). "And what a find has Paramount in this naive and charming Charlotte Henry. This child should go far—and she deserves to.... For here is Alice as you have pictured her. An Alice wafting through her fantastic dream world, just as your imagination told you she would."

Charlotte perhaps did her job too well. She was so good as Alice that she became identified with the role and could never shake her star making portrayal.

She was born Charlotte Virginia Henry on March 3, 1914, in Brooklyn, and for a while received her education in a convent. She took up modeling and became interested in acting, appearing in school plays. By 1927, her parents had divorced and Charlotte lived with her mother and grandmother. (Her father remarried and had a son.)

At the age of 14, Charlotte was cast in the Broadway show *Courage* (1928–29) with Junior Durkin. After it closed, she and her mother moved to Hollywood, where Charlotte film-debuted in *Harmony at Home* (1930) and then reprised her Broadway role in the 1930 screen version of *Courage*. She returned to New York to do the play *Hobo* (1931), but then it was back to Hollywood for roles of varying size. She made a favorable impression as Huck's (Junior Durkin) love interest in *Huckleberry Finn* (1931); played the title character in 1932's *Lena Rivers* (ads proclaimed her a "New Screen Sensation" who "will win the heart of the nation"); and starred again with Durkin in *Man Hunt* (1933).

But things started to get tough; she had trouble obtaining screen work, and the "big, bad wolf [was] hovering," remarked Philip K. Scheuer. Enter Paramount: In

A more contemporary portrait of Charlotte Henry than her fans were used to seeing in the 1930s.

1932, they were readying their big production *Alice in Wonderland* and conducting an extensive search for an actress to play the title role. A fresh-from-England Ida Lupino was considered, but wiser heads prevailed. (According to Scheuer, England's Pearl Hay, not Lupino, was Charlotte's only serious competition.)

Charlotte was doing the Pasadena Playhouse play *Growing Pains* when she made her Paramount test for Alice. Everyone was struck by the little blonde teenager, feeling she "resembled more closely than any other candidate, the 'child of pure unclouded brow and dreaming eyes of wonder' as idealized by Lewis Carroll and Sir John Tenniel, his illustrator" (*Salt Lake Tribune*). Harrison Carroll reported that Charlotte was so shocked when they chose her to play Alice that she cried for 15 minutes. She explained to Hubbard Keavy that she was "so worked up, thinking for days about getting the role, that I just had to cry."

The publicity for *Alice in Wonderland* (1933) was considerable, and the accepted idea was that Charlotte was a newcomer who had only previously acted as a film extra and was an unsophisticated, naïve child. "Charlotte's screen career has been brief," wrote Keavy, "largely because of her immature appearance. Her mother never could convince casting directors that Charlotte was capable of playing anything but youngsters." After a flurry of press interviews during the making of *Alice*, Harrison Carroll announced that the "ordeal of her first screen appearance has the youthful actress on the verge of a breakdown" and Paramount nixed all further requests. She was "ordered" to eat her lunch in her dressing room and to "lie down and rest as much as possible."

(*Left to right*): **Stan Laurel, Felix Knight, Charlotte Henry and Oliver Hardy in a publicity photograph from** *Babes in Toyland* **(1934).**

Alice in Wonderland featured an all-star cast (Gary Cooper, W.C. Fields, Cary Grant, Charlie Ruggles, Jack Oakie, Richard Arlen, etc.) so heavily made up as Carroll's book characters that they were mostly unrecognizable. Charlotte's unaffected, "shy girlish charm" (*Salt Lake Telegram*) was just right for the part and even though many critics didn't like the movie, they loved her.

Charlotte participated in an extensive personal appearance tour to promote the movie, but ultimately it did not do as expected at ticket windows. And she found herself typecast. The studio had worked hard to meld character and actress together in filmgoers' minds, without thought of how it would affect Charlotte's future.

Before *Alice*'s box office receipts came in, there were plans to headline Charlotte in talkie remakes of Mary Pickford pictures and star her as Cinderella and as Lovey Mary in a sequel to *Mrs. Wiggs of the Cabbage Patch*. None of this happened and the brass ring she had caught with *Alice* was wrenched from her hands. Many compared her to Betty Bronson, who hit it big with *Peter Pan* (1924) but never received a suitable follow-up, eventually fading into obscurity.

Paramount loaned Charlotte to 20th Century Pictures (*The Last Gentleman*), Universal (*The Human Side*) and Hal Roach (*Babes in Toyland*). In the latter, she portrayed Bo-Peep opposite Laurel and Hardy. Today, movie fans associate Charlotte more with this role than that of Alice. But at the time, it did nothing to slow her Hollywood decline.

Charlotte as Alice in *Alice in Wonderland* (1933) (courtesy John Antosiewicz).

In March '34, even though Charlotte was still active in movies, columnist Len G. Shaw was asking his readers to "try to recall the last time you heard mention of Charlotte Henry, who skyrocketed to fame so spectacularly, and then dropped from view."

Her Alice association was referenced whenever columnists and reviewers mentioned her. A common comment came via Kaspar Monahan, who said of her performance in *The Last Gentleman* (1934), "A lovely looking child, she fails to impress in this picture, for she acts as though she were still in wonderland."

Charlotte found herself having to start over. In April 1934, she appeared in a San Francisco stage production of *Ah, Wilderness!* starring Will Rogers. The new year of 1935 had Paramount dropping her option. She told George Shaffer,

I have learned that it is a sad mistake for a girl to be made a star when she is too young or too inexperienced. I never want to be put into a part of such prominence again until I have merited it by my work…. So here I am on a bottom rung again, laying a real foundation with study and experience. I want to go up again, of course, but only when the public wants me. The American motion picture public is pretty smart. It measures a star by her work.

It wasn't long before Charlotte found herself on Poverty Row, where the stardom she craved was lost in a haze of supporting parts and leads in the Bs *The Hoosier Schoolmaster* (1935), *Forbidden Heaven* ("[She] has much of Janet Gaynor's winsome wistfulness"—*Hollywood*), *The Return of Jimmy Valentine*, *The Gentleman from Louisiana* (both 1936), *God's Country and the Man* and *Young Dynamite* (both 1937). "We'd like to toss a bouquet to lovely little Charlotte Henry," wrote a New Hampshire film exhibitor about the 1935 movie *Three Kids and a Queen*. "Why can't we see more of her?"

She was a sweet, competent actress but always seemed to play younger than her years. It's a shame she didn't get more "grown-up" assignments like Republic's *The Mandarin Mystery* (1936), where she and Eddie Quillan (as Ellery Queen) bantered romantically. She had a supporting role in Fox's *Charlie Chan at the Opera* (1936), now one of her best-known pictures. Serial fans also recall her as the ingénue lead in the low-budget *Jungle Menace* (1937) with Frank Buck. The chapterplay's co-director Harry L. Fraser recalled in his autobiography that one of his leading lady's more harrowing moments involved a boa constrictor. (Fraser also *mis*remembered that his leading lady was Betty Bronson, "so cute and whimsical as Peter Pan, such a delicate little lady, I almost hated to put her through the killing paces of the Columbia serial.") From Fraser's autobiography:

As the script called for, Betty was tied hand and foot by the villain, at the bottom of a big tree in the jungle…. Two cameras covered the action: a full close-up of the girl's face on one, while the other camera showed the snake and the girl. But in shooting, I was careful to keep the snake out of Betty's sight until we were ready to go for a take. I felt that if she ever actually had a glimpse of that huge boa constrictor, she would never be able to do the scene. I protected the shot by placing the reptile crew and the snake's owner and trainer (a woman who performed with the boa during the circus season) out of her line of vision.

The impression we were creating was that nobody could predict exactly what would happen when the seven-foot crusher discovered its victim. Would he slide across her body, or would he wrap her in his steel-like coils, crushing the life out of her in a minute? That was the suspense which would later thrill and horrify moviegoers from coast to coast. But, as we filmed it, it was real-life action, fraught with danger, even if we were using a supposedly tame circus snake.

The scene proceeded smoothly. The snake moved slowly. Its slither was perfect for cutting, just the right speed, until four feet or so of its huge reptile body was hanging over the girl's horror-stricken face. And the horror was real, because that was Betty's first look at the snake. Later she confided to me, "I never felt so helpless and frightened in my life."

Finally, the full length of the snake slipped into camera's view, leaving the hold he had maintained on the tree. He missed dropping on Betty by inches. Now came the climax. What would he do? The snake crew stood by, ready to act quickly if there was an emergency. The snake was in no hurry. Slowly he slithered across the girl's body, while she screamed and struggled. He turned, looking for a spot to slip under her to make his first wrap. I motioned to the reptile crew to get ready, and a split-second later gave them the signal to move in. But now, the maddened snake fought them and did its best to coil around one of the men. Before that happened, however, I had cut, and we had a good cliffhanger with our terror-stricken heroine to close the episode.

By the end of '37, Charlotte had left movies. "Wonder whatever became of Charlotte Henry, who almost became a star in Paramount's not too successful *Alice*," asked Hubbard

"Tweedledum and Tweedledee agreed to have a battle! / For Tweedledum said Tweedledee had spoiled his nice new rattle": Alice (Charlotte Henry) watches as the two *Alice in Wonderland* characters (Jack Oakie [*left*] and Roscoe Karns) get ready to rumble (courtesy John Antosiewicz).

Keavy. She was in Memphis and thereabouts with her own stage show, *Charlotte Henry's Hollywood Revue.*

The following year, it was claimed that film studios had closed their doors to her. She complained that in Hollywood she had been "billed as a child actress. That was all right as far as [Alice] was concerned, but it left me typed, definitely typed. My biggest job now, just as it has been for the past two or more years, is to prove that I am quite capable of playing serious adult parts."

Financial woes forced her to go to work for the WPA theater circuit in such shows as *Big Blow* and *Blossom Time*. "The project has aided me in at least two ways," she told Robert J. Rhodes. "I had to have a job. I know nothing except acting. The project provided me with a job. I needed more stage experience, and I am getting it. I know there must be a few rough edges to my acting. But the project work is helping me in polishing them off. Soon I hope to be in a position to again pound on studio doors."

To support herself and her mother, Charlotte did stock across the country and in Vancouver, B.C., and appeared in ads for Cadillac—at the same time she was taking the bus to work. When she did return to Hollywood, it was as an extra. In May 1940, columnist Harold Heffernan ran a story about RKO cashier Harry Peale. In the story, he handed an $8.25 check, a day's work for an extra, to Charlotte Henry. "It's things like this that get you down," the cashier said. "To think that only a few years ago I was handing this same girl ... cheques each week running into the thousands. She was a big timer then."

Approached on the set of *The Howards of Virginia* (1940), Charlotte remarked, "What's the use of talking about it? That doesn't help and so I've taken a philosophical view of the past. I know that I had a lucky break and it helps me to know that this opportunity comes to very few people. I want to look forward and to the hope of better things, not backwards." Other pictures in which she did extra work include *Lucky Partners* and *Dance, Girl, Dance* (both 1940).

Charlotte got a lot of press at this time and in one syndicated story she made it seem as if being an extra was her own idea instead of a necessity: "I decided recently to do extra work, play bits or anything that keeps me active and permits me to earn some money. I want to save enough money to go to New York, then come back to Hollywood and be a success.... One good stage role back there and Hollywood might stop remembering me as Alice, and give me a chance to show what I can do."

A brunette, almost unrecognizable Charlotte got a break when she replaced Cecilia Parker as Warren Hull's love interest in the East Side Kids comedy *Bowery Blitzkrieg* (1941). Producers William Pine and William Thomas, who had known her when they were Paramount press agents, gave her small parts in their productions *Flying Blind* (1941) and *I Live on Danger* (1942), and claimed in their publicity that Charlotte looked like a "young Hedy Lamarr." A bit of a stretch, but it's good to know that she still had friends in Hollywood looking out for her.

In 1942, she permanently said goodbye to movies. She later said she "simply lost interest." According to the *Los Angeles Times*, the high spot in that year's Beaux Arts revue, *Naughty, Naughty*, was Charlotte's "quaint little song about Hollywood, in which she dons her *Alice in Wonderland* dress and blond wig." The following year, Hedda Hopper was telling her readers that Charlotte was "playing little theaters around the Middle West." A week later, Hopper dropped the bombshell that "little Charlotte Henry, of *Alice in Wonderland*,"

was in San Diego performing in a "burlesque house under her own name." This brief fling with strip-teasing ended without any more notice and it was reported that Charlotte was managing an apartment house.

On January 6, 1947, in San Diego, she married used car dealer Charles Jackson. Jackson was out of the picture by '49 and Charlotte went to live with her mother. Money was obviously still an issue because it was back to the Burly Qs: Dorothy Kilgallen wrote that Charlotte "has startled Hollywood by

Eddie Quillan (as Ellery Queen) and Charlotte Henry investigate a clue in *The Mandarin Mystery* (1936).

opening in a strip tease act that puts Margie Hart in a class with Maggie O'Brien by comparison. And her act is preceded by a short strip of celluloid showing her as Alice." Columnist M. Oakley Stafford was particularly upset by this news: "When I heard that ethereal little Alice of *Alice in Wonderland* film fame, Charlotte Henry, was doing a daring strip tease in theater work, I felt like weeping. Does theater count so much, that to stay in it at any cost, is worth the price?" Charlotte did appear in a legit stage production of *John Loves Mary* in San Diego.

Charlotte Henry and William Bakewell in the Columbia serial *Jungle Menace* (1937).

While Charlotte never denied the stripping stories, she did balk at the claims she was supporting her "invalid mother" by working as a seamstress in a San Diego burlesque house. "Says she can't thread a needle, and Mom feels fine," wrote Dorothy Kilgallen.

Sometime after this, Charlotte opened up an employment agency with her mother. She was then an executive secretary for Charles F. Buddy, the Roman Catholic Bishop of San Diego, a job that lasted 15 years.

According to Richard Lamparski, Charlotte spent 18 months in the early '70s on a grand jury, and when *Alice in Wonderland* aired on TV the jurors started asking her questions about it. "Alice reaches out and shadows my existence, even today," she sighed.

About two years after her mother's 1971 death, Charlotte wed Dr. James J. Dempsey, a dentist she had known since the mid–1960s. This marriage lasted until the 66-year-old Charlotte's death on April 11, 1980, from cancer at La Jolla's Scripps Hospital. She is interred at Holy Cross Cemetery.

Two years after Charlotte's death, her half-brother, Reverend Robert E. Henry, Jr., was convicted of child molestation. He served a prison sentence.

Charlotte Henry Filmography

1930: *Harmony at Home, Courage, On Your Back.*
1931: *Huckleberry Finn, Arrowsmith* (uncredited).
1932: *Forbidden, Murders in the Rue Morgue* (uncredited), *Lena Rivers, Rebecca of Sunnybrook Farm* (uncredited), *A Hockey Hick* (short), *Rasputin and the Empress* (uncredited).
1933: *Man Hunt, Alice in Wonderland.*
1934: *The Last Gentleman, The Human Side, Babes in Toyland.*
1935: *Laddie, The Hoosier Schoolmaster, Forbidden Heaven, Three Kids and a Queen.*

1936: *The Return of Jimmy Valentine, Hearts in Bondage, The Gentleman from Louisiana, Charlie Chan at the Opera, The Mandarin Mystery.*
1937: *Jungle Menace, God's Country and the Man, Young Dynamite.*
1940: *Lucky Partners* (uncredited), *The Howards of Virginia* (uncredited), *Dance, Girl, Dance* (uncredited).
1941: *Bowery Blitzkrieg, Flying Blind.*
1942: *She's in the Army, I Live on Danger.*

Rita Johnson

Rita Johnson's courageous Hollywood story deserves to be better known. Although she was acknowledged as a perfect Other Woman on screen, she was actually a versatile actress who played a variety of roles (supporting and leads) in the 1930s and '40s. In 1948, she had not achieved stardom but she was busy, well-known and well-liked. The events that followed an "accident" with a hair dryer changed the course of her life and cut short her successful career.

The daughter of a Worcester Street Railway Company motorman, Rita Ann Johnson was born in Worcester, Massachusetts, on August 13, 1913. At age four, she developed a speech impediment; elocution lessons sparked her interest in acting. She wanted to appear in school plays, but the head of the drama department felt she had no talent. Throughout high school, she took acting lessons from a dramatic coach.

After graduation, she studied piano at the New England Conservatory of Music at her parents' insistence. Not happy, she dropped out and eventually got involved with various stock companies.

On radio, her perfect diction came in handy and she was called one of the airwaves' most versatile actresses. She had roles on *John's Other Wife*, *The Court of Human Relations*, *The Wonder Show*, *Columbia Workshop*, *The March of Time*, *Joyce Jordan, Girl Intern*, etc. Johnson also worked as Walter Winchell's "Girl Sunday" and as an advertising model.

Stock work came in Boston (notably with the Louise Galloway Players), Brookfield and Falmouth, Massachusetts, and Milwaukee, Wisconsin. During these early years, she acted alongside Rosalind Russell, Conrad Nagel and Florence Reed. In

An early MGM portrait of Rita Johnson.

New York, she had small roles in Theater Guild stage productions. The *Boston Globe* reported that Johnson also did bit parts in movies made in New York, but gave no specifics.

Samuel Goldwyn saw her performance on Broadway in George M. Cohan's *Fulton of Oak Falls* (1937) and screen-tested her for his upcoming screen version of *Dead End*. For a while, it looked as if she would get the part of society girl Kay, but Wendy Barrie was cast. MGM saw her test, requested she do another (scenes from *The Good Fairy* and *Paris Bound*), and then signed her to a contract. Her first assignment was the lead in *London by Night* (1937), acquitting herself well opposite George Murphy.

During the early days of filming her first movie, it was announced that Johnson would test for the chance to replace Jean Harlow. The beloved Blonde Bombshell had died on June 7, 1937, while working on *Saratoga* with Clark Gable. The plan was to rewrite the script with a new type of personality taking over. One weird idea was to keep Harlow in the picture and then when her scenes ran out, have Lionel Barrymore come on screen and tell the audience that she had died and that another actress would finish the movie for her. Gladys George, Virginia Bruce and Virginia Grey also tested, but Johnson got the most publicity. As Walter Winchell commented, "No matter who gets the difficult assignment—there will be a public breathlessly waiting to complain and compare, etc." Ultimately, MGM decided to keep Harlow's footage and complete the film with doubles (Lee Arlen, Mary Dees) hiding their faces. Rita said she hadn't wanted the part and was relieved when she didn't get it. "It was too big an assignment for me," she told Mayme Ober Peak. "Everyone advised me not to do it, it would be very unwise. It was big enough initiation for an actress to be given a lead in her first film, even though the part wasn't very large. But it was beneficial and gave me something to live up to. I have to prove myself."

Louella Parsons mentioned Rita's lead in *London by Night*, her test for *Saratoga* and a new part in *Live, Love and Learn* (all within her first month in Hollywood) and concluded that she was "destined to become one of Metro-Goldwyn-Mayer's important stars. No actress in a long time has come to the front with such dizzy rapidity."

If only. Instead of *Live, Love and Learn*, Johnson was cast in a supporting part as Maureen O'Sullivan's friend in *My Dear Miss Aldrich* and what amounted to a bit as one of Rosalind Russell's bridesmaids in *Man-Proof*. (Johnson inexplicably gets better billing than Nana Bryant, who has a major supporting part.)

During this time, Johnson was involved with brawny actor Broderick Crawford, and columnists kept reporting that they were secretly married or about to tie the knot. Winchell went so far as to say they were expecting a baby! (That must have *thrilled* MGM.) Actually, even though they dated from 1937 to 1940, the two never made it legal, nor had a baby.

According to Mayme Ober Peak, Johnson was "getting discouraged at MGM" until she was borrowed by Universal (for *Letter of Introduction*) and RKO (*Smashing the Rackets*). While these were still supporting parts, they were better than what Metro had been giving her.

It was back to MGM and roles that did little for her: *Rich Man, Poor Girl* (sister of Robert Young), *The Girl Downstairs* (rich girl thrown over for scullery maid) and *Honolulu* (fiancée of Young). *Girl Downstairs* director Norman Taurog told Milton Harker that Johnson had the makings of "another Ina Claire."

Things picked up considerably with the excellent, frisky part of star Ruth Hussey's wisecracking, likable jailhouse pal in *Within the Law* (1939). She again threw around the quips in the Jeanette Mac-Donald musical *Broadway Serenade* (1939) as a showgirl involved with producer Frank Morgan; her scenes with predatory Virginia Grey were a hoot.

Announced for a top role in *Northwest Passage*, she instead got the lead in the Jacques Tourneur–directed *They All Come Out* (1939) with Tom Neal. Initially intended as a *Crime Does Not Pay* short, it was deemed worthy of expansion to a feature. Both Johnson and Neal gave sincere performances. She followed that up with a lead in *6,000 Enemies* (1939), a B mystery with Walter Pidgeon.

This short foray into leading lady parts was broken by a rather brief supporting one in *Stronger Than Desire* (1939). Society girl–murder suspect Johnson has designs

From left: **Rita Johnson, Eve Arden and Ann Sheridan admire man-about-town Charlie McCarthy in** *Letter of Introduction* **(1938).**

on her married counsel (Walter Pidgeon) and tries to vamp him. After he spanks her to "curb her animal instincts," she responds by kissing him—leading to an affair.

According to *The Los Angeles Times*' Edwin Schallert:

> MGM is taking recognition, rather belated, it would seem, of the talents of Rita Johnson, who has done various good performances in the more or less "B" class of pictures.... Miss Johnson's record in *They All Come Out* and *Stronger Than Desire*, quietly convincing performances, is to assure her of a "break," if all goes well, in the series of films starring Walter Pidgeon, which will be taken from the "Nick Carter, Detective" stories.

Johnson's first in the mystery series, *Nick Carter, Master Detective* (1940), was also her last: The series continued without her for two more entries with other actresses opposite Pidgeon.

Her roles were continuing to vary in size. A substantial part in *Congo Maisie* (1940) was followed by a small, fourth-billed dramatic role of a woman who regrets giving up her baby in the Eddie Cantor starrer *Forty Little Mothers* (1940). The Group Theatre in New York wanted her for Clifford Odets' *Night Music* (1940), but she had to turn it down due to picture commitments.

While *Night Music* was a flop, MGM came through, giving Johnson her most prestigious role to date: Mrs. Edison in *Edison, the Man* (1940) starring Spencer Tracy. Because of this film, Johnson got a lot of long overdue attention. Edwin Schallert thought she "certainly succeeded in maintaining unusual dignity in her portrayal," while Harriet Parsons praised her "gracious, womanly performance.... I have heard it compared to Greer Garson's unforgettable Mrs. Chips."

"Metro-Goldwyn-Mayer should at last be awake to Rita Johnson's possibilities," wrote Harold W. Cohen. This sentiment was echoed by many—including Johnson. *Rage in Heaven* (1941) with Robert Montgomery was mentioned as her next, but instead she was thrown in the silly crime comedy *The Golden Fleecing* (1940) with Lew Ayres. MGM assigned her supporting parts in *Maisie Was a Lady* and *Ziegfeld Girl*. She turned down the former (she felt it wasn't important enough) and then asked for and received her release from her contract.

In an interview with Mayme Ober Peak, Johnson denied being difficult. "It is not true ... that I 'walked out' on *Maisie* and was suspended for it. I didn't walk out; I was ill with intestinal flu and also had a throat infection. I had two nurses." She understood MGM's need to keep their players busy, "but after working at MGM for four years, and most of the time in B pictures, I felt I had earned something better. I won the feminine lead in *Edison, the Man*. After that they put me in *Golden Fleecing*. I couldn't see any progress. I'm a business investment to myself now."

On November 25, 1940, just six months after she broke up with Broderick Crawford, Johnson, 27, married stockbroker F. Stanley Kahn, 42, in New York.

In theory, being a freelancer seemed like a sound "investment," but Johnson soon found that the important roles she thought she would get as a result of *Edison, the Man* would not materialize. But Columbia's *Here Comes Mr. Jordan*, Universal's *Appointment for Love* (both 1941) and Paramount's *The Major and the Minor* (1942) cemented her reputation as one of the screen's best menaces and Other Women. William A. Seiter, who directed her in *Appointment for Love* and *The Affairs of Susan* (1945), pinpointed Johnson's "brittle, barbed almost feline voice-qualities" as one of her assets in such roles.

Previously, Johnson had played basically good girls without any malice toward the leading ladies. She told columnist Charles R. Moore there were

Mr. and Mrs. Edison (Spencer Tracy and Rita Johnson) in *Edison, the Man* (1940).

Rita, one of the screen's best Other Women, attempts to come between married couple Charles Boyer and Margaret Sullavan in *Appointment for Love* (1941).

plenty of "compensations for the 'other woman' type of roles," specifically: "Some of the best and meatiest lines are handed to us, and usually we have at least a couple of really big scenes." She insisted that if she had a choice of playing a "bad woman in a top grade picture or of taking the lead in a second class film," she would "naturally … grab the role of the hellion."

If major movies were what she wanted, she got them from 20th Century–Fox, the Technicolor dramas *My Friend Flicka* (1943) and *Thunderhead—Son of Flicka* (1945). In both she played Nell McLaughlin, wife of Preston Foster and mother of Roddy McDowall. She was set to play a Nazi in *Ministry of Fear* (1944), but illness forced Paramount to replace her with Hillary Brooke.

On June 29, 1943, Johnson was granted a Reno divorce from Kahn. Their relationship was a tumultuous one. They remarried on December 30, 1943, but all was not well.

Johnson's career bumped along with mostly supporting parts in a variety of parts. (Contrary to "conventional wisdom," she was not confined to playing Other Women.) "I like to think I'm going to keep on acting and not worry too much about the roles," she told columnist Patricia Clary. "I love to act. Meanies, goodies, anything, just so long as I have a chance to stand up before the cameras and really work." She had a lead in the B western *Michigan Kid* (1947) with Jon Hall. After Universal made it, they tried to unload it onto Poverty Row company PRC, but ultimately opted to release it themselves.

Johnson is perhaps best-known today for supporting roles in two classic films noir: *They Won't Believe Me* (1947) as the sympathetic, long-suffering wife of Robert Young, and *The Big Clock* (1948) as Charles Laughton's blackmailing mistress. Even in the latter,

Johnson was able to project a likability, although she is at her best confronting Laughton and spewing some pretty harsh words before meeting her untimely demise.

In March 1947, after being separated from husband Kahn for two years, Johnson went to court to shed him for good. She testified that he treated her like a child, was "critical, irritable, fault-finding, and remained away from home for long periods." She made the rounds of the nightclubs with Howard Lang, Sammy Colt (Ethel Barrymore's son), Lawrence Tierney, writer Mike McCausland and others.

In August '48, she organized a unit to entertain veterans at rehabilitation hospitals. "Hats off to her," wrote Harrison Carroll. "Many of the stars are forgetting the boys these days."

She was an established, busy featured player with offers in Italy, possible plays on Broadway and a likely role coming up in *Knock on Any Door*.

Earlier, in 1939, after she was involved in a car crash, Johnson supposedly took out a $100,000 insurance policy in case an accidental "mishap" affected her career. "Rita Johnson, kissing, and tossing over her left shoulder, a pin she spied on the *Innocent Affair* stage," read a widely circulated publicity item in May 1948. "She's so superstitious she makes a wish if the hem turns up when she's putting on a dress."

She could have used some luck.

On September 6, 1948, Johnson was found dazed and disoriented in her apartment by her friend, actress Mary Ainslee, who had come to pick her up so they could go together to a party. Before blacking out, Johnson claimed that her 40-pound beauty parlor hair dryer had fallen on her head. Ainslee called Johnson's doctor, who examined her on the scene and said she had a large lump on her head, a bruised lip and a concussion.

Initially, her injury went untreated because Ainslee claimed they were "unable to get an ambulance." Rita's doctor further stated that he "tried without success for more than two days to get hospital accommodations." Finally admitted to St. Vincent's Hospital, Johnson underwent emergency surgery to remove a blood clot in her brain. She was in a coma and oxygen tent for 16 days. Her brother William wanted the police to investigate her mishap. Narcotics detectives were tipped off by an unidentified man that Johnson was "taken from her apartment under unusual circumstances." Nothing came of this.

Although there were old bruises covering her body, the incident was deemed an accident. Her old boss Walter Winchell was one of many who felt it was suspicious: "Hollywood wonders if Rita Johnson's concussion was caused by

A gun-toting Ray Milland protects Rita in a publicity shot from *The Big Clock* (1948).

a former flame (screen actor-tough guy; not a writer), famed for knocking his darlings cold." (There was another rumor floating around that she was romantically involved with a gangster.) Winchell asked in another column, "The Movietown police aren't going to let Rita Johnson's slugger get away with almost killing her, are they?"

When she did awaken, she was initially unable to speak or walk. Recovery was slow. When she was fit enough to be interviewed by the police, she said she couldn't remember anything about the incident.

Rumors continued to swirl: one, that she was in an automobile crash; two, she fell in her bathtub. Her personal doctor was cut off from seeing Johnson after he offered the press the latter reason for her accident.

Columnists splashed a lot of gossip ink on her, starting with Edith Gwynn: "Rita Johnson's hospital room is filled with roses. But they oughta be daisies. Because 'daisies don't tell!'" Dorothy Kilgallen wrote, "Now that Rita Johnson is well on the road to recovery, a screen actor known for his prankishness is sleeping nights."

"Despite the recurring efforts of certain columnists to treat Rita Johnson's case as a dark mystery," wrote Jimmie Fidler, "L.A. police are completely satisfied that her injuries were inflicted, accidentally, by a heavy hair dryer."

The press scapegoat seemed to be bad boy Lawrence Tierney. The actor, known for his public brawls and drunkenness, was to many the logical choice. His nephew Michael Tierney recently countered:

I know of no instance of Larry hitting a woman. He had hundreds of fistfights with men but as far as I know he never hit a woman. I could be wrong, but so far, I have seen no evidence. He did stalk, bully, seduce, charm, etc. For example, he never hit my mother, whom he had a child with. He would have her driving him all over Los Angeles holding her captive in the car while he visited friends and drank in bars but that's about it. Harmless but exhausting.

George Murphy and Rita Johnson menaced by the Umbrella Man in *London by Night* (1937)

Johnson refused to discuss the matter publicly,

but family members later alleged it was Rita's on again-off again boyfriend Broderick Crawford who caused her injuries. When they were seriously dating in the late 1930s and early '40s, there were a few reports of injuries to Johnson: a swollen jaw, cut forehead, etc. They were attributed to "accidents."

"Publicity helps careers, when you're able to work," Johnson told Alice Mosby in 1952. "If I could have stepped out of bed into a picture, I'd have been hot stuff. But I was unable to work for a year."

Her first job after the accident was a recurring role on TV's *Taylored Lady*, a "fashion featurette" series starring Estelle Taylor. She also guested on some local TV programs. She reportedly turned down a chance to act on the New York stage because of a "couple of good picture offers" (Sheilah Graham). The only one mentioned was Douglas Sirk's *Two Hearts in Three-Quarter Time*, to be filmed in Vienna, but that highly touted project never got off the ground. Instead, she got a supporting part in the Ella Raines movie *The Second Face* (1950).

Work also came via radio, including multiple episodes of *Family Theater*. Unable to support herself and still harboring physical problems because of her accident, Johnson lived with her parents, who had moved from Massachusetts to California to help her.

During this rough patch, she said, "Sometimes I drive alone to the top of the hill. I shake my fist at the city and I say, 'Hollywood, city of bright lights, I'll lick you yet.'"

Things brightened up in 1952 with more radio (*Broadway Is My Beat*), lively parts on the television series *Mr. & Mrs. North* and *Rebound*, and the unsold pilot *Career for Cathy*. "I'm doing exciting things in TV," she told Sheilah Graham, but it still wasn't enough to make a living. What might have helped: In late May 1953, it was announced that Johnson was "signed, sealed and delivered" as Robert Young's wife in the upcoming TV series *Father Knows Best*. It is unclear why she was not cast, but it certainly would have helped her career blues.

She wondered at the time if the notoriety of the Hair Dryer Accident had caused the sudden drought in acting roles. The sad truth was that she was having trouble remembering her lines and her sense of balance was off. (Back in the 1930s, publicity claimed that Johnson had a photographic memory and could memorize a page of dialogue after just a glance.)

It couldn't have been easy for Johnson to act during this time, but she valiantly forged ahead and in 1954–55 did episodes of *The Lone Wolf*, *Your Favorite Story*, *The Christophers*, *The Man Behind the Badge*, *The Adventures of Ozzie and Harriet*, etc., and essayed a few small movie roles. Boyd Martin singled out her performance as Dick Powell's psychologist in *Susan Slept Here* (1954) as one of the picture's funniest scenes. Martin called Johnson a "first-rate comedienne," adding, "Hollywood needs more actresses and fewer glamour darlings, although Miss Johnson is plenty glamorous as far as I am concerned." Her part in *Unchained* (1955), as the warden's wife, was cut before release. Johnson made her last screen appearance in *All Mine to Give* (1957).

The following year brought a new vocation: running a Hollywood Blvd. dress shop. She bought old clothes from her movie star friends and resold them.

By the late '50s, Johnson had developed a drinking problem. For two weeks in 1965, her niece Barbara Coulter, who considered Rita "a wonderful person … very sensitive and kind," visited her. In 2013, she told writer Matt Weinstock she was stunned to find "empty bottles, including one in the back of the toilet. She would pretend she was drinking water in front of me, but her voice would get a little more slurry, and I could tell it was vodka. She'd walk down to the corner store on North Orange Drive and come back with a brown bag."

A few months later, on October 31, 1965, Rita collapsed in the West Hollywood apartment she was sharing with her widowed mother. Fifteen minutes after being admitted to Los Angeles County General Hospital, the 52-year-old died. A hospital spokesman said the possible cause of death was a cardiac arrest due to "acute subdural hemotoma (head injury)." Her mother stated that Rita had not been "troubled by the old injury recently." An autopsy showed that Johnson had also suffered from liver disease and "alcohol-induced encephalitis."

She is interred at Culver City's Holy Cross Cemetery.

Rita Johnson Filmography

1937: *London by Night, My Dear Miss Aldrich.*
1938: *Man-Proof, Letter of Introduction, Smashing the Rackets, Rich Man, Poor Girl, The Girl Downstairs.*
1939: *Honolulu, Within the Law, Broadway Serenade, 6,000 Enemies, Stronger Than Desire, They All Come Out, Nick Carter, Master Detective.*
1940: *Congo Maisie, Forty Little Mothers, Edison, the Man, The Golden Fleecing.*
1941: *Here Comes Mr. Jordan, Appointment for Love.*
1942: *The Major and the Minor.*
1943: *My Friend Flicka.*
1945: *The Affairs of Susan, Thunderhead—Son of Flicka, The Naughty Nineties, Pardon My Past.*
1947: *The Perfect Marriage, Michigan Kid, They Won't Believe Me.*
1948: *Sleep, My Love, The Big Clock, An Innocent Affair, Family Honeymoon.*
1950: *The Second Face.*
1954: *Susan Slept Here.*
1956: *Emergency Hospital.*
1957: *All Mine to Give.*

Mayo Methot

"If I can't be a second Sarah Bernhardt, I won't be anything," an eight-year-old Mayo Methot told the Salem, Oregon's *Capital Journal* in 1912.

Long before she was "Sluggy," one-half of the Battling Bogarts, Methot was an experienced, well-regarded stage actress with much to offer the theater world. In movies, she may not have been leading lady material, but she was sufficiently skillful to have gone on for years as a character actress. Her 1938 marriage to Humphrey Bogart pretty much ended that: She chose to make his career more important. In addition to this, she was plagued by demons that ultimately destroyed her.

Today, if Methot is remembered at all, it is for being the almost homicidal, irrational alcoholic with whom "poor" Bogie was stuck with before he met the true love of his life, fourth wife Lauren Bacall. While that duo "had it all," Methot has gotten a dirty deal from historians. To define her as simply an erratic ex of a superstar is unfair, because there was much more to the lady.

A direct descendant of President Zachary Taylor, she was born Mayo June Methot on March 3, 1904, in Chicago. Her paternal grandmother Minnie Holman was a soprano who enjoyed a bit of renown on the concert stage and as a comic opera singer. Minnie was married to salesman John Samuel Methot and had two children.

Minnie's hubby was "handsome, active, witty, attractive—and, alack-a-day" (*Quad-City Times*). A big drinker, he was jealous of anyone's attentions toward his wife. In 1888, when Minnie filed for divorce, the *Quad-City Times* reported her allegations:

[John] would fly into a passion and drive her out of the room. Once he dragged her on the floor by the hair and tore her music to pieces. One evening he kicked the dishes off the table, rushed into the parlor and kicked the lamp off the piano, and then

Badass Mayo Methot looking as if she could take everyone in the room.

kicked his wife off the piano stool. He then assaulted her with a razor, and would have killed her but for the interference of the boarders.

Abandoning the family, he became a "habitual drunkard" and by the time of the divorce suit was a resident of the Washingtonian Home for the Cure of Inebriates in Chicago.

Minnie's daughter Mayo ("our" Mayo's aunt) had a career on the legit stage: She traveled with Richard Mansfield's acting troupe for several years before settling down to a domestic life. Her brother John Dillon, a sea captain known as Captain Jack, commanded cargo ships. He was not without his drama: In 1903, he wed Beryl Evelyn Wood, who was pregnant with their daughter Mayo at the time of the nuptials. All fine and good, except he had married another woman two years earlier and was now a bigamist. To make the union legal, Captain Jack and Beryl tied a proper knot on May 26, 1910, in another marriage ceremony in Chicago.

By 1911, Captain Jack and his family had moved to Portland, Oregon. (Beryl worked as a police reporter for *The Oregonian*.) Little Mayo showed theatrical talent early and at the age of seven made her stage bow as a boy in a production of *Sapho* (starring Florence Roberts, who also did a 1913 movie version, *sans* Mayo). She followed that up with roles in *Mrs. Wiggs of the Cabbage Patch* and *Alias Jimmy Valentine* with Portland's Baker Players.

"In addition to a beautiful face and a slender, graceful little body," wrote the *Capital Journal* in 1912, "Mayo has a fine memory that is regarded as astonishing. When but very young, she committed to memory and used frequently to recite the death scenes from *Romeo and Juliet*, and other heavy passages far beyond her baby comprehension. Her grasp of what is required of her during rehearsals of plays is held to be unusual...."

The eight-year-old garnered praise as David in *The Awakening of Helena Richie* (1912) in Oregon and on tour (with her mother in tow). "Of Mayo Methot's fascinating prowess as the child too much praise cannot be given," wrote the *Statesman Journal*. "She is beautiful of body and mentality, her acting is not acting in any sense of the word meaning because she is natural.

A blonde, glamorous Mayo from the early 1930s.

Every movement, every gesture of her agile child's body, every lilt of the eager baby's voice held not one trace of the affected."

A hit with locals, she was seen as part of the Baker Players in *Salvation Nell, The Builders* and *Mary Jane's Pa* (all 1913). She also played the latter in Vancouver, British Columbia, Canada. "Little Mayo Methot won the hearts of the audience completely with her impersonation of Mary Jane and was greeted with great applause," wrote the *Vancouver Sun.*

Given the official title of the Portland Rosebud, she welcomed important people to the city and also traveled to express the good wishes of the people of Portland. In June 1913, she went to the White House to present a message and bouquet of white roses from Oregon Governor Oswald West to President Woodrow Wilson. Later that month, Wilson wrote a note to the governor: "My Dear Governor West: I was very much charmed with little Miss Mayo Methot. She presented the roses with delightful grace and simplicity, and it was altogether a very refreshing incident. I appreciated the note, also, very sincerely, which she brought from you. Cordially yours, Woodrow Wilson."

In 1914, after appearing on stage in *As a Man Thinks, A Fool There Was* and *The Littlest Rebel*, Methot joined other Baker Players in making her film debut in *Forgotten Songs*, produced by Portland's American Lifeograph film studios.

When she not acting at the Baker Theater, Methot was involved in school recitals and vaudeville and performed with other theater groups. She portrayed Alice in Wonderland and, for the Portland Shakespeare Club, was Puck in *A Midsummer Night's Dream*

Wholesome Mayo poses for the cameras.

(1915). The *Oregon Daily Journal's* Vella Winner called her "perfectly cast" and opined, "[A] gayer and more elfish little sprite could not be imagined. She dodged about the trees and about her royal charges with all the abandon of boyish youth, danced in her supreme glee and when the occasion demanded, said her 'lines' like the little veteran that she is."

There were only a couple of stage roles in 1916 (*The Littlest Rebel* and *On Trial*) because she was attending Miss Catlin's School. Rumors that the teenager would go to New York to try for a stage career or enter movies were denied by Methot, who preferred to continue at Miss Catlin's. She also expressed a lack of interest in film, as she enjoyed "spoken drama."

When her father wasn't away at sea, he taught Mayo about boats ... and how to take care of herself. In February 1918, she was riding with Captain Jack in an automobile when they saw George Abdie, 18, on the curb making faces and blowing kisses to 13-year-old Mayo. Her father stopped the car, got out and slapped the boy so hard he broke his jaw. In court, he was fined $10, which was later remitted when the captain appealed the case, saying he was just protecting his daughter. The judge agreed and remarked that it should serve as a warning to future mashers that that kind of behavior would not be tolerated.

In 1919, Mayo graduated from Miss Catlin's and rejoined the Baker Stock Company. "Portland has always known her and loved her as a child," wrote the *Oregon Daily Journal*, "and now Portland stock lovers will watch her develop into something more than merely a clever child actress." Verna Felton, Lillian Foster and Leona Powers were the leading women from 1919 to 1922 and with them Mayo did such diverse plays as *Come Out of the Kitchen*, *Walk-Offs* ("Mayo Methot is a delightful little Russian model and is gaining the poise of an experienced actress"—*Oregon Daily Journal*), *Eyes of Youth*, *Hobson's Choice*, *It Pays to Advertise* (playing a French adventuress), *Pollyanna* ("[She] wears boys' clothes this week and becomes the sweetheart of Pollyanna. It was quite evident she wasn't a boy from her mannerisms and voice, but she was well liked"—*Oregon Daily Journal*), *The Brat*, *Nothing But the Truth*, *The Trail of the Lonesome Pine*, *Remnant* ("lends a touch of refinement and womanliness that the play grievously requires"—*Oregon Daily Journal*), *Big Chance*, *The Five Million* (as a French war bride), *Lombardi, Ltd.*, *Peg o' My Heart*, *A Prince There Was*, *Parlor, Bedroom and Bath*, *Way Down East*, *A Tailor Made Man*, *The Little Shepherd of Kingdom Come*, *That Girl Patsy*, *The Ouija Board*, *Turn to the Right*, *Smooth as Silk*, *Three Live Ghosts*, *Up in Mabel's Room*, *Rebecca of Sunnybrook Farm*, *Forever After*, *The Haunted House* and *A Temperance Town*.

In March 1921, Wallace Reid was in Portland and, according to columnist Earl C. Brownlee, urged young Mayo "to consider a career in the pictures." The Methots were old friends of the Reid family, particularly Wallace's father, playwright-actor Hal Reid, who had died the year before.

Locally, Methot appeared in director-producer-writer Robert C. Bruce's *And Women Must Weep* (1922), a one-reeler filmed on the Oregon coast and advertised as a "Wilderness Tale." Playing her husband was John M. La Mond, a cinematographer who worked with Bruce's production company. Filming on the picture finished in June 1921; on September 28, Methot and La Mond married in Vancouver, Washington.

She continued with the Baker Players until April 1922, and then went with her husband to San Francisco. In the summer, the couple was back in Oregon to again work for Robert Bruce: *While the Pot Boils*, *Mixed Trails* and *By Lantern Light*. It is possible she worked on even more of Bruce's films.

In November '22, she went to New York with the intention of doing Broadway. Newspapers were calling her "one of the beauties of the Pacific coast" and were enthused with her talent. There was mention of an unnamed movie to be made by the New York–based India Pictures Corp., but it is unknown if this became a reality. She did have a role in the William Randolph Hearst–produced film *Unseeing Eyes* (1923) starring Lionel Barrymore, with cinematography by her husband. From there she did stock in Malden, Massachusetts.

Methot remarked to Lloyd S. Thompson,

I went the rounds of the theatrical offices and spent much time sitting on people's doorsteps. Finally, I got a small part in an unimportant play [the 16-performance Broadway flop *The Mad Honeymoon*]. It was my good fortune that George M. Cohan came to see that play. A few days later he sent for me, and almost before I realized it, I had been given the leading role in *The Song and Dance Man* [1923].

Reviewing the Cohan show, the *Boston Globe* called her "blonde, petite and pretty, in addition to being a clever ingénue." Some were comparing her in looks to Lillian Gish.

When *Song and Dance Man* ended in March 1924, Methot did more stock and joined the Atlanta Baldwin Players as leading lady to John Litel, notably appearing in *Getting Gertie's Garter*. In October '24, she and the Mutual Welfare League performed the play *The Haunted House* before a captive audience at Sing Sing prison and then she did the show for three weeks in Philadelphia.

There were more shows that never reached New York, and then she finally returned to Broadway in *Alias the Deacon* (1925), a modest hit—something that was rare for her as she often went from one show to another. In 1926, Methot appeared in the plays *Fool's Bells* with Donald Meek; *Americans All* with Wallace Ford; a return engagement of *Alias the Deacon* in New York and Chicago; and *The Jazz Singer* with George Jessel.

She was Ann in Broadway's *What Ann Brought Home* (1927). It was produced and directed by Earl Carroll but without his usual naughtiness, the show lasted less than 100 performances. The curtain also came down on her marriage to John La Mond. On October 5, 1927, she filed for divorce, charging incompatibility, non-support and desertion, they had been separated for more than a year.

Later that month, she was on the New York stage as the daughter of a Dutch farmer in *The Medicine Man*. The verdict of the *Brooklyn Eagle*: "[Methot] seemed at first rather too fresh from the beauty parlor and far too cultured for her surroundings, but she warmed up as the play progressed and was most convincing in the last act." Her divorce from La Mond was granted on December 29, 1927.

More out-of-town plays failed to make the grade before she again landed on Broadway in *The Song Writer* (1928), but that also flopped, and it was followed by more shows that went nowhere. She and Grant Mitchell suffered through another New York misfire, *All the King's Men* (1929); she did *Hokus Pocus* in Connecticut; and had a dismal eight-performance Broadway run in *Now-a-Days* with Melvyn Douglas.

Up to now, Methot was regarded as a capable comedy and dramatic actress; even when a show was a bust, which was often, she was always well-reviewed. She had done some musical numbers here and there but was not considered a singer. Then composer Vincent Youmans heard her at a party and cast her in his new musical *Great Day* (1929). Methot, "dainty and demure" (*Pittsburgh Courier*), got one of the best numbers in the show, a standard that long survived the short run of the play: "More Than You Know," music by Youmans and lyrics by Edward Eliscu and Billy Rose. Most agreed that although hers was not a powerful voice, she put it over convincingly.

The *Hartford Courant*, lamenting her poor track record with Broadway shows, called Methot "one of the most beautiful actresses on the American stage and much sought after by producers." Alas, *Half Gods* (1929) was another failure. In 1930, while still in New York, she made her first talkie, the short *Taxi Talks*, which also featured Spencer Tracy in one of his earliest roles as the cab driver.

Arthur Hopkins, who had produced and directed *Half Gods*, was more than satisfied with Methot's performance in it, and when he needed a replacement for Joanna Roos in Broadway's *Torch Song* (1930), he cast Mayo as the jilted singer who joins the Salvation Army. "It is a mixture of realism and broad caricature," wrote John Chapman, "with a fat theatrical role for Mayo Methot that left last night's crowd in their seats at the second intermission, cheering her." He also praised her torch singing: "When her heart breaks over a man, it breaks, and does something to your own, too."

Torch Song was immediately bought by MGM. There was some talk that Methot would repeat her role on the screen, but when it went before the cameras (renamed *Laughing Sinners*), it starred Joan Crawford.

After *Torch Song*'s modestly successful Broadway run, Methot went to visit her mother in Portland (her father died in 1929 after an unspecified operation).

In 1931, Method recreated her *Torch Song* role at San Francisco's Alcazar and Los Angeles' El Capitan theaters. "It is good to be back in the West," she told the *San Francisco Examiner*'s Lloyd S. Thompson. "New York is a fine, exciting place, but every so often I get homesick for real mountains. They don't have any mountains in the East, you know—they just imagine they have." Interviewer Thompson found Methot to be

> a rather diminutive young lady with a laughing eye and a mouth rather strikingly like that of Lillian Gish. When I talked to her, she was anticipating a happy week prowling through the city's art galleries. In New York she spends her off Sundays in Carnegie Hall at the symphony concerts—Debussy is her favorite composer, with Wagner a close second. She is a spirited conversationalist and a thoroughly intelligent and likable person.

The same good reviews she got on Broadway for *Torch Song* were heaped on her in California and Thompson mentioned that "many of her scenes brought her bursts of spontaneous applause." The *Los Angeles Times*' Philip K. Scheuer wrote that she had a "rare talent for putting over a scene. Miss Methot is not a spectacular performer, but she seems to have caught a good deal of the anguish and helplessness [of her character]. We are really moved to a sort of cosmic pity for her and ourselves."

Due to her popularity in *Torch Song*, Methot was signed to appear with Chester Morris and Alison Loyd (aka Thelma Todd) in the film *Corsair* (1931). The bootlegging drama, directed, produced and co-written by Roland West, was meant to showcase his real-life girlfriend Todd as a dramatic actress. But ninth-billed Methot had the meatier female role as Sophie, tough cookie secretary who double-crosses her boss, bootlegger Fred Kohler, with the help of boyfriend Ned Sparks. Two of her scenes stand out: saying goodbye to Sparks before he leaves for a dangerous mission, and when she tries to manipulate Frank Rice into helping her warn Sparks of impending danger.

After viewing the rushes, West signed Methot to a personal contract to do two more films for him. This seemed like a big break, but *Corsair* was the last movie West ever did.

On November 28, 1931, at Riverside, California's Mission Inn, Methot wed Percy T. Morgan, Jr., described as a Beverly Hills oil man.

Now based on the West Coast, Methot concentrated on movies. She was a glamorous standout in the Thatcher Colt mystery *The Night Club Lady* (1932), where she played the title character, and *Vanity Street* (1932). The *Daily News*' Kate Cameron praised her "proper amount of hardness and slickness" in the former. One of her best roles came in *Virtue* (1932) as Carole Lombard's prostitute pal, in love with no-good Jack La Rue.

Her underplaying made her a natural for the screen but the variety she had on stage now gave way to typecasting. She was so perfect as tough wisecrackers that Hollywood had a hard time seeing past that. Still in her twenties, she looked and acted much older, and leading roles were not offered; she had to be content with character parts. Although many times Methot's screen time was limited, she could be counted on to make indelible impressions in her brief vignettes. One outstanding example is also one that went against the norm of her standard screen character: In her frazzled bit in *The Mind Reader* (1933), her desperation is palpable as she confronts Warren William on giving her bad advice. Her realism always set Methot apart from other hard-boiled dames. In the same year's *Good-bye Love*, she had some comic moments as Sidney Blackmer's ex and gets drunk with his intended, Verree Teasdale.

In October 1935, Methot returned to Broadway for the lead in *Strip Girl*, a comedy the *New York Daily News*' Burns Mantle called "coarse, crude and calloused. Probably as profane an exhibit as the theatre has revealed." He had nothing but praise for Methot, writing that she was "magnificently true to character, without apology and without fear. She played Dixie as she saw her, and she came through with her superiority to her material definitely and unmistakably established." After only 33 performances, the play closed the following month.

Marked Woman, which started filming at Warner Bros. in December '36, was one of Methot's best all-around movies, and she blended well with the other actresses (Bette Davis, Isabel Jewell, Rosalind Marquis, Lola Lane) playing "hostesses," aka D girls, involved with gangsters. Unfortunately, Methot's boozing had taken its toll on her looks and in the

Prosecutor David Graham (Humphrey Bogart) tries to persuade (*left to right*) "hostesses" Florrie (Rosalind Marquis), Estelle (Mayo Methot), Gabby (Lola Lane) and Mary (Bette Davis) to testify against gangsters in *Marked Woman* (1937).

film there are cracks made at her expense: "Kind of old, aren't you?" one of the characters asks her. "I need young dames here … the kind men go for in a hurry."

Methot and the film's male lead, Humphrey Bogart, started seeing each other. At the time, both were married but separated from their respective spouses.

On February 5, 1937, in Los Angeles, she filed for divorce from Percy Morgan, after being separated for almost a year. One of her complaints was that he wouldn't permit her to accept a stage engagement in New York City (probably *This Our House*). Morgan also reportedly became "sarcastic and abusive" when she changed the furniture around "to give the house a little different atmosphere." Morgan was being called a finance company executive, but would soon join with his brother to co-found the Cock 'n' Bull restaurant on the Sunset Strip.

At the time, Bogart had started divorce proceedings against his second wife, actress Mary Philips. It was already established that he and Methot would marry when both were free.

As the date of the Bogart-Methot nuptials drew nearer, columnist Sheilah Graham asked him if he was looking forward to the wedding. "You don't think I'd get married, if I wasn't," he told her "crossly" (her word). "I've had a whole year to make up my mind." His son Stephen Bogart later claimed that Bogie *was* having second thoughts, but felt obligated to marry Methot.

On August 20, 1938, they wed at the Bel Air home of scenarist Melville Baker. Mayo was so "broke," Gloria Stuart told authors A.M. Sperber and Eric Lax, she had to borrow a dress to wear for the ceremony because, Stuart said, "Bogie didn't buy her one."

The two had much in common, including a love of the sea, but they fought before the marriage and spent their wedding night apart after a post-vows brawl. Bogart's pet nickname for her was "Sluggy," which also became the name of their boat. Outside their house was a sign that read Sluggy Hollow.

With her new marriage, Methot lost interest in her career and she decided to concentrate on Bogart's. His first two tries at matrimony had failed because his wives continued to act and he didn't want that to happen again. Mayo was famously talking him up to producers, trying to get him out of gangster roles and advance him. This was the period before he was a star; some have claimed that Methot helped him a great deal with his low self-esteem as he struggled with Warner Bros.

But the tempestuous twosome fought continually, many of the battles fueled by alcohol to dangerous levels. There have been famous stories about Methot stabbing Bogie, waving a pistol at him, and setting fire to the house. Reportedly, he knew she was going to strike when he heard her humming "Embraceable You."

Neighbor Cynthia Lindsay, a writer then married to actor Russell Gleason, told Sperber and Lax that one night she saw from her window quite a scene being played out on the Bogart roof across the street: "We heard this ruckus, and there was Mayo with a noose around her neck, running across the top of the building—on a kind of balcony on the lower part of the roof. He was chasing her like a dog on a leash." Reportedly, Bogart was yelling, "I'm going to hang you!" Lindsay said everyone thought it was funny and no one believed they would actually hurt each other.

Fists, however, were the Bogarts' chosen weapons. The Battling Bogarts would often have scuffles that spilled out of their home and onto the lawn. Newspaper columns omitted their more serious domestic disturbances, but gleefully reported the nightclub and bar brawls. Drunks would pick fights with Bogie to see how tough he really was, but instead had to fend off the scrappy Methot. During one encounter, Bogart hid under a table with David Niven and reassured the actor, "Don't worry, Mayo's handling it."

At the end of '41, Methot described their relationship to Dee Lowrance:

> If you're too tame, you're half dead. Bogey and I like excitement. We need it. And we get it in these workouts of ours. The thing I'd like to stress though—to be serious a minute—is that they aren't what I'd call hangover fights. Ours never leave a nasty taste in the mouth. One minute we're mad, the next we're over it. We never hold grudges or go on those silent sulks that are so bad.

For his part, Bogart tempted the fates by being unfaithful, and he delighted in incurring her wrath. His son Stephen later noted, "Dad told the Mayo stories with great relish."

On the *Dodge City* (1939) train junket, according to Jimmy Starr, who claimed he witnessed it, Methot caught Bogart making plans for a rendezvous with an actress and

The Battling Bogarts take a tea break from their famous brawls.

hit him over the head with her high-heel shoe. Bogart threw her into a compartment and "slapped her around. I could hear the smacks."

Methot's frustration and jealousy escalated, and not without cause. Authors writing about the couple always put the blame on her, labeling Bogart as a victim of an irrational, mentally disturbed wife, but it takes two to tango; Bogie was very much a part of the problem, and thought nothing of instigating fights in front of dinner guests. (Reputedly, too, he was proud of the black eyes she inflicted on him.)

In a syndicated column supposedly penned by Methot, she wrote, "I didn't marry Humphrey Bogart of the screen. I married a man who behaves like a man and who offers me excitement as well as security and fun along with my food. And I like it."

Gloria Stuart and her husband, writer Arthur Sheekman, were friends of the couple; Stuart wrote in her autobiography, "Sadly, Mayo usually had bruises on her face—left or right cheek, chin. It seems unconscionable today to remember that we used to remark, 'They must get their jollies that way.'" Stuart also recalled Bogart ripping Methot's low-cut gown "right down to as far as it would go" in front of everyone just because she talked back to him. Another time, he shoved her into a bunch of chairs in a restaurant and made her cry.

According to Stephen Bogart, Methot was diagnosed as a paranoid schizophrenic, and a psychiatrist wanted to institutionalize her. Just how reliable was a medical diagnosis of this sort back in the 1940s? She was worried that her husband was cheating and was

Mayo flanked by Hugh Herbert (*left*) and Hobart Cavanaugh in *We're in the Money* (1935). Although she was 10th billed, Mayo's scenes as "Miss Griwatz" have been cut from modern prints.

violent when she was drunk. In any case, Bogart refused to commit her, allegedly saying, "My wife is an actress. It just so happens that she is not working right now. But even when an actress isn't working, she's got to have scenes to play. And in this case, I've got to give her the cues." Whatever emotional issues Methot had were exacerbated by her husband: "He played with her emotions," agent Sam Jaffe told Sperber and Lax. "I know he did it, because he told me so." Methot even tried suicide a few times as her mental health declined.

In 1940 and '41, Methot joined her husband on a tour of movie theaters, where they did songs and skits. "My own career? Pouff!" she remarked to Mildred Martin. She claimed she didn't mind giving up acting: "I get fun out of going over scripts with Bogie. I get a thrill out of previews of his pictures. Besides, I found out long ago it was better to be home waiting for him than to get back late from the studio and find Bogey doing a little foot-tapping. It's that sort of thing which ruins so many Hollywood marriages." That, and showing up unexpectedly on sets and giving the fish-eye to his female co-stars.

During World War II, they made a ten-week tour of North Africa and Italy entertaining troops. In a bar in Italy, they met up with director John Huston, who was making *The Battle of San Pietro*. A soused Methot insisted on singing, despite protests from everyone. Her off-key, pathetic performance allegedly inspired Claire Trevor's attempts at singing in Huston's Bogart-starring *Key Largo* (1948).

"Hollywood wags are insisting that Mrs. Bogart will return to this country with a black eye and a Purple Heart!" read an Erskine Johnson item that would never go over today. "Women should be beaten; it's good for them," Bogie reportedly told columnist Inga Arvad.

The Bogarts' relationship dissolved even further as Bogart's star rose courtesy of *High Sierra*, *The Maltese Falcon* (both 1941) and *Casablanca* (1942). But as Louise Brooks later wrote, "Except for Leslie Howard, no one contributed so much to Humphrey's success as his third wife, Mayo Methot … who set fire to him"—and Brooks didn't mean with a lit match. She added, "Those passions—envy, hatred, and violence, which were essential to the Bogie character, which had been simmering beneath his failure for so many years—she brought to a boil, blowing the lid off all his inhibitions forever."

Methot went with Bogart on location for *Sahara* (1943), and Bruce Bennett told Sperber and Lax that he thought she "was a very unhappy woman." He remembered that the couple was "constantly needling each other," and the sounds of shouting, breaking glass and shoved furniture were always coming from their suite.

The beginning of the end came when 44-year-old Bogart met 19-year-old Lauren Bacall on the set of *To Have and Have Not*, which started filming in February 1944. By October, the Bogarts announced they had separated and were headed for a divorce. After two weeks, they decided to give their marriage another go but then broke up again.

Methot had hoped a reconciliation would last but Bogart had had enough of the fighting—their conflicts were becoming more severe—and he wanted to marry Bacall. Methot resisted at first, unable to let Bogart go. Some columnists, such as Sheilah Graham, acted as if Mayo was standing in the way of the great love Bogart and Bacall shared. Graham went so far as to call Bogie "henpecked." There was no way Methot, whose looks had been ravaged by drink, could compete with the glamorous Bacall, a woman 20 years her junior. After more break-ups and make-ups, Methot finally gave in. "The real trouble with Humphrey Bogart and Mayo Methot was probably combat fatigue," wrote Jimmie Fidler.

In March '45, Methot, given a nice settlement by Bogart, headed for Nevada, and was granted a divorce on May 10. On the 21st of that month, Bogart married Bacall. They co-starred in four films together and their romance became legendary. (Bacall's solo career got off to a rocky start with 1945's *Confidential Agent*. Jimmie Fidler: "Ha! A local wit, after seeing Lauren Bacall in *Confidential Agent*, opined that the picture must have been directed by Mayo Methot!")

Methot moved to New York and tried to revive her Broadway career. But she had been away too long. She was seen around with Larry Golob, a publicity man who worked for Warners' Eastern office. "Mayo Methot is driving everyone in New York slightly screwy— going here, there and everywhere with a press agent who's a dead ringer for Humphrey Bogart," wrote Hugh Dixon. In 1946, Methot moved back to Portland, where her mother still lived. She invested her money in apartment buildings and kept a low-profile.

On June 9, 1951, 47-year-old Methot died at Portland's Holladay Park Hospital. She had recently undergone surgery for cancer and the cause of death was reportedly complications from a bout with the flu. This was the official story. According to *NW Examiner* reporter Carol Wells, Methot's body was "found in a motel room in Multnomah Village, where it had lain undiscovered for several days," but this fact was covered up by Mayo's mother, once a news reporter herself, because the death was actually a suicide.

Whatever the nature of her death, Methot was hardly destitute as other sources have claimed. She had real estate properties that produced a $3600 annual income ($34,786.11 in 2019 money) and $1400 in personal property. She had also left $50,000 ($483,140.38 now) in trust for her mother. (When her mother died in 1956, her will created a Mayo Methot Scholarship at Miss Catlin's School. Mayo's library of classic books was also willed to the school.)

Bogart heard the news of Mayo's death when he was on location for *The African Queen*. When Bacall told him, Bogart was quiet for a long time, then remarked, "Too bad. Such a waste." She asked him why, and he said that Mayo had real talent, but had "just thrown her life away." On alcohol, yes, but, to be fair, also on him.

But maybe he did feel a little guilty: For years, a dozen roses were delivered each week to Methot's marker in her family's crypt in Wilhelm's Portland Memorial Mausoleum. The roses stopped coming one week after Bogart's death on January 14, 1957.

Mayo Methot Filmography

1914: *Forgotten Songs.*
1922: *And Women Must Weep.*
1923: *While the Pot Boils, Mixed Trails, By Lantern Light, Unseeing Eyes.*
1930: *Taxi Talks* (short).
1931: *Corsair.*
1932: *Squaring the Triangle* (short), *The Night Club Lady, Vanity Street, Virtue, Afraid to Talk.*
1933: *The Mind Reader, Good-bye Love, Counsellor at Law.*
1934: *Jimmy the Gent, Registered Nurse, Harold Teen, Side Streets, Mills of the Gods.*
1935: *The Case of the Curious Bride, We're in the Money, Dr. Socrates.*
1936: *Mr. Deeds Goes to Town* (uncredited), *The Case Against Mrs. Ames.*
1937: *Marked Woman.*
1938: *Women in Prison, For Auld Lang Syne* (short, uncredited), *Numbered Woman, The Sisters.*
1939: *Should a Girl Marry?, Unexpected Father, A Woman Is the Judge.*
1940: *Brother Rat and a Baby.*
1944: *Report from the Front* (short, uncredited).

Marjie Millar

"Marjie Millar is a new screen personality, and her fine work in this picture indicates that she, too, is going places in a film career," wrote Jimmie Fidler in 1953 about the female lead in Martin and Lewis' newest comedy, *Money from Home.*

Don't feel bad if you've never heard of Millar. Her movie-TV career lasted all of five years: three movies with the likes of Dean Martin, Jerry Lewis, Shirley Booth, Robert Ryan and director Daniel Mann, plus recurring roles on TV with Jack Webb and Ray Bolger. Then bad luck tripped her up.

The younger of two children to an automobile distributor, of Scottish English descent, she was born Marjie Joy Miller in Tacoma, Washington, on August 10, 1930. She was four when she twirled a baton in a daffodil festival parade. A year later, Marjie won a Shirley Temple lookalike contest at the local Roxy Theater. As a young girl, she was the official mascot drum major of the Afifi Temple band and patrol and participated in the Pasadena Rose Bowl parade.

Starting in 1941, 11-year-old Marjie became known in Tacoma as the Sweetheart of the 41st Division because she sang for soldiers at Fort Lewis. She had her own radio series, *This Song Is Yours,* aired over KMGH. She spent many hours singing and dancing for troops during World War II.

About her budding career, she said, "I really loved the work, but my parents were smart. They would not allow me to make a childhood profession of it, much as I liked it. They allowed me to be a child, to play with the other children, to choose my fun, my subjects, and my college."

While in high school, she appeared in plays at the Tacoma Little Theatre. Her interest in acting continued when she attended Stephens College in Columbia,

Marjie Millar, a Hal Wallis discovery slated for stardom (courtesy C. Robert Rotter/Glamour Girls of the Silver Screen).

Missouri. There she was a member of the National Collegiate Players and studied with famed actress Maude Adams. While in college, Marjie acted in numerous plays, choreographed stage musicals, and worked in radio. At KSD in St. Louis, she acted in and directed radio programs including the series *Musical Silhouettes*.

On July 22, 1950, in Pierce, Washington, Marjie married James Sidney Rollins III, a University of Missouri student who hailed from an important political family. The union was dissolved shortly thereafter.

In 1951, she graduated from Stephens with degrees in drama and psychology. Returning to Tacoma, she taught at the Lewis Harter Dance Studios, acted on the local stage and did radio.

While visiting Los Angeles the following year, wholesome blonde beauty Marjie found that she could make money as a model. Magazine ads and covers followed. She met Mrs. Darryl F. Zanuck at a party and this led to a 20th Century–Fox screen test. The studio passed on her. Now named Marjie Millar, she screen-debuted in 1952 in "The Rivals," an episode of TV's *Fireside Theatre* with Robert Paige.

Paramount's Hal B. Wallis got hold of her Fox test and signed Marjie to a personal contract, and she made her screen bow in Wallis' *Money from Home* (1953). "Right in the middle of a love scene, Dean [Martin] will start looking at me cross-eyed and then I'm lost," she laughed to Emily Belser. "But don't get me wrong—I love acting!" Millar was a pretty and pleasant love interest. Martin sang Frank Loesser and Burton Lane's "Moments Like This" to Millar as they romantically danced outside—one of the dismal movie's few highlights.

On August 16, 1953, Millar was with some friends for the weekend at drugstore magnate Sam Sontag's home in Shelter Cove. They borrowed Conrad Hilton's 19-foot boat. Geary Steffen (Jane Powell's ex-husband) was water skiing behind the craft when Boni Buehler, a former airline hostess and aspiring actress, fell overboard. The backwash from the vessel forced her into the propeller. One of the passengers felt a thud and cut the motor. Steffen rescued Buehler, breathing air into her mouth as they rushed to Santa Ana Hospital. Buehler suffered devastating injuries: her left arm was sheared

"Besides being talented, Marjie Millar is about the most beautiful starlet to be seen on the screen in recent memory," wrote one critic (courtesy C. Robert Rotter/ Glamour Girls of the Silver Screen).

off an inch from her shoulder, and her left leg had to be amputated close to the hip.

Buehler had been Millar's college roommate and they were sharing a Hollywood apartment with another actress, Nancy Hadley. Millar remained loyal to her throughout her recovery and admired her perseverance.

Millar's second film for Wallis was the Shirley Booth starrer *About Mrs. Leslie* (1954). "She's utterly fascinating to work with," Millar told Erskine Johnson about recent Oscar winner Booth. "I've never seen anyone use their hands to help express emotion the way Shir-

Marjie made her film debut as Dean Martin's love interest in *Money from Home* (1953) (courtesy C. Robert Rotter/Glamour Girls of the Silver Screen).

ley does. She studies everything she does. She reads all the off-stage cues. She offers to help you with your lines, and then she thanks you."

In the film, Millar was likable as an aspiring actress who gets her priorities straight when she falls for Alex Nicol, but it was Booth's show all the way and Millar's screen time was limited. "Both Miss Millar and Mr. Nicol are stardom bound," wrote the *Bridgeport Telegram*. "Besides being talented, Marjie Millar is about the most beautiful starlet to be seen on the screen in recent memory, [and] both have an acting talent far beyond their youthful years."

Based on these two films, it was predicted that Millar would become a star. It's unclear what happened to her deal with Wallis. Some sources say that Paramount wanted to take over her contract and she balked at that.

When director Elia Kazan was contemplating a film version of Paul Osborn's play *Morning's at Seven*, he was hyped about Millar's possibilities in the lead. Unluckily for her, the project and his enthusiasm fell by the wayside.

Millar signed on as Ray Bolger's co-star in the TV series *Where's Ray-*

Sassy portrait of Marjie (courtesy C. Robert Rotter/Glamour Girls of the Silver Screen).

mond? (1954–55), which gave her an opportunity to show off her dancing skills. Bolger described her to James Devane as "a sort of June Allyson with sparkling eyes," and said one of the reasons she was cast was because she had "wonderful coordination for dancing." Columnist Walter Ames wrote, "I don't know who did the casting for Ray, but they certainly gave him an eye-opener for a partner in charming Marjie Millar. Without any help from her sponsor's products, I'm sure she could come close to winning any beauty contest she

Marjie and Alex Nicol played the secondary love interests in the Shirley Booth vehicle *About Mrs. Leslie* (1954) (courtesy C. Robert Rotter/Glamour Girls of the Silver Screen).

entered. In addition, she dances with Bolger with the greatest of ease."

On April 23, 1955, in Tacoma, she married photographer John Florea, 14 years her senior. Boni Buehler was her maid of honor. There was no honeymoon as Millar had to testify in court in Buehler's case against (among others) Conrad Hilton.

After her gig with Bolger, Millar was seen mostly in TV commercials. In September '55, she had the female lead in the Republic crime quickie *When Gangland Strikes*. "So maybe her career is on the upgrade again," wrote Eve Starr. "And she's a girl who really deserves it." But all that eventuated were roles on such TV series as *Star Stage*, *The Millionaire* and *The Bob Cummings Show*.

At the end of '55, it was announced that Jack Webb cast Marjie as Sharon Maxwell, a secretary in the Records and Identification Division, in his TV series *Dragnet*, effective January 1956. "She will be brought along slowly," wrote Eve Starr, "not appearing in every episode, but will eventually emerge as Sgt. Friday's best girl.... Webb is certain she'll give his show the lift it seems to need, which, coupled with the new starting time, should start the drums beating all over again for *dum-de-dum-dum*." The viewer response was "encouraging," wrote Steven H. Scheuer, who added: "The fans don't resent her as was feared." Millar labeled her character "aggressive ... I keep asking Joe for dates. I provide a contrast to Joe's stoic, hard-beaten manner."

Her agent, however, wasn't happy with the smallish size of her *Dragnet* role. He wanted to take her out of the series and get her one of her own, even mentioning a situation comedy that would pair her with football player Elroy "Crazylegs" Hirsch.

The lessening of her *Dragnet* role was based on fan reaction: Although they had liked her at first, the idea of a love interest for Sgt. Friday wore thin. "I believe Marjie Millar is a very fine actress and did a good job," Webb told Marie Torre, "but the TV audience seems to prefer the straight dramatic half-hour without the love interest." She exited the show in June '56 amid reports that she was pregnant. (There was no baby. Perhaps she used pregnancy as an excuse to leave the show.)

Her only known acting role in 1957 was an episode of *The O. Henry Playhouse* starring Thomas Mitchell. An unimportant supporting part in the chiller *Back from the Dead* (1957) went to Evelyn Scott when Millar was too ill to accept.

In May '58, Marjie was involved in a car accident that left her with multiple bruises and cuts. Since her injuries did not seem serious, the hospital released her. A couple of months later, she awoke to find that the small scratch on her ankle was inflamed and "became a hole you could put your fist in," Eve Starr later gruesomely related. Feverish and unable to move, Millar lingered in bed for two days until a neighbor suspected something was wrong and checked on her. Her husband was nowhere to be found.

At the hospital, Millar almost died when gangrene developed. Doctors were afraid that the infection would spread and that they would have to amputate her leg. For the next year she underwent a series of skin graft operations in an attempt to save her leg; she was told that she would never dance again.

During this ordeal, in August 1958, she divorced Florea, whom she claimed "showed her no love and affection" for more than a year and neglected her. He only visited her twice when she was in the hospital. She received $400 a month, medical expenses and half the proceeds from the sale of their Pacific Palisades home.

Bedridden for about three years, a depressed Marjie developed a serious drinking problem. Her family intervened and persuaded her to move back to Tacoma.

Millar underwent numerous operations, but she found new purpose in her hometown after looking up her old dancing instructor, Lewis Harter. While the surgeries continued, she, through therapy, was able to dance again. Millar started teaching children dance, drama, modeling, baton and song styling. She said, "I just couldn't get used to the idea of going through life with a limp. I can't stand people having to feel sorry for me. I was determined to walk right and dance again. And … well … it happened…. I think I've grown up a lot, am more sensitive and tolerant of others."

"Anyway, that's why you haven't heard anything about Marjie Millar until now," Eve Starr told her readers in 1961. "A very courageous girl who has kept her troubles to herself and let the rest of the world go about its own business."

While publicly Millar showed a positive outlook, she still battled alcoholism. Near the end of 1959, she met Tacoma native John Dennis McCallum, the writer of numerous books. His next project was to be a biography of Millar entitled *Talk About a Girl*. According to the *Port Angeles Evening News*, "McCallum believes the story of Miss Millar's

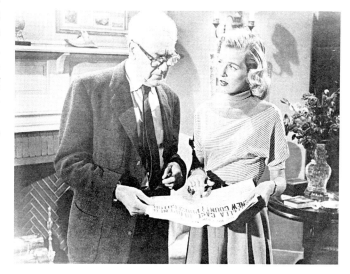

Raymond Greenleaf and Marjie Millar as father and daughter in the crime thriller *When Gangland Strikes* (1956) (courtesy C. Robert Rotter/Glamour Girls of the Silver Screen)

remarkable ability to persevere when most people accept defeat, will inspire others hand-icapped to greater effort toward a return to normal life. This is the theme of the book he hopes to complete this year."

On June 11, 1961, in Clallam County, Washington, she and McCallum married. The book was never published but together they produced and co-starred on a local Tacoma five-days-a-week television show called *The Voice of the Sound* and traveled around the state of Washington with a series of lectures, one of which was called "Hollywood—A Detached View."

On May 28, 1961, Millar was staying at Port Angeles' Aggie's Motel when she slipped getting out of the bathtub and cut her leg in two places. In May 1962, she filed a motion for a jury trial in her $10,108 personal injury suit against motel owners James and Aggie Willis. Her attorneys contended that the two scars in the front of her leg between the knee and the ankle were "permanent and disfiguring, constituting a substantial detriment to the plaintiff as a dancer." The suit's outcome is unknown.

On November 21, 1964, just after she got her final divorce decree from McCallum, Millar wed husband #4, Lt. Comdr. Charles Candoo, a former high school classmate, and they relocated to San Diego. Charles spent about a year in Japan on Navy duty while Millar stayed home.

On April 16, 1966, 35-year-old Millar died at San Diego's Coronado Hospital of cirrhosis of the liver. She had also been suffering from chronic pancreatitis.

In 1969, her ex-husband McCallum dedicated his book *Going Their Way* to "Marjie—a Very Special Memory."

Marjie Millar Filmography

1953: *Money from Home.*
1954: *About Mrs. Leslie.*
1956: *When Gangland Strikes.*

Mary Nolan

"What a story! Everything but the bloodhounds snappin' at her rear end." This line, from *All About Eve* (1950), best describes Mary Nolan's life. If ever there was a poster girl for Hollywood Hard Luck Ladies, it's Nolan. Jimmie Fidler wrote that she had "a genius for choosing the wrong kind of friends and a talent for getting herself into trouble. She lacked the strength of character that she needed to protect herself from the consequences of her own beauty. Fame and success and money, in her case, were not blessings but misfortunes." She destroyed two careers with three different names and was dead before the age of 50.

The youngest of five children, she was born Mary Imogene Robertson on December 18, 1902, in Hickory, Graves County, Kentucky. (The year 1905 is the most often given, but on her U.S. passport application in 1924 she put 1902 as her year of birth.) In 1904, when Mary was still an infant, her mother died. Her father, in poor physical and financial shape, found he could not care for Mary and sent her to live with a foster family. From there, she was shipped to a St. Joseph, Missouri, orphanage where she acquired the nickname "Bubbles."

Mary's early years were filled with upheaval and tragedy, shuttled back and forth between relatives and the orphanage and having to cope with the deaths of her mother, father (in 1911), sister Myrtle and a newborn nephew (both in 1912). As a teenager, she went to live with her sister Mabel and her husband in New York City. She modeled for artists James Montgomery Flagg, Norman Rockwell and Charles Dana Gibson.

In 1922, she made her stage debut as a chorus girl in *Daffy Dill*. Unaware that the show's star, 43-year-old Frank Tinney, was already married, Mary began an unhealthy relationship with him. (In her 1941 memoir, she claimed

Mary Nolan lights up in *Shanghai Lady* (1929).

to be 14 when she and Tinney met. She was 19.) "It was the perfect love match," DeWitt Bodeen later wrote. "He was a sadist with a violent temper; she was a masochist, who kept taunting him to beat her some more. Which he always did." Mary, in the first of her series of 1941 memoirs, wrote of Tinney, "Drink wrecked his life. In the years we were together I don't believe I ever saw him entirely sober. He lived on whiskey. Two to three quarts were his daily rations."

As Imogene "Bubbles" Wilson, she made a splash in the 1923 and '24 editions of the *Ziegfeld Follies*. Considered one of the loveliest of all the Ziegfeld Girls, she was called "the most beautiful blonde I ever glorified" by impresario Florenz Ziegfeld himself. Columnist Mark Hellinger noted, "Only two people in America would bring every reporter in New York to the docks to see them off. One is the president. The other is Imogene 'Bubbles' Wilson."

During the run of the 1924 *Follies*, fights between Mary and Tinney grew more intense and she attempted suicide. Days later, Tinney accused her of cheating on him with Hellinger, who had been interviewing her in her apartment. Tinney allegedly inflicted a beating on her. "He was a maniac," she wrote in 1941. "He couldn't have known what he was doing. He beat me horribly, with me screaming, kicking and clawing with all my might. But I was powerless against him." Her eyes swollen and her lips bleeding when the police finally arrived, she had Tinney arrested for assault. Filing a $100,000 civil suit against him, she called Tinney the "man who has left a trail of maimed women across the continent" (quoted in several newspapers).

In court, the lady claimed that Tinney subjected her to regular physical abuse; she said she had attempted suicide several times because she was tired of being beaten. The case went to the grand jury, but the charges were ultimately dropped. Tinney and his attorney accused her of merely seeking publicity.

After the trial, Mary didn't help her case when she got back together with Tinney. It certainly didn't do wonders for her career (or his, for that matter). "I dismissed Miss Wilson from the cast of the *Follies* this afternoon because she promised me that she would not have anything further to do with Frank Tinney," Ziegfeld said. "She broke her promise and I discharged her on account of the notoriety and also to prevent a possible disruption of the morale of my cast."

In September 1924, Mary set sail for England. "I am very unhappy and I want to go away," she told reporters. "I may stay away forever. From now on, I will lead a quiet life." The main reason for her departure: A month earlier, Tinney had taken off for England, where he had accepted stage engagements. When

Florenz Ziegfeld called Mary "the most beautiful blonde I ever glorified."

Mary arrived, they reconciled, but their relationship was no better and the abuse reportedly continued. She claimed his jealousy ruined her chances of appearing in movies and on the London stage.

Finally leaving Tinney for good, she moved to Germany. Here, billed as Imogene Robertson, she starred in a series of films. This success prompted a 1927 offer from producer Joseph Schenck and United Artists to make movies in America. Initially she declined, but she had been living lavishly in Germany and was having money problems; they were worsened by the cost of an operation she underwent in Berlin. (She later alleged it was the result of injuries inflicted by Tinney.)

While she had been accepted as a movie star in Germany, her notoriety here had not died down. The protests from people like Will Hays about her suitability in Hollywood put a scare into Schenck and UA. It was suggested she cancel her contract; when she balked, their solution was to change her name from Imogene Wilson to the plain Mary Nolan. "Of course, they were trying to tell me in a polite way that Imogene Wilson and everything associated with that name would be booed from the screen all over the land," she wrote in 1941. "They had given me a new identity, a fresh start, in an effort to bury my past."

She only made a couple of movies for UA, not the best parts, and only one with billing, *Sorrell and Son* (1927). Signed by Universal, she starred in 1928's *Good Morning, Judge*. In her first two films for the studio, she was credited as Imogene Robertson, but then started using the name Mary Nolan again.

Mary's most noteworthy film was made on loanout to MGM, director Tod Browning's *West of Zanzibar* (1928), as a girl caught in the middle of a paralyzed magician's (Lon Chaney) vengeful scheme against his late wife's ex-lover.

Movie stardom seemed to be in the cards for the young actress … but it wouldn't last.

Involvement with another married man, MGM executive Eddie Mannix, had devastating consequences. From 1927 to '31, she claimed, they lived together as man and wife at the Ambassador Hotel. Like Tinney before him, he reportedly abused Mary; a 1931 beating was so severe that she ended up at Good Samaritan Hospital for emergency abdominal surgery. She alleged that he attacked her again while she was recovering in the hospital and she eventually was "forced to undergo 20 operations."

Believing Maizie (Mary Nolan) to be the product of his late wife's affair with another man, magician Flint (Lon Chaney) introduces her to a life of debauchery in *West of Zanzibar* (1928).

During her long recuperation period, Mary became addicted to narcotics. Her *Young Desire* (1930) co-star, William Janney, stated in a 1991 interview with Michael G. Ankerich that the film was "a mess" because of her. "She took dope and practically everything else. She was supposed to have had all these [diseases] and it scared me to death when she would stick her tongue down my throat during our love scenes and rub herself all over me. I would go to the dressing room and gargle with Listerine because I was terrified she was going to give me something."

At this point, Mary needed drugs to help her get through scenes. In 1930, her drug use was investigated; one of her nurses claimed that Mary was "constantly under the influence of illegal drugs" and her arms full of hypodermic needle punctures. Supposedly the narcotic officers found no evidence to support these claims, and the investigation was dropped. Nolan later claimed that Mannix was instrumental in putting the heat on her. Universal fired her from the film *What Men Want* (1930) and her contract was terminated. "That Nolan girl has torn Universal limb from limb," wrote *Photoplay*. "She has passed fighting talk to everyone from Carl Laemmle down to the boy who waters the elephants. She has demanded, raged, stormed and caused more trouble than a hundred ordinary actresses." Nolan accused the studio of sabotaging her career.

Between 1931 and 1933, Mary found work mostly at the Poverty Row outfits, getting leads in *Enemies of the Law* (1931) and *Docks of San Francisco* (1932) and supporting parts in others. On March 28, 1931, she married Wallace T. Macrery. It was claimed that just before they tied the knot, the groom lost millions in the stock market. In fact, he was a page boy on the Stock Exchange and just "played" the role of the millionaire stockbroker. Before their marriage, he was serving as Nolan's secretary. In a psychiatric report, quoted in the *Evening News* in 1937, Dr. Anne L. Clark wrote that Macrery was "a suave, polite youth, suggesting the gigolo type."

He and Mary opened a Beverly Hills dress shop. This did nothing to ease her debts—in fact, it added to them—and she filed for bankruptcy. Her assets were $3,000, liabilities $93,000. The Macrerys got into legal hot water when they failed to pay their employees. Convicted of several labor law violations, they were ordered to pay $1,300 and sentenced

Mary, seen here with Ralf Harolde, is a carnival dancer who longs to start a new life in *Young Desire* (1930).

to 30 days in jail. While all this was going on, in August '31, Wallace was creating more trouble: Hannah Menihan, a Hotel St. Moritz manicurist, accused him of calling her to his room "for the wrong kind of service." Menihan remarked to detectives: "He should have called the gymnasium, and then some Lonely Hearts association." Once she was in the room, she alleged that he "began to make violent love to her, and then began sparring with her, and finally knocking her down." Her complaint charged him with beating her and "attempting criminal assault upon her." The case was settled out of court. In June 1932, Mary supposedly filed for divorce, citing their money difficulties, but it never happened.

The following year, she made her last film, Allied Pictures' *File 113*, in which she co-starred with an equally down-on-his-luck Lew Cody. She began taking singing engagements in New York and Pennsylvania, performing in cheap venues. "Mary Nolan, once Ziegfeld's 'American Beauty,' now sings sad songs in a little roadhouse," wrote columnist Paul Harrison.

In 1933 and '34, she was in trouble with the law for passing bad checks and accused of stealing $2,000 from a booking agent: The agent heard her sing at the Green Gables Tavern in Hazleton, Pennsylvania, and took her back to her hotel; he later noticed that his cash was missing. Both charges were dropped. Around this time, there were multiple hospital stays for operations for an "abdominal ailment."

Nolan sought work wherever she could, with stints in vaudeville and more seedy nightclubs and bars. "I don't like nightclubs, but I have to live," she told Joseph Mitchell in 1935. "I'm not a singer, but I have to make a living." Mary claimed she was studying English. "I am going back to Hollywood and I want to be physically and mentally in perfect health when I go. And, also, I want my English to be perfect. I am only 28 [she was 31]. I'm not old. I can make a comeback." She also revealed her interest in Christian Science. "No matter what goes wrong, when I read the words of Mary Baker Eddy, I am peaceful."

She never got another chance at Hollywood. A role in a British film, she claimed, fell through when she lost her voice for several weeks. According to columnist George Tucker, in 1936 she "warbled lachrymose songs [in a] cheap little Brooklyn honky-tonk." One tune was the "cruelly factual one about 'Out in the Cold Again.'" Her gigs were on the fringes of New York; none of her appearances were at any upscale establishments, just remote places. She also performed her act in Detroit and Pittsburgh.

Also, in 1936, she sued the man she blamed for her health issues, former boyfriend Eddie Mannix (now MGM's vice-president). According to Mary, not only did he assault her, he used his industry influence to put the skids under her career. Mannix countered that Mary had accepted $3,000 from him to pretty much leave him alone. In October, the $500,000 suit was settled, but the terms were secret.

Life was at its lowest, with alcoholism, illness and poverty plaguing her. In May 1937 she spent a night in debtors' prison for a long-ago $405.87 debt to the Wilma Gowns dress shop. Mary's hysterics and convulsions got her sent to Bellevue Hospital's psychiatric ward. Afterwards, she was quoted by the *Fresno Bee* as explaining: "The shock of my recent arrest and brief imprisonment for an old debt put me under a severe nervous strain. I am gaining strength daily, and am sure that in the near future, I shall be a strong healthy woman…. I'll do anything to earn an honest living, although I still believe that it is in Hollywood that I belong."

Newspapers printed shocking photos of Nolan looking dissipated and much older than her 34 years. Her manager Al Reinis secured her a nightclub job and an agreement had been reached to pay off her debt. Mary told reporters that she and the devoted Reinis would be married, but in reality she was still wed but separated from Wallace Macrery and would continue to be until she died. "Isn't it wonderful to have one person [Reinis] who believes in you and tries to help you no matter what happens? All of my fair-weather Broadway friends, for whom I did everything when I had plenty of money, have forgotten me now. But I have one person on whom I can rely, and, believe me, I'm not going to let him down."

Hollywood, unfortunately, did not care.

"Mary Nolan, whose name has become synonymous with bad luck, suffered new hardships yesterday," wrote the *New York Daily News* on June 3, 1937. Just three weeks after her confinement at Bellevue, the landlord of the cheap rooming house where she was staying hollered cop and she was removed by stretcher. Members of the Ziegfeld Girls Club arranged with the Actors Fund to move the "very sick" Mary to the Brunswick Home in Amityville, New York. "She was too proud to ask aid," someone from the Actors Fund told Dale Harrison, "even when she needed it desperately."

By August '37, Mary was out and about and claiming she was "maliciously libeled" when a "well-known Harlem weekly," the *Amsterdam News*, alleged that she had once been married to Dr. Eugene Nelson, a "colored Hollywood physician." After all she had been through, she said *this* story had damaged her reputation and she wanted $25,000

Reformed diamond thief Mary Nolan and miner John Gilbert fall in love in *Desert Nights* (1929).

to mend it. The newspaper actually had her confused with another *Follies* girl, Helen Lee Worthing. Nolan's case was dismissed.

In August 1937, her estranged husband Wallace Macrery also hit hard times. He was working as an usher in New York when he was arrested and sentenced to three years in prison for breaking into a restaurant and stealing $60 worth of cigarettes and liquor. "You are a member of a good family," the judge lectured the "stooped and seedy" man in court. "You received a good education. But Hollywood has ruined you. You can continue your Hollywood education in the penitentiary."

On October 19, 1937, Mary's manager Al Reinis brought her back to Bellevue Hospital after she overdosed on sedatives. A little less than a month later, she left on a stretcher, heading again to the Brunswick Home. According to the *New York Daily News*, alcoholism, narcotic poisoning and internal complications were the problems plaguing her.

In 1938, she was seeking $25,000 from Wilma Gowns for the arrest back in May '37. Mary insisted that because of her incarceration, she "had been compelled to forego contracts as an actress and entertainer." When she didn't show up for the court date, the case was dismissed.

A year later, she was back in Hollywood and living with sister Mabel, in denial about how substance abuse and hard living had ravaged her beauty. "I am a competent actress, and there should be a place for me here. I want to go back to work" (*St. Louis Star and*

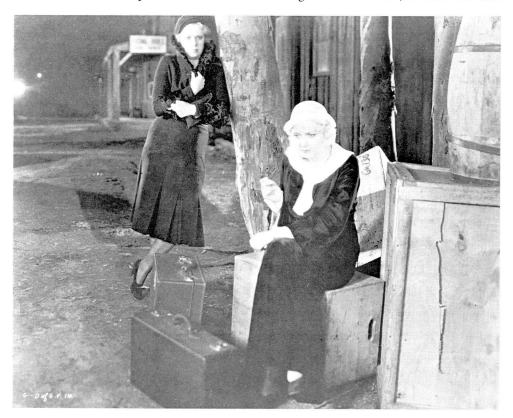

Gangster's moll Belle (Mary Nolan, *right*) contemplates a better future, as her friend Rose (Marjorie Beebe) looks on, in *Docks of San Francisco* (1932).

Times). For a time, she managed a bungalow court. In 1941, she sold her life story to *The American Weekly*, which netted her a little money.

In April 1944, Walter Winchell informed his readers that Mary was working as a private nurse in Hollywood. A month later, he was reporting that she was "so ill and in sour luck again on the Coast." Winchell was back in June '45 stating that Mary "had completely cured herself" and was working as a nurse in a sanitarium for "similar sufferers."

Life, however, remained difficult and she existed in poverty-level conditions. Mabel (with whom Mary had been living) later told the *Los Angeles Times* that Mary's only possession at this time was an antique piano previously owned by Rudolph Valentino: "I think she worshiped Rudy's memory. She clung personally to this piano and always kept Rudy's picture on the music rack. I think it reminded her of her own greatness and helped her profoundly in her discouragement."

In April 1948, under the name Mary Wilson, she was brought to Hollywood Receiving Hospital, suffering from malnutrition (she was down to 70 or 90 pounds; sources vary) and a chronic gall bladder disorder. She was transferred to Cedars of Lebanon Hospital, her stay paid for by the Motion Picture Fund.

Louella Parsons: "I can tell you one of the things which added to Mary Nolan's serious condition is that she was bitterly disappointed when a book publisher told her he has decided not to publish her memoirs, *Yesterday's Girl*."

Throughout the year, she was in and out of the hospital with the same issues and had to be fed intravenously. In the fall, she complained of abdominal pains and her doctor left some additional sedatives for her to use if the pain continued. On October 31, 1948, 45-year-old Mary Nolan was found dead in her bungalow. Newspapers reported that a bottle of morphine sulphate was found near her body. Mabel told the press that the cause of death was a bladder ailment, but an autopsy confirmed that Mary had overdosed on sedatives.

Her funeral was attended by 50 friends and family members. Dr. Walter Raymond, pastor of the Unity Church, said he had hoped that in the Hereafter, "[she] would find the life that is truly indestructible." She is buried at Hollywood Forever Cemetery.

"As I ran over my life in retrospect, I realized that I had too much, too young," Mary reflected in 1941. "It spoiled all natural instincts. It has been said that beauty is a gift, money a blessing, and success a crowning glory, but success robbed me of happiness. I didn't misuse these things that were given me. They misused me."

Mary Nolan Filmography

1925: *Wenn die Liebe nicht wär'!, Das Parfüm der Mrs. Worrington, Die Feuertänzerin, Die unberührte Frau, Verborgene Gluten.*
1926: *Fünf-Uhr-Tee in der Ackerstraße, Unser täglich Brot, Die elf schillschen Offiziere, Wien, wie es weint und lacht, Das süße Mädel, Die Welt will belogen sein, Die Abenteuer eines Zehnmarkscheines, Die Königin des Weltbades, Die Abenteuer eines Zehnmarkscheines.*
1927: *Erinnerungen einer Nonne, Halloh–Caesar!, Topsy and Eva* (uncredited), *Sorrell and Son, Die Mädchen von Paris.*
1928: *Good Morning, Judge, The Foreign Legion, West of Zanzibar.*
1929: *Silks and Saddles, Desert Nights, Charming Sinners, Shanghai Lady.*
1930: *Undertow, Young Desire, Outside the Law.*
1931: *Enemies of the Law,* × *Marks the Spot, The Big Shot.*
1932: *Docks of San Francisco, The Midnight Patrol, Beautiful and Dumb* (short), *Broadway Gossip No. 3* (short).
1933: *File 113.*

Susan Peters

According to *Variety*'s December 29, 1943, review of *Song of Russia*, "[I]f it achieves nothing else, [it] at least establishes the stellar value of a comparative newcomer; this is Susan Peters' most important role to date. It reveals her as one of the finest young dramatic actresses to emerge from Hollywood in some time. The word-of-mouth on her performance, beauty and expressive underplaying should make her a 'must' in any future Metro plans."

She was unquestionably headed for stardom, having also gotten an Academy Award nomination for her first big role in *Random Harvest* (1942).

A gun-related accident on New Year's Day 1945 changed all that, leaving Peters unable to walk. It was thought her acting career was over.

Peters, described by *The New York Times* as a "charming but an extremely stubborn and self-willed person," refused to give up. She presented herself to the public as handling her disability with good humor and strength and earned the nickname "Hollywood's Unconquerable Star." Yet, pushing herself to continue might have been her downfall because she compromised her already frail health.

The older of two children of French-Irish descent, she was born Suzanne Carnahan in Spokane, Washington, on July 3, 1921. Her great uncle was General Robert E. Lee. Not long after her birth, the family moved to Portland, Oregon, and then back to Washington. On July 25, 1926, in Leavenworth, Washington, her construction engineer father, 33 years old, was killed in an automobile accident.

In 1943, *Variety* called Susan Peters "one of the finest young dramatic actresses to emerge from Hollywood in some time. The word-of-mouth on her performance [in *Song of Russia*], beauty and expressive underplaying should make her a 'must' in any future Metro plans" (courtesy C. Robert Rotter/ Glamour Girls of the Silver Screen).

Her mother went to work in a dress shop. When money became a problem, it was decided to send teenage Suzanne to Los Angeles to attend school and live with her paternal grandmother, Madame Maria Patteneaude, one of the city's leading dermatologists.

In an April 1943 *Boston Globe* article, the actress wrote that she first became interested in medicine on a summer visit back to Washington: "A little boy who lived near us was a victim of infantile paralysis. [My brother] Bob and I visited him every day. I couldn't understand why he couldn't be cured until Mother explained it to me. That's when I determined to study medicine. This remained my goal until financial reverses stepped in to block the way."

Just before Suzanne entered Hollywood High, her mother and brother came to live with her and Madame Patteneaude.

High schooler Suzanne was taking a drama class when Hollywood talent scout Lee Sholem became convinced of her screen potential. (It struck Suzanne as funny that "a studio representative would pick the poorest student in a high school dramatic class as a potential star....") Deciding that acting would be an easy way to make extra money to get to medical school, Suzanne went along with the idea. But despite Sholem's interest, others were not impressed by her ability. A test for the movie *Our Town* (1940) was not a success.

Writer and family friend Salka Viertel arranged for Suzanne to meet with director George Cukor, which led to a bit in *Susan and God* (1940). Suzanne auditioned at Max Reinhardt's School of the Theater and was given a three-month scholarship.

Susan wearing a flamingo bathing suit (courtesy C. Robert Rotter/Glamour Girls of the Silver Screen).

There are two versions of how she got the attention of Warner Brothers producer Henry Blanke: He either saw her in *Susan and God* or in Reinhardt's production of *Holiday*. A screen test resulted in a Warners contract. She started in small, mostly uncredited "conditioning parts," wrote Harrison Carroll, "implying that better jobs are coming." She was also a "test girl," helping other youngsters get contracts. "The next two years were tedious, hard-working ones," she wrote in *The Boston Globe*. "But I shall always be grateful for every moment of them.... No stock company, vaudeville circuit or dramatic school could give me the training I received by making these tests. Every one presented a new play, a different type of leading man and a lesson in acting."

The Warner years were not a total bust. *Santa Fe Trail* (1940), where she was billed 24th, was her first credited role (as Suzanne Carnahan). As the blonde-wigged Boston schoolmate of

Olivia de Havilland, she catches the eye of George Custer (Ronald Reagan) at a dance. In real life, she was engaged to another *Santa Fe Trail* cast member, Bill Marshall. An elopement to Salt Lake City didn't go as planned when she chickened out at the last minute.

After this, Warners wanted to change her name to Sharon O'Keefe. When she heard their choice, she told Frederick C. Othman she "howled," adding, "[T]he Warner Brothers were very nice. They sent me a list of 50 names and told me to choose my own. I picked Susan Peters." Under this name, she had the ingénue leads in *Three Sons o' Guns* (1941) and *The Big Shot* (1942), as well as a loanout to RKO for *Scattergood Pulls the Strings* (1941).

The *Dayton Daily News'* Evelyn Hart, reviewing *The Big Shot*, called Susan an "attractive little actress who might be groomed for those roles Olivia de Havilland is getting tired of." In fact, Peters more closely resembled newcomer Joan Leslie and their competition for roles at Warners always ended with Leslie getting the nod.

She was considered for parts in *Sergeant York*, *They Died with Their Boots On* (both 1941) and *The Male Animal* (1942), losing out on the latter when she was stricken with appendicitis. Her illness also kiboshed a planned wedding to actor Phillip Terry.

Peters' failed screen test as the mentally unstable Cassie in *Kings Row* (1942) prompted Warners to release her from her contract—"which is a polite way of saying they fired me," she told Frederick C. Othman. Discouraged, she thought of going back to her original plan of being a doctor; after all, she told Frank Chapman,

> I had never really wanted to be a screen actress anyway and the disappointments of those two years were anything but encouraging. I was through and really didn't care much. I have seen hundreds of girls hanging on to the fringes of Hollywood when they should have quit. They hang on, bit parts, infrequent extra work, and their hold growing more and more precarious year by year. That was not for me. People who do that just beat their brains out for nothing.

Then her agent told her about a role MGM was casting in *Tish* (1942). She met with its director, S. Sylvan Simon, and to her surprise was given the part of a young girl who secretly marries and dies in childbirth when she thinks her husband has died.

Her love interest in *Tish*, which began filming in April 1942, was 21-year-old Richard Quine. "They had several love scenes together," wrote Sidney Skolsky. "Then they began to play the scenes offstage and without a script." That was bad news for Quine's wife of four months, showgirl and model Susan Paley, who traced their marital rift to the early stages of his filming *Tish*.

Director Mervyn LeRoy and producer Sidney Franklin ran some of Peters' rushes from *Tish* and were struck by her dramatic ability. They had been having

An atypically sultry portrait of Susan (courtesy C. Robert Rotter/Glamour Girls of the Silver Screen).

trouble casting the part of Kitty, the young girl amnesiac Ronald Colman almost marries, in *Random Harvest* (1942).

"Susan Peters is getting raves because of her work in *Random Harvest* with Ronald Colman and Greer Garson at MGM," wrote Edwin Schallert. "Some say that she'll steal the high honors. She is of the Teresa Wright school of younger players." Critics were particularly affected by the way she played the scene where she realizes Colman loves another: "I'm not the one. I am nearly the one, Charles, but 'nearly' isn't enough for a lifetime."

Peters had some good moments in *Dr. Gillespie's New Assistant* (1942) playing a newlywed who uses an elaborate ruse to hide her past from her husband. Quine had a role in the picture as an Australian intern.

Random Harvest had reaped Peters an Oscar nomination for Best Supporting Actress (she lost to *Mrs. Miniver*'s Teresa Wright), but MGM seemed unsure how to cast her. Although in her early twenties, she had a mature screen presence and should have been given roles that reflected that.

A powerful role in the wartime drama *Assignment in Brittany* (1943) was incongruously followed by the frivolous *Young Ideas* (1943), where she tries to break up her mother's new marriage. There was talk she would replace Ann Rutherford in the Andy Hardy series; MGM even tacked a brief scene onto the end of *Andy Hardy's Double Life* (1942) to "introduce" her. But wiser heads prevailed. According to columnist Frank Chapman, these were Peters' future plans: "I'll not act after I'm thirty. I don't want to live the rest of my life in a goldfish bowl. I want to marry, live in a small town and have children."

In October '42, Mrs. Richard Quine went to court for a divorce, citing his "aloofness," her age (she was 27, he was 21) and his "infatuation for another woman" as the main reasons for the split. In March 1943, with Quine set to go into the Coast Guard, he and Susan had to wait until his divorce was final to tie the knot. "I admit I am in love with Richard," Peters told Louella Parsons, "and proud of it, but of course, you can't make any plans with the war

Richard Quine and Susan Peters met and fell in love while filming *Tish* (1942).

on." Louella noted, "Susan is so straightforward and never tries to evade a question put to her, and she is a fine little actress."

Also, in 1943, Peters was named one of *Motion Picture Herald*'s Stars of Tomorrow.

MGM considered co-starring Robert Taylor (one of their biggest stars) and Susan in *The Last Time I Saw Paris* and *Gentle Annie*. The movie they ultimately made, *Song of Russia* (1944), would come back to haunt both MGM and Taylor (who claimed the assignment was forced on him). When it was made, the Soviets were our allies but by the late '40s it was a different world and all the House Un-American Activities Committee could see were Communistic elements. It was actually a simple story of a Russian pianist (Peters, in a role Greta Garbo turned down) and an American conductor (Taylor). Producer Joseph Pasternak anticipated problems and told Louella Parsons at the time, "It's a love story laid in Russia with no reference being made to politics." Peters later told columnist Jim Morse, "The government asked us to make that one. That's when we were all supposed to be pro–Russia. We changed from pro–Russia to anti–Russia so fast that I just keep my peep shut. I don't want to get mixed up in politics."

On November 7, 1943, at Los Angeles' Westwood Community Church, Peters married Richard Quine.

Her next at MGM was to be an adaptation of Millen Brand's 1937 novel *The Outward Room*, a story about a mentally unbalanced girl who escapes from an institution and tries to rebuild her life. The role would be a heady one, testing her abilities more than any of her previous parts. The director was Jules Dassin, and Susan's co-star would be Robert Young. The new title was given variously as *Secrets in the Dark* and *Strangers in the Dark*.

Then Brand's ex-wife, poet-novelist Pauline Leader, threatened to sue MGM for $500,000, alleging that the main character was based on her and "it would damage her because there is an illicit love affair and a baby born out of wedlock." Louella Parsons made a salient point: "Of course, I wonder if Mrs. Brand knows there isn't a chance of an illicit love affair nor an illegitimate baby in any movie these days? Papa Hays and his office would say 'No! No!'"

Russian pianist Susan Peters is romanced by American conductor Robert Taylor in *Song of Russia* (1944).

In April '44, Peters underwent an emergency abdominal operation which was described in news reports as being "of a serious character." (At the time, *Variety* said she had her appendix removed; modern sources blame a miscarriage.) *Secrets/Strangers in the Dark*, which had been filming for at least ten days, was halted pending her recovery. The film was eventually shelved due to Peters being "critically ill" (so said Louella) and the threatened lawsuit.

As she was recovering, several projects floated around the studio for her including *Death in the Doll's House* (which was later filmed in 1950 as *Shadow on the Wall*). Finally, in late summer 1944, Peters—still not entirely well after her operation—joined Lana Turner and Laraine Day as WACs in training in *Keep Your Powder Dry*. She played the most level-headed and sweetest of the trio. Perhaps alluding to the blandness of her role compared in her co-stars, Peters told Mayme Ober Peak on the set, "I'm tired of playing sweet roles. I want good parts … that's why I'd like to be a character actress, because they get the good acting plums of the year. I won't be happy until I'm the best one of the business. When I find I'm just fair, I'll quit." Ober Peak concluded the interview by stating, "Susan Peters is a natural. She's so real and brings such reality to her roles that few people think she's acting. It's an art few develop."

In mid–December '44, with Quine stationed in the Coast Guard's public relations department in San Diego, Peters was thinking of joining the voluntary port security force, an auxiliary of the Coast Guard.

On January 1, 1945, Peters was out duck hunting with her husband, his cousin Tom Quine and his wife Mary Lou in the Lake Cuyamaca region, east of San Diego. Peters went to retrieve the barrel of a partly dismantled .22-caliber rifle that was left behind underneath a bush. According to the Associated Press, "The trigger, in an exposed condition, caught on a branch and discharged a shell which had not been removed from the firing chamber when the stock was separated from the bolt-action rifle." The bullet pierced Peters' upper abdomen and lodged into her spine. During the ride to the hospital, she felt she might die, but then thought, "It isn't the right time. I have too many things to do yet." The slug was surgically removed at San Diego's Mercy Hospital.

"I don't know anyone who has worse luck than Susan Peters," Louella Parsons wrote on January 4. "She was sick for so long and still hasn't fully regained her health, and now the accident in San Diego.… At first it seemed as if she wouldn't have the strength to pull through, but today she was better. It will be a long time before she'll be able to return to the studio. She's been off the screen for a year now, and it's a pity because she is such a promising young actress."

By January 9, it was being reported that Peters was paralyzed from the waist down, but there was still hope. "The doctors say that although paralysis is there now, Susan is improving rapidly and eventually will be able to walk again," her mother told reporters. "The upper part of Susan's body is not affected, her mind is very alert and she is quite cheerful."

One of her lungs was damaged and she was getting constant blood transfusions. A three-week–long high fever weakened her eyes. By the end of January, she was awaiting a transfer to Hollywood's Cedars of Lebanon. A special chair was being made for her and she hoped by then to be able to sit up.

A local radio station announced they would stage a benefit for Peters upon hearing that MGM immediately took her off the payroll after the accident. Louis B. Mayer responded by insisting that Peters was being kept on salary. "We expect Susie will be back here on the lot and we certainly don't want one of our brightest stars an object of charity. Besides, that would not be necessary even if we didn't help, but we feel she's entitled to her salary, and we are giving it to her gladly, and any other help she needs."

As Peters was convalescing in the hospital, Lou Costello sent her a 16mm movie projector with a note (recounted by Erskine Johnson): "I don't know you but I'd like to make your life in the hospital more pleasant. Seeing movies kept me from going crazy when the docs kept me in bed." Distributor Scotty Brown gifted her with a print of *Counsellor at Law* (1933), in which a teenage Richard Quine played a role.

In May '45, *Keep Your Powder Dry* was released. "She is thus the most likable and the most admirable of the trio, and leaves the best impression on the audience," the *Baltimore Sun*'s Donald Kirkley wrote. At that point, it was uncertain if Peters would ever be able to go before the cameras again.

By June, Peters was optimistic that she would be walking pretty well in three months, telling Bob Thomas, "I took three steps in my braces yesterday. And it's only been a week since I had them on for the first time. The first time I tried them, the doctor said I could only stand for three minutes. But I surprised him and stood for ten. The next time I was feeling pretty cocky and fell on my face." Asked if she would continue acting, Peters replied, "Why, of course. Just let them try and stop me. The doctors won't let me discuss any business at this stage, but I'd like to do some radio work for a while. Then I'll go back to the movies." She wanted to tour military hospitals to show boys in similar conditions that they could walk again. "I am convinced that anyone can walk, no matter what may be the matter with them." Ultimately, she was too frail for the braces and she had to give up on them.

She later amended her thinking, telling Mary Morris that she was "planning my life as though I'll never get out of this wheelchair. Then whatever happens for the good is a birthday present." She believed in hope but "I also think you've got to think the way you are." Quine constantly encouraged her and reinforced her faith that she could carry on. "I don't know what I would have done without his support and help," she told Edwin Schallert. "He is the true believer about everything coming out all right."

On September 4, 1945, she made her first acting appearance after the accident: the *Theatre of Romance* radio series' adaptation of "Seventh Heaven" with pal Van Johnson. "I was pretty scared to face that audience in a wheelchair," she admitted to Virginia MacPherson, "and my hands were shaking so hard I could hardly hold the script. But I did it!" Initially, her doctors didn't think she was up to the challenge but she argued for the chance. "They decided it'd be good for me, I guess. Or else, they just gave in to keep me quiet."

There were promises of roles at MGM, including *The Barretts of Wimpole Street*, *The Romance of Rosy Ridge* and *Ballerina* (renamed *The Unfinished Dance*), but the studio never came through. Jimmie Fidler couldn't understand this since he claimed Peters, who had no new pictures out, was "ahead of all but three stars on the MGM lot in fan mail received."

Meanwhile, she wrote articles for *Photoplay* and did more radio (*Theatre of Romance*'s "Love Affair" with Van Johnson; *Lux Radio Theatre*'s "Johnny Eager" with Robert Taylor; *Encore Theatre*'s "Dark Victory" with Franchot Tone; *Suspense*'s "They Call Me Patrice"; and *Family Theater*'s "The Awakening" with hubby Quine).

Peters was trying to lead a normal life, learning to drive a hand-controlled car, taking flying lessons, going fishing and hunting, and making personal appearances. She also continued to visit handicapped soldiers in hospitals to boost their morale.

After Quine was discharged from the Coast Guard, he went back to his contract at MGM. Peters' 53-year-old mother died of heart disease on December 4, 1945, which was a big blow as she was a constant presence when Susan was recovering in the hospital.

In January 1946, Peters and Quine decided they wanted to adopt. "I think it will be the best thing in the world for us to have babies in the house," Quine told John Todd. "Susan loves babies. Whenever she has a chance, she goes over to Laraine Day's to take care of her baby. If we had our own, it would give Susan something to concentrate on all the time." On April 17, 1946, they adopted ten-day-old Timothy.

In June 1946, she underwent a series of operations "which doctors hope may completely cure her paralysis," wrote Jimmie Fidler. She was back in the hospital in September. Nothing changed; she remained in her wheelchair.

When she was finally well enough to make a movie, it was not with MGM (she bought her way out of her contract) but an indie produced by Irving Cummings for Columbia. For her participation, she would be sharing in the profits; Peters explained to Bob Thomas, "The only way for me to make pictures is with a percentage. My lawyer has arranged it so I will be paid over a period of ten years. It's like an annuity."

The film, *The Sign of the Ram*, started shooting in July '47. "Of course, I will have to arrange the schedule so it isn't too tiring—perhaps work a five-day week," she told Bob Thomas. "I'm terribly excited about it and a little bit frightened. It's been so long." Her brother and aunt, a registered nurse, were on the set to help her throughout the shoot.

Troubled Christine (Peggy Ann Garner) is emotionally manipulated by stepmother Leah (Susan Peters) and it almost leads to murder in *The Sign of the Ram* (1948).

She was particularly thrilled about the departure the part would afford her: "It's a mean woman, and that's the role I'd like to play. I couldn't stand to play one of those starry-eyed, good little girls." She didn't expect many other movies in her future. "It would be hard to find roles for me—in my condition."

A wheelchair-bound Peters gave an edgy performance in *The Sign of the Ram* as a troubled woman manipulating her husband and stepchildren; outwardly sweet, she is actually controlling and devious. She scoffed at Bob Thomas' suggestion that she should be nominated for an Oscar: "The shooting schedule isn't long enough for an Academy Award performance." Alas, the movie was not a favorite with critics (because of her character's unsympathetic nature) or at the box office. The *New York Times*' Bosley Crowther thought she was "worthy of a more substantial token of respect" than she receives in *The Sign of the Ram*.

It was back to radio with appearances on *Family Theater* (with Robert Mitchum), *The Radio Reader's Digest* and *Studio One*. She was disappointed when a role she really wanted, in *Walk Softly, Stranger* (1950), eventually was given to Alida Valli.

She took a trip to New York with her brother, seeing the sights and a few Broadway plays. Quine got a contract with Columbia to produce and direct; it would be the start of a whole new career for him. The couple was making plans to build a house and contemplating another adoption.

Louella Parsons praised Quine's devotion to Peters and how he "let his own career go" to care for her. It was, said the columnist, "one of Hollywood sweetest stories."

But it didn't last: By March '48, the couple separated and she and Timothy went to live on her brother's ranch near San Luis Obispo. Quine, referencing reports of their "perfect marriage," remarked, "[People] put us both on a pedestal and we couldn't live up to this ideal." To Louella Parsons, he stated, "[For] a long time she has been asking for her freedom. She has said again and again that she is much happier alone. When she went to New York without me, she said she knew how much better off she is by herself." He emphasized that the divorce was Peters' idea, not his.

Peters explained to Louella, "I think it's better that we separate. He's really a noble guy, but he's entitled to a normal life, which he can't have with me. Many times, he's been offered jobs that he couldn't take, because he couldn't leave me or take a chance. I want him to be free to have his own career which has been sadly hampered." Quine's response: "I'm not a hero—I'm just an ordinary, plain guy, and I wish that Susan would feel we could continue together."

Sheilah Graham was the first columnist to imply that Peters was romantically interested in a fellow paraplegic, lawyer Bill Hamilton, something Peters denied. "My doctor thought it would help me to meet Mr. Hamilton," she told Harrison Carroll. "It has, too. I have been inspired by what he has been able to do since he was hurt 14 years ago." It was probably her association with Hamilton that prompted Peters to take law classes at UCLA.

On September 10, 1948, she was granted a divorce; she received custody of their son, $300 a month for his support and a dollar a month alimony for herself. She testified that she and Quine disagreed on everything, adding, "Then my husband would refuse to speak to me for days and I became so emotionally upset I couldn't eat."

The following month, she was in Detroit raising money for the Community Chest. "Some might say that I have had more opportunities to rebuild my life than others," she told reporters. "And, by golly, that's undoubtedly true. But, don't you see, that's why I'm here. That's why we have the Community Chest. It provides money and facilities so less fortunate persons can get treatments—both physical and mental—so they can rebuild their lives."

Beginning on January 16, 1949, she hosted a local Sunday night television program called *Mabel's Fables*. Sheilah Graham reported an incident that happened when Peters called a "big studio" to ask if she could use some of their actors on her series. Someone in charge told her, "If we let you, it would be just out of pity for you." Remarked Graham, "Susie hung up and cried silently. That really was brutal."

Starting in June '49, against the wishes of her doctor, she toured the straw-hat circuit in the plays *The Glass Menagerie* and *The Barretts of Wimpole Street*. "If I waited [for] approval, I'd never do anything," she remarked to Harrison Carroll. Her brother, his wife and a nurse traveled with her.

After the success of her eastern tour, Peters took a slight break, during which she appeared on Ed Sullivan's *Toast of the Town* TV show competing in a ping-pong match with two world champions. Then she went back on the road with *The Barretts of Wimpole Street*. "I cherish my independence," she told Bob Thomas. "So I had to find a way to make a living and keep my little family together." While she was touring, her son remained in California with friends.

She put on a cheerful front for reporters, telling them what fun she was getting out of life, although doing split-weeks and one-nighters took a physical toll on her and doctors urged her to undergo another operation. "They said I would never be able to stand the ordeal of this tour," she told Peggy Starr. "The nervous strain of playing one-night stands and continuous travel. But I am standing it fine. I have sat up 20 hours at a time." But she admitted she needed to conserve her energy for her performances because of her lack of sleep.

She continued her grueling *Wimpole Street* tour into the early months of 1950. Consistently getting good reviews and box office, she was praised for the emotional depth and "wringing emotional quality" (*Pittsburgh Post-Gazette*) she gave to the character of invalid Elizabeth Barrett Browning. From March to May 1950, she switched to *The Glass Menagerie*, which she did with "beauty, simplicity and warmth" (Paul Jones, *Atlanta Constitution*).

When she got back to California, she weighed around 80 pounds and hoped a rest would do her good before going back to the touring grind. True to her word, in July '50, she was performing *The Glass Menagerie* in stock and *Wimpole Street* on the Subway Circuit.

Fatigue cut her tour short in September and she returned to California. Richard Quine allowed her to stay at his house while he moved in with friends. Doctors urged her to undergo another spinal operation because she was in such intense pain, but she held off, hoping therapy would be better. In February '51, she returned to stock in *Wimpole Street* but had to cancel performances due to illness.

Peters gave up the road when NBC offered her the TV role of Susan Martin, a paralyzed attorney who practices law in her hometown of Martinsville, Ohio, in the 15-minute, five-day-a-week *Miss Susan*. Because there was no available space in New York, the production was moved to Philadelphia. Peters told Elizabeth Toomey,

I really always wanted to be a lawyer, but it would take me several years, so this television serial is as close as I'll get to that, I guess…. I go to see these boys in paraplegic wards of the veteran hospitals, and some of them are so bitter. For the life of me, I can't think of anything to be bitter about. I'm doing the things I want to do.

On July 6, 1951, three years after she won her interlocutory degree, Peters and Richard Quine finally divorced. The final degree should have been entered a year after their divorce was granted but her lawyers claimed they "never received instructions to take the legal step after informing her of her rights." It was issued on Quine's request because he wanted to remarry. Meanwhile, Peters was engaged, to Col. Robert Clark, who was doing overseas duty in Germany.

Miss Susan ran from March 12 to December 28, 1951. Her daily schedule was from 10:00 a.m. to 6:00 p.m., a routine that wore her down and adversely affected her health. She became so ill she had to leave the show. Reports said she was recuperating "from the agony" (Erskine Johnson) of her TV show in Denver; others that she was resting after surgery at her brother's ranch. She was unable to work, although some columnists were saying she was reading scripts in May '52.

In June, Erskine Johnson wrote that she had been hospitalized in Exeter, California, after a "delicate skin graft operation." It was reported that she would soon go out on the road again with *Barretts of Wimpole Street.*

The truth, according to her doctor, was that Peters "wouldn't allow anyone to help her…. In the last few months, I felt she had lost the will to live." In August, frail, exhausted and suffering from depression, she told her physician, "I'm getting awfully tired. I think it would be better if I did die."

Death came to the valiant 31-year-old Susan Peters on October 23, 1952, at Visalia Municipal Hospital. The primary causes were kidney failure due to a chronic kidney infection and bronchial pneumonia. Her doctor said she battled internal infections for years. Several days before her death, she stopped eating and drinking, which hastened her demise. She was buried at Forest Lawn.

Timothy began living with Quine before Susan's death. Timothy's daughter Shannon told this author,

My dad never talked about Susan. I know my mom said that she didn't treat him very well towards the end, but I'm sure that had more to do with her deteriorating health than anything else. I never really knew what his life was before; he kept everything very much to himself when it came to that.

Richard wasn't really a good father [to Timothy]. He was more into movies and his career and couldn't pay attention to anything else. My dad had become very much self-reliant at a very early age and was also exposed to drugs and alcohol at parties which made him an addict at a young age.

Dad was not close to Richard at all. I know he was kicked out at 16 or 17 and pretty much was on his own from there. He spent a lot of time in jail for multiple things. He did mostly labor, warehouse jobs, but he was extremely smart and read a lot. My dad had a lot of charisma and was friendly, but also had a bad temper and could be very mean. He was an alcoholic–drug addict, and it ultimately led to his death in 2007. He chose to overdose and was successful.

I'm sorry I don't know a whole lot about Richard and Susan, but I know my dad was very traumatized and damaged.

As for Richard Quine: On June 10, 1989, a day before his fifth wife's birthday, the 68-year-old shot himself in the head with a shotgun. Modern sources paint a dramatic picture of him, tormented by memories of his ex, Susan Peters, killing himself with the same gun that crippled her 44 years earlier. While he probably did have lingering regrets about Peters, the truth was he was depressed and in poor health.

Susan Peters Filmography

1940: *Susan and God* (uncredited), *Young America Flies* (short, uncredited), *Money and the Woman* (uncredited), *Always a Bride* (uncredited), *Santa Fe Trail.*
1941: *The Strawberry Blonde* (uncredited), *Meet John Doe* (uncredited), *Here Comes Happiness* (uncredited), *Scattergood Pulls the Strings, Sockaroo* (short), *Three Sons o' Guns.*
1942: *The Big Shot, Tish, Dr. Gillespie's New Assistant, Random Harvest, Personalities* (short, uncredited), *Andy Hardy's Double Life.*
1943: *Assignment in Brittany, Young Ideas.*
1944: *Song of Russia.*
1945: *Keep Your Powder Dry.*
1948: *The Sign of the Ram.*

Lyda Roberti

According to her discoverer Lou Holtz, Lyda Roberti's success was

due to the fact that she is a natural wit and can adapt herself to any spontaneous bit of business that occurs on the stage. She has worked with me through three different productions now and has proven her ability beyond a doubt. Unlike most stage comics, she needs little rehearsing and practically no part to make good. Give her a few lines, a suggestion or two and she carries an entire scene, including ad-lib stuff. I can always rely upon her for a comeback that is funny no matter what I say when I stray away from the written lines.

Roberti's brand of breathless, kinetic energy was simply irresistible and best show-cased in such films as *Million Dollar Legs* (1932) and *College Rhythm* (1934). The fun-loving 28-year-old Lyda was so full of life tearing up the screen in the latter that it is hard to accept that she would be dead less than five years later.

Portrait of an effervescent Lyda Roberti (courtesy C. Robert Rotter/Glamour Girls of the Silver Screen).

Born Lyda Pecjak on May 20, 1906, in Warsaw, Poland, she was the second of three children to the German circus clown Roberti and his Polish bareback-rider wife. (Both of Lyda's siblings used the Roberti surname in their professional careers: Mary aka Manya acted on stage and in movies and Robert was a musician.)

According to publicity, Lyda "could walk a slack wire, ride horses bareback, do aerial stunts on a trapeze and wrestle with a trained lion when the average child was just beginning to go to school." It's difficult to determine if many of the stories Lyda told of her childhood were true or a publicist's fancy.

The family traveled extensively with a circus act through Russia, Egypt, France, Germany and Turkey. Lyda and her family were supposedly "caught in Russia by the revolution" and ended up in Shanghai, where in the early 1920s Lyda and Manya sang and danced in nightclubs; Lyda's specialty was a burlesque number called "The Dying Swan." When the show they were in went broke, the stranded sisters worked as waitresses. "For interminable weeks we served tourists and natives," Lyda later recalled to the *Baltimore Sun*. "Then Manya met a young American, married him and came to the United States. I saved enough for my own passage and followed." Her first work was as a chorus girl in a stage show at the Paramount Theater in Los Angeles.

The "petite Polish dancer and singer" appeared in "piquant and quaint numbers," wrote the *Oakland Tribune*, by herself and with the orchestra of Horace Heidt and with Larry Ceballos. In 1928–1929, her association with the latter led to a brief foray in films, the shorts *Undersea Revue* and *The Roof Garden Revue* (where she sang and did some acrobatic dancing). Billed as "The Irene Bordoni from Poland," Lyda was a member of Fanchon and Marco's revues, but broke her contract because she was required to buy her own costumes and pay for her own transportation. She later claimed that she lost out on a chorus job in Broadway's *Fifty Million Frenchmen* (1929).

At the end of 1930, she toured movie houses in the *Black and Silver Revue* and received praise for her "personality prattle." On the road, she was noticed by producer and comic actor Lou Holtz, who engaged her for his Broadway-bound *You Said It*, a "slick and urbane musical comedy of college life without the faintest suggestion of football or baseball complications" (*Philadelphia Inquirer*).

Lyda, as a "rather rough and very ready 'Polak' town girl" (*Los Angeles Times*), didn't have a very big role, but when *You Said It* opened in Philadelphia on Christmas night, 1930, she was an unqualified sensation. Before its Broadway opening (January 19, 1931), Walter Winchell was dubbing her the "find" of the season: "She is from Poland and her dialect is contagious, but so is her talent." Her big number "Sweet and Hot" (pronounced "Swit ahndt Hawt"), written by Harold Arlen and Jack Yellen, stopped the show every night. "It isn't exactly opera," remarked David P. Sentner, "but Lyda sizzles it so naively that it is worth walking miles down the aisle to see. The boys in the orchestra trenches called for so many encores that Lyda was embarrassed. Lyda looks so cute when she is embarrassed."

Most agreed it was a routine show at best, but it was the perfect vehicle to propel Lyda to stardom. "Blond, thin and awkward, with a peculiar Polish accent, she was a riot," wrote Sidney

Columnist Mae Tinee praised Lyda's "grinning, irrepressible, sweet-tempered dim-wittedness" (courtesy C. Robert Rotter/Glamour Girls of the Silver Screen).

Skolsky. "She is by no means a finished performer. She doesn't work according to the formula and will go a long way if she is lucky enough not to learn it. Her charm lies in the fact that she is naive."

It wasn't long before ads called her "The Polish Blonde Broadway Has Gone Wild About!" The *Chicago Tribune*'s Burns Mantle, praising her sense of fun, reported that "offers have already been made by the ever-active scouts of the cinema for her services." Paramount was interested, but she stalled all offers because she felt a sense of obligation to Holtz for her big break. (Sister Manya, who was her understudy in the show and went on when Lyda was ill, signed a movie contract first—with Fox.) Lyda stayed with *You Said It* until it ended its run in July '31.

She subsequently joined Holtz, Ethel Merman, Kate Smith and William Gaxton in a vaudeville act that had a record-breaking run at the Palace Theater. Earl Carroll wanted to hire Lou and Lyda but they were contractually tied to a *You Said It* tour. They would have been better off with the *Vanities*: There were high hopes when the *You Said It* company arrived in Chicago in September '31, but they were dashed rather quickly. Some blamed poor business on the material (its ethnic humor didn't go over in the Windy City) and it closed.

Lyda was now free to accept Paramount's contract. In her first, *Dancers in the Dark*

Lyda in a rare serious moment. Paramount glamour at its best (courtesy C. Robert Rotter/Glamour Girls of the Silver Screen).

(1932), she was Fanny Zabowolski, comedy relief with Eugene Pallette (hilariously pronouncing his character's name of Gus as "Goose"), and breathlessly sang Ralph Rainger's "I'm in Love with a Tune." According to columnist Mollie Merrick, at a *Dancers in the Dark* studio preview, Lyda "put over such a clever song and dance that a professional audience was enthusiastic enough to applaud her work right in the middle of the picture. Which ought to be a hint to Paramount to do something about it."

In February and March 1932, Lyda was back with Holtz in his 1932 *Vaudeville-Revue*, which also boasted Harry Richman, Hal LeRoy, Mitzi Mayfair, Benny Baker, Gloria Grafton, Larry Adler, etc. Harold Arlen, who worked in the revue as well, wrote her a song called "You Got Me, Baby."

Her second for Paramount

was the one that really put her on the map: the zany *Million Dollar Legs* (1932) starring Jack Oakie and W.C. Fields. A fourth-billed Roberti plays the greatest woman spy of all time, Mata Machree, the Woman No Man Can Resist, a parody of Mata Hari and Garbo. She is introduced on screen glamorously slinking down a long staircase singing Robin and Rainger's "It's Terrific (When I Get Hot)."

Loaned out to Goldwyn, she was Eddie Cantor's flirtatious love interest in the bull-fighter comedy *The Kid from Spain* (1932). Ads called her "the Willowy Sex Menace," but reviewers complained she was in too little of the movie despite her second billing. The score was so-so, but Lyda got the best number, a duet with Cantor on Kalmar and Ruby's "Look What You've Done."

Soon after she wrapped her scenes, Lyda was off to New York to co-star on Broadway with Jack Buchanan in the highly anticipated George and Ira Gershwin musical *Pardon My English* (1933). (Before it opened, Buchanan was replaced by George Givot.) The hit of the show was Roberti and her song "My Cousin in Milwaukee." During previews, Arthur Pollock wrote, "Miss Roberti puts more punch into her songs than any of the others, and manages to be broadly entertaining. The girl abounds in what might be called fetching animal spirits." Lyda's song "My Cousin in Milwaukee," plus "The Lorelei" and "Isn't It a Pity?" were the only things to survive the show, which closed after 43 performances in February 1933.

Paramount gave her two non-musical roles in *Three Cornered Moon* (as an unglamorous maid unable to understand much English) and *Torch Singer* (1933). In the latter, Lyda gave a quiet, charming performance as a widow who gives birth in a charity ward and befriends unwed mother Claudette Colbert. "It's a pity Lyda Roberti had so little to do," wrote the *Pittsburgh Post-Gazette*'s Harold W. Cohen, "but then the movies have never made the most of this girl anyway." True enough.

In March-April '33, she made personal appearances in Chicago and Philadelphia. Reviewers approved of her "wicked wiggle" and her "seezzling" manner (*Philadelphia Inquirer*). She was announced for parts in MGM's *Meet the Baron* and Paramount's Bing Crosby musical *We're Not Dressing*; she was replaced by Ethel Merman in the latter.

Instead, Lyda headed back to Broadway for *Roberta* (1933–34). It featured one of Jerome Kern's best scores and Roberti socked out two tailor-made tunes, "Something Had to Happen" (with Bob Hope) and the marvelous "I'll Be Hard to Handle." Arthur Pollock was grateful Lyda could be "relied upon to provide the robust quality the others lack. [She] dashes about and shakes her hips and sings strong nasal notes and is animation itself." Pollock also said that he looked forward to the day when she had a "nice role written for her and isn't asked to be the complete life of the party." Burns Mantle was more realistic: "Lyda Roberti, the wild one, clowns in, clowns out, which is what she is hired to do."

Pollock's comment that she "tries too hard" was an indication that Roberti was pushing herself. It was reported that she was very ill near the end of the run and might leave the cast.

Paramount gave the impish Roberti one of her best parts in *College Rhythm* (1934), where she gloriously put over the show-stopping title song and "Take a Number from One to Ten," both of which she recorded for Columbia. Paramount was thinking of teaming Roberti with W.C. Fields in a musical version of the Rip Van Winkle story.

Loaned to Fox, she gave a somewhat tame performance in *George White's 1935 Scandals*. As a short-tempered chorus girl (named after her real-life sister Manya), she is

From left: Bob Hope, Ray Middleton, Lyda Roberti and Sydney Greenstreet in the original Broadway production of Jerome Kern's musical *Roberta* (1933).

paired with Cliff Edwards and they duet on "I Got Shoes, You Got Shoesies" and they were included with stars Alice Faye and James Dunn on "Hunkadola."

Friends nicknamed the platinum blonde blue-eyed Roberti "Greenie." According to Iola Ellis' "Minute Biography," Lyda enjoyed fencing, "is effervescent and alive ... with a priceless sense of humor.... [She] laughs at the world.... It laughs right back."

An optimistic outlook would come in handy. Roberti had been romantically linked to Lou Holtz and *The Kid from Spain*'s assistant director Robert Golden. When she lost her appendix in late February, while recuperating at California Lutheran Hospital, she also lost her heart: Another patient, recovering from a car accident, was pilot and radio executive Hugh "Bud" Ernst. On June 25, 1935, the day after Ernst got his final divorce decree from his wife, he and Lyda eloped to Yuma, Arizona. Their honeymoon was delayed because Lyda was working on *The Big Broadcast of 1936* (where she sings Rainger-Whiting-Robin's "Double Trouble") and then when her doctor cited her "weakened condition" (presumably due to the aftereffects of her appendix operation) and ordered her to rest in the hospital.

In late July '35, she was able to make their honeymoon trip. When she and Ernst arrived at their boat, she refused to take off her sunglasses. The press speculated that she might be concealing a black eye from her new husband, an allegation she denied. Roberti said it was simply the case of the glare of the sun hurting her eyes. Ernst had another story: His wife had a stye. "We've had several spats," Lyda said, "but are perfectly happy." Walter

Winchell added another story: "She got it, it appears, doing publicity shots for Paramount on the Coast. While leaning on a ledge, Lyda fell one story, hurting her head too."

She was set to go to Broadway for a new edition of *George White's Scandals* with Bert Lahr and Cliff Edwards and sing "I've Got to Get Hot." Not long after that announcement, Winchell wrote, "Lyda Roberti is in a hosp, but for a mysterious reason!" A month later, she felt well enough to appear in a preview of the new *Scandals* in Virginia, but following her performance she became ill and was ordered to rest for two days before the company advanced to Newark, New Jersey. "Chronic laryngitis" was blamed when Gracie Barrie took over Roberti's role there and subsequently on Broadway.

Leaving Paramount, Roberti signed with Hal Roach for a comedy series with Patsy Kelly; Lyda was taking the place of Kelly's old castmate Thelma Todd, who had died. Roberti complained that Paramount had "sexed her up" and she felt her real forte was slapstick comedy—something she hoped Roach would let her do. She and Patsy teamed in the 1936 shorts *At Sea Ashore* and *Hill-Tillies* and the feature *Nobody's Baby* (1937). (Of the latter, columnist Margaret Miles wrote, "Roberti is the possessor of an intriguing accent, has a fresh manner and is chubbily cute.")

Lyda was offered a role as a countess in Paramount's *Champagne Waltz*, but turned it down "on the grounds it was too small for an actress of her caliber," wrote Sheilah Graham.

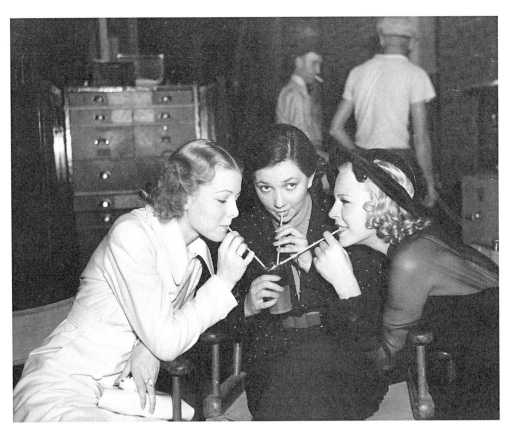

Three on a Soda: (*Left to right*) Rosina Lawrence, Patsy Kelly, and Lyda Roberti during a break in filming of *Nobody's Baby* (1937).

In May '36, Roberti sought to annul her marriage to Ernst, giving no details on the reason. Their relationship continued to be on again-off again and they never made their separation legal.

Lyda and Patsy Kelly were to join Oliver Hardy and Vincent Price(!) in *Road Show*, but Roach scrapped those plans. (He filmed it later with another cast.) Columnist Mae Tinee was one of many who liked the Roberti-Kelly combination and thought Lyda's "grinning, irrepressible, sweet-tempered dim-wittedness" mixed well with Patsy's "good-hearted, desperately earnest bungling."

Alas, they were never paired again. Roberti did contribute a song to *Pick a Star*, in which Kelly was featured. The song, Fred Stryker and Johnny Lange's "I've Got It Bad," has some presciently ominous lines involving needing a physician and being in a "bad condition" because of a bad heart.

Parting with Roach, Roberti made Columbia's *Wide Open Faces* (1938) with Joe E. Brown and Jane Wyman. It is a straight comedy role, a bit slight, as Alan Baxter's moll, and she vamps Brown in an attempt to learn where stolen loot is hidden.

On March 10, 1938, she filled in for an ailing Martha Raye on Al Jolson's radio show. Two days later, 31-year-old Roberti died at her Sunset Blvd. apartment with her husband Ernst at her side. Her doctor told the press she had suffered a severe heart attack the night before and he had given her "heart stimulants." Another report said her death was attributed to "chronic nephritis," an inflammation of the kidneys. For the past two years, she had curbed her screen work because of a heart ailment and she had had "frequent"

Lobby card of Joe Penner (*left*), Lyda Roberti and Jack Oakie in *College Rhythm* (1934).

heart attacks during that time. (A weird rumor circulated that she died of a heart attack while bending over to tie her shoes, but this was apparently untrue.)

Her funeral attracted more than 400 friends. Eulogist Ernest Holmes praised her charitable activities; her favorite songs were played by Salvatore Santaella's trio; and James Newill sang "The Rosary" and "Abide with Me." Roberti was interred at Forest Lawn. (Her gravestone has a 1912 birthdate.)

Bud Ernst later married twice more, to Mary Pickford's niece Gwynne and actress Betty Furness. He committed suicide in 1950.

Lyda Roberti Filmography

1928: *Undersea Revue* (short).
1929: *The Roof Garden Revue* (short).
1932: *Dancers in the Dark, Million Dollar Legs, The Kid from Spain.*
1933: *Three Cornered Moon, Torch Singer.*
1934: *College Rhythm, Hollywood Rhythm* (short).
1935: *George White's 1935 Scandals, The Big Broadcast of 1936.*
1936: *At Sea Ashore* (short), *Hill-Tillies* (short).
1937: *Nobody's Baby, Pick a Star.*
1938: *Wide Open Faces.*

Peggy Shannon

In 1931, ex–Ziegfeld Girl Peggy Shannon thought she got the greatest break of her life when she was contracted to replace ailing star Clara Bow in Paramount's *The Secret Call.* It was a heady beginning for the screen newcomer. Little did she know how the comparisons to Bow would haunt her throughout her short life, even though the only similarity they shared was red hair.

Ten years later, when Shannon died, some headlines were not so kind: "Peggy Shannon, Who Sought Clara Bow's Place, Is Found Dead"; "Peggy Shannon Dead; Failed in 'It' Role"; and "Failure in Films Discovered Dead." All obits pointed out how she "failed" as Bow's successor—as if that was ever one of her goals. There was more to Shannon than being Bow's shadow.

Born Winona Sammon on January 10, 1907, in Pine Bluff, Arkansas, of Irish descent,

A striking portrait of Peggy Shannon.

she was the daughter of a real estate agent who later became a hotel and restaurant owner. Sister Carolyn was born in 1920. Winona attended Annunciation Academy, a Catholic school in Pine Bluff.

In 1919, she met ten-year-old actress Madge Evans, who was passing through Arkansas on a personal appearance tour, and from then on, Winona was adamant that she wanted to become an actress.

In 1923, while visiting New York City with her mother and sister, 16-year-old Winona was offered a job as a chorus girl by Florenz Ziegfeld. She dropped out of Pine Bluff High School to accept. Ziegfeld changed her name to Peggy Shannon and she appeared in the *Ziegfeld Follies of 1923* (1923–24). The press painted her as a simple country girl, a "sweet but wild little devil with red hair streaming and green eyes shining" (*San Francisco Chronicle*), who hunted possum, rode horseback, ran barefoot and climbed trees on her family's farm. Peggy was "a breath of the little old hometown on Broadway."

By 1926, Peggy had joined Earl Carroll's *Vanities*. In February of that year, she was named as co-respondent in Beatrice W. Bourne's suit for separation against her husband Arthur K. Bourne II, president of the Singer Sewing Machine Company. Mrs. Bourne alleged that her husband and Peggy had lived together as man and wife for a year.

On February 26, 1926, in New York, Peggy wed actor Byron Alan Davis, who was appearing in the show *White Cargo* in Philadelphia. Davis had gained notoriety in July 1925 when he was shot behind the right ear by ex–*Vanities* girl Edith Parker, who claimed to be his common-law wife. When the case went to trial in April 1926, Parker testified that Davis "frequently beat her and kept all the money she earned" (*Variety*) and gave her morphine. On the day of the shooting, she heard Davis and two other men "plotting to attack" her. Parker's self-defense plea earned her an acquittal, and she had some advice for Peggy: "I feel very sorry for the new Mrs. Davis and hope she will not live the life I did with Davis. I also hope she will not have to support him, as I did for nearly two years. If she sticks with him long enough, she will have to keep him." It was a lesson Peggy had to learn herself.

In 1927, Peggy was an extra in her first film, *Foreign Devils*. Moving away from the chorus, Peggy became a part of the Rivera Players at Brooklyn's Werba's Rivera Theatre playing supporting parts in *The Little Spitfire*, *An American Tragedy*, *The Barker*, *Tenth Avenue* and *Jimmie's Women*. On– and off–Broadway, she appeared in *Piggy*, *What Ann Brought Home*, *High Gear* (all 1927), *Back Here*, *Pipe Dreams* (both 1928), *Now-a-Days*, *Cross Roads*, *Girl on the Barge* (all 1929), *Damn Your Honor* (1929–30), *A Smart Woman* (1930) and *Life Is Like That* (1930– 31), and was briefly under personal contract to William A. Brady. In October 1930, Peggy started in the play *Blind Mice*, but was replaced after only a couple performances by Mildred MacLeod. In 1930 and '31, she made two Warner Bros. Vitaphone shorts, *The Gob* and *The Meal Ticket*.

March 1931 saw her on Broadway in *Napi*, a play directed and co-starring Ernest Truex. It did not last, but Paramount became interested in her. They brought her to Hollywood, ostensibly to play the lead in *Is Zat So?* These plans changed a week after her arrival when she was given what was

Peggy showing off her legs and a saucy attitude (courtesy C. Robert Rotter/Glamour Girls of the Silver Screen).

thought to be a big break: replacing star Clara Bow, who had suffered a nervous breakdown, in *The Secret Call* with Richard Arlen.

Paramount went all-out promoting their new star—perhaps too far. She was called the "New It Girl," with newspaper ads noting that Peggy had red hair just like Bow. Good publicity at the time, it would taint Peggy's career for years to come.

Her next two assignments were as replacements for others, Mary Brian in *Silence* and Carman Barnes in *The Road to Reno* (both 1931), yet she was still being compared to Bow. Columnist Robbin Coons claimed that Peggy was even being made up to resemble Clara as closely as possi-

Even in this sexy shot Peggy exhibited a down-to-earth likability.

ble and that Peggy "would like to break away and be herself—and rightly."

The studio co-starred her with Arlen again in *Touchdown!* (1931) and Charles "Buddy" Rogers in *This Reckless Age* (1932), but stardom did not come and they loaned her to Poverty Row outfit Tiffany for *Hotel Continental* (1932). *Variety*'s Ruth Morris thought Peggy's initial "stroke of good luck" would prove her "undoing" and did not see a bright future ahead for her if Paramount continued to

publicize her as a personality equal to the original It Girl. [She] has red hair, but in all other matters she is the direct opposite of the inflammable Clara. Miss Shannon's manner is thoughtful and well-bred. Her neatly ordered features couldn't begin to cope with the facial exaggeration of Clara Bow pantomime. Her temper is held firmly in check by a serene manner and a bright, restrained smile. She registers as a sane, likable and agreeably talented ingénue who suffers by an unfortunate comparison with someone whom she doesn't in the least resemble.

Sailor Peggy (courtesy C. Robert Rotter/ Glamour Girls of the Silver Screen).

Peggy, believing herself "on a treadmill," according to Robbin Coons, "working hard, but apparently getting nowhere," asked for her release. She lamented the parts given her, insisting to *Photoplay*'s Frances Kish that she was "really a comedienne. That's the sort of thing I always did on the stage."

Fox signed her for two pictures, *Society Girl* and *The Painted Woman* (both 1932), opposite James Dunn and Spencer Tracy respectively, but then she became a free agent. "I have always thought it unfair to Miss Shannon that she should have been launched on her screen career as the successor to Clara Bow," remarked Louella Parsons. "Neither her ability nor her personality made it necessary to exploit her as a substitute."

Publicity noted that Peggy was "the champion soda pop drinker of Hollywood. The titian-haired actress drinks pop instead of coffee. She takes a bottle when she rises, has it with her meals. A case of it is kept on the set at all hours. She has consumed as much as 15 bottles of pop in 10 hours, and she prefers strawberry." In reality, she preferred beverages of the alcoholic sort and it began to take its toll.

Leads came via the Bs, supporting parts in As. Nineteen thirty-three's *Deluge*, about the dog-eat-dog world that results from an apocalyptic earthquake and flood, was a standout.

Peggy's collection of rabbit's feet could not stop her film career from declining, and in 1934 she returned to Broadway for *Page Miss Glory*. She appeared in the movies *Night Life of the Gods* (she "steps out as a comedienne here and promises much if the producers will heed the possibilities disclosed by the young actress"—Edward E. Gloss), *Fighting Lady* and *The Case of the Lucky Legs*.

A 1936 contract with Columbia resulted in nothing. Movie roles were few; she went out on tour with Ernest Truex in *Larger Than Life* (1936) and did some radio. She toured in the Ed Wynn–produced play *The Light Behind the Shadow,* but during its run on Broadway (where the play was renamed *Alice Takat*) she was replaced by Ruth Conley. Depending on what source you believe, it was either due to a makeup or tooth infection. At the Pasadena Community Playhouse, she did *We Dress for Dinner* (1937) and co-starred in an industrial film for Standard Oil with Robert Armstrong.

Richard Arlen and Peggy Shannon on the set of *The Secret Call* (1931), the movie in which she replaced Clara Bow.

Nineteen thirty-eight was not a good year, as she was involved in three accidents; her shoulder was dislocated when a door slammed on her, and one of two car accidents resulted in a lacerated nose and cuts on her legs.

There was talk of a comeback in 1939 when she co-starred with Lee Tracy in *Fixer Dugan* and (unsuccessfully) tested for the Belle Watling role in *Gone with the Wind*. Unfortunately, her movie career did not improve and *Fixer* was her last leading part. Her best chances during this later period came via the *Our Gang* shorts *Dad for a Day* (1939) and *All About Hash* (1940). In both, she played Robert Blake's mother.

On July 8, 1940, after a rough 14 years, she obtained a divorce from Alan Davis, testifying that she supported him: "He was just lazy—he played all the time." She also alleged that he struck her in front of guests. Her friend Wynne Gibson verified the charge, saying the slap was "over something very inconsequential." Davis' treatment caused Peggy's weight to drop from 116 to 92 pounds.

Her last movie, the George O'Brien western *Triple Justice*, was released in September 1940. The following month, Peggy wed cameraman and studio carpenter Al Roberts in Mexico. She was cast in Monogram's *Roar of the Press*, but was replaced at the last minute by Dorothy Lee.

In March '41, Peggy was in the news when it was reported that a "chance encounter" with Alan Davis at a cocktail bar to talk over old times led him to go to her house to confront Roberts. A minor scuffle erupted before police were called. Davis' chauffeur was arrested on suspicion of stealing two wristwatches, but Roberts declined to press charges.

Less than two months later, May 11, 1941, Roberts returned from an overnight fishing

Sidney Blackmer carrying Peggy Shannon to safety in *Deluge* (1933) (courtesy Tom Weaver).

trip to find Peggy, barefoot and dressed in a sun suit, slumped over their kitchen table, an empty glass besides her and a burned-out cigarette between her lips. She had been dead for about 12 hours. An autopsy on the 34-year-old determined the causes: a liver ailment "resulting from excessive alcoholism" and a combination of low vitality, a rundown condition and a heart attack.

She was interred at Hollywood Forever, her headstone reading, "That Red Headed Girl."

Nineteen days after her death, on May 30, Roberts placed flowers on her grave. Returning home, the 39-year-old shot himself in the head with a rifle. His body was found slumped in the same kitchen chair Peggy died in. His suicide note stated, "It happened that I am very much in love with my wife, Peggy Shannon. In this spot she passed away. So in reverence to her you will find me in the same spot." Peggy's mother called for an investigation into their deaths, but nothing came of it.

On December 11, 1943, Peggy's ex-husband Alan Davis died (he had an abscess on one lung) at the age of 41. *Variety* wrongly reported that he "leaves a widow, Peggy Shannon, film actress."

Peggy Shannon Filmography

1927: *Foreign Devils* (uncredited).
1930: *The Gob* (short).
1931: *The Meal Ticket* (short), *The Secret Call, Silence, The Road to Reno, Touchdown!*
1932: *This Reckless Age, Hotel Continental, Society Girl, The Painted Woman, False Faces.*
1933: *Girl Missing, Deluge, The Devil's Mate, Turn Back the Clock, Fury of the Jungle.*
1934: *Back Page.*
1935: *Night Life of the Gods, Fighting Lady, The Case of the Lucky Legs.*
1936: *The Man I Marry, Ellis Island.*
1937: *Romancing Along* (short), *Stan, Youth on Parole.*
1938: *Girls on Probation* (uncredited).
1939: *Blackwell's Island, The Adventures of Jane Arden, Fixer Dugan, The Women* (uncredited), *Dad for a Day* (short, uncredited), *The Amazing Mr. Williams* (uncredited).
1940: *Cafe Hostess, The House Across the Bay, All About Hash* (short), *Triple Justice.*

Rosa Stradner

"Fasten your seat belts, it's going to be a bumpy night!"

Few things in Hollywood history are as iconic as Bette Davis' Margo Channing uttering those words in writer-director Joseph L. Mankiewicz's Oscar-winning *All About Eve* (1950). That incident and the character of Channing were partly inspired by his wife, Rosa Stradner.

At parties at the Mankiewiczes, "it was a predictable event," their son Christopher remarked, "that my mother would hit the martinis and there would be a big scene. That cocktail party in *All About Eve*—it could not be more typical of almost any party given at our house. It seems so clear to those of us who were there that the inflections, the over-the-top dialogue, seem lifted out of our dining room." Christopher and his brother Tom agreed that the scene where Bill pins Margo on a stage bed and "tells her to stop the paranoid outbursts" sounded like their parents fighting. "The main difference," Tom added, "is that Mother had severe mental problems, which Margo Channing did not have."

However, helping (and inspiring) her husband with his screenplays just wasn't satisfying to the actress inside of her.

The daughter of a factory worker-engineer, she was born Rosa Stradner in Vienna, Austria, on July 31, 1913, and lived as an infant in Trieste and Isonzo, Italy. After World War I, she was educated in a convent.

She acted in school productions and one publicity item claimed that she was 15 when she debuted on a professional stage in Zürich, Switzerland, in a "small comedy part" (*Detroit Free Press*). At age 19, she auditioned for Max Reinhardt and was

Rosa Stradner displayed a "special sort of dignity," wrote columnist Alice L. Tildesley.

given a contract. By this time, she said, "I had put in seven years of dramatics. Each year I had read at least three English plays...."

For the next few years, Stradner appeared on the Berlin stage; her diverse repertoire included Shakespeare, Ibsen, Molière, Dreiser and O'Neill (more than 50 plays, classical and modern). According to the *Orlando Sentinel*, Italian Prime Minister Benito Mussolini was so taken by the young actress that he saw one of her plays three times and presented her with a bouquet.

Starting in 1933, she also made a few movies. At the Berlin premiere of one of her films, another admirer, Joseph Goebbels, offered her a 15-year contract to make films for Nazi Germany. When she said she preferred making Viennese movies, the Reich Minister of Propaganda replied, "In that case, you'll be working for us eventually. It's only a question of time."

In 1934, Stradner wed Karlheinz Martin, who had been directing her at the Volksbühne (People's Theatre). Twenty-seven years her elder, he was a well-regarded Germany stage and film director.

Official stories claim that Stradner was discovered by MGM's Louis B. Mayer and Benny Thau as they made a 1937 European trip and looked for talent; director-producer Victor Saville, actress Hedy Kiesler (aka Lamarr), singers Ilona Hajmássy (aka Massey) and Miliza Korjus and writer-director Walter Reisch were also found on that trip and were on the same ship with Stradner that headed for America. According to Tom Mankiewicz, it wasn't that simple: "She and my Austrian grandmother ... fled Austria and the Nazis in the mid–30s. My grandfather and uncle, Fritz, stayed behind to fight for their country. No one ever found out what happened to the old man. Fritz became an SS officer and was executed against a wall in Aachen, Germany, by Allied troops."

Rosa Stradner and Hans Söhnker in a publicity photo for the Austrian film *Diener lassen bitten* (1936) aka *Dinner Is Served.*

Stradner in costume for the Austrian film *Der König lächelt-Paris lacht* (1936).

Foto: Hammer-Tonfilm

Not coming to America with Stradner was her husband. There were conflicting reports on their relationship—he was either back in Austria or "tucked away" in Hollywood somewhere. But all agree on one thing, that there was a divorce soon after she arrived.

More than a few columnists stated that the real reason Stradner was signed by Metro was to keep MGM's German-born contract star, two-time Oscar-winner Luise Rainer, in line. The studio had been having problems with the difficult Rainer, who was turning down assignments. Columnists briefly fostered the notion of a rivalry between the two. "It seems that Rose Stradner … was on the stage in Vienna at the same time Luise Rainer was appearing in that city," wrote Grace Wilcox. "In fact, the two were more or less rivals. Unless I am mistaken, they are likely to be rivals on the screen and I'm betting on Miss Stradner. She is most interesting and 'different' looking." Added Alice L. Tildesley, "But there is no similarity between them. Luise is small, dark, vivid; Rose is tall, with blue eyes and brown hair, with a special sort of dignity. There is no one in the least like her in Hollywood." Less than two weeks after her arrival in America, Stradner was given one of Rainer's discards, *The Last Gangster* (1937).

The studio hatched a short-lived plan to change her screen name to Andrea Marlow or Andra Marlo, but finally simply substituted Rose for Rosa.

Based loosely on Al Capone, *The Last Gangster* is the story of ruthless underworld czar Joe Krozac (Edward G. Robinson), nicknamed "Napoleon Joe." He returns from a European trip with a new wife, starry-eyed Talya (Stradner), who is unaware of his business

Newly released from prison, Joe Krozac (Edward G. Robinson) confronts ex-wife Talya (Rosa Stradner) and her husband Paul North (a mustachioed James Stewart) in *The Last Gangster* (1937).

and penchant for murder. In early scenes, Stradner subtly plays her naïve character with a hesitant English accent, still learning the language, and confused about her surroundings. She becomes pregnant just as Joe is busted for income tax evasion. After Joe lands in Alcatraz, Talya realizes that he is not the man she thought he was and only married her to get an heir. She divorces him and marries a newspaperman (James Stewart). Starting a new life, she distances herself from the Krozac name to raise her son respectably. Meanwhile, Joe counts the days of his ten-year sentence and vows to track down her and their son.

Robinson dominates the proceedings, with his "unerring instinct for making a human being out of a screen shadow" (*Kingsport Times*). Stradner has a decidedly lesser part, but handles it with skill, making a believable transition from lovesick to disillusioned wife and again when she finds happiness with another man.

> In her first appearance before American screen audiences, Rose Stradner, MGM's new Viennese "find," proves herself not only lovely to look at but an actress of distinguished talent. In the difficult [assignment], she brings to the role a sincerity and dramatic depth that should endear her to American audiences and raise her to [the] front rank along with her contemporary, Luise Rainer.
> —*The Kingsport Times*

Paul Harrison thought her role "had enough drama to attract wide critical approval" and felt sure that MGM "has more important parts in mind for her." Initially, MGM felt she showed a lot of promise, and were impressed by her "haunting beauty," thoughtfulness, intensity and command of the English language.

Stradner came on the Hollywood scene during a period when studios were importing foreign stars. In 1937 and '38, there were Annabella, Danielle Darrieux, Olympe Bradna, Isa Miranda, Franciska Gaal, Della Lind (aka Grete Natzler), Miliza Korjus, Ilona Massey, Tilly Losch, Luli Deste and Hedy Lamarr. It is saying a lot that Stradner was considered to be the one in the group destined for great things. "She has two advantages over all the other recent glamour importations—a distinguished background in the theater, and a better command of English," wrote Paul Harrison.

At a time when MGM was even having difficulty placing Lamarr, Stradner just sat around doing nothing after *The Last Gangster*. RKO wanted to borrow her for *The Saint in New York*, but that deal fell through. In 1938, when MGM was preparing a new version of Rafael Sabatini's novel *Scaramouche*, Stradner and Fernand Gravet (aka Gravey) were purportedly going to be the leads.

After those plans stalled, Metro dropped Stradner's option. Austrian-born Lamarr, who created a sensation on loanout in *Algiers* (1938), came back to MGM a star and the studio scrambled to find stories for her. Stradner could never compete with the more glamorous and charisma-loaded Lamarr. (As far back as 1933, Stradner was abruptly replaced by Hedy in a Vienna stage production of *Sissy*; Rosa sued the producers for breach of contract.)

Stradner was in New York looking for stage properties when Columbia expressed interest in her. "I am awfully glad to hear Harry Cohn signed Rose Stradner in New York and is sending her back to Hollywood," Louella Parsons wrote. "I saw her in only one picture, *The Last Gangster* … but she was charming and it was surprising that she didn't do more." Parsons would remain an ardent Stradner booster.

In February '39, Stradner went to work on Columbia's psychological crime thriller *Blind Alley* starring Chester Morris as an escaped killer who holds a family hostage in their own home as he awaits transportation. Sixth-billed Stradner played the wife of the psychologist (Ralph Bellamy) who delves into the criminal's mind in an effort to weaken him. Although tame compared to its source (a 1935 play by James Warwick), the film packed its own punch and had especially strong acting. The top female role went to the amazing Ann Dvorak as Morris' tough but loving moll; her quiet, affecting scene talking heart to heart with Stradner is one of Rosa's best chances in the movie. Stradner's sensitive, restrained performance was one she could be proud of, and it should have proved to Columbia that she was able to handle bigger parts.

In New York, on July 28, 1939, Stradner married producer and writer (later director) Joseph L. Mankiewicz. The two had met at MGM while she was making *The Last Gangster*. With her once promising Columbia contract now a memory, Stradner quietly retired to a domestic life.

Except it wasn't so quiet—not by a long shot.

The Mankiewiczes' two sons, Christopher (born 1940) and Tom (1942–2010), later entered the movie business. Tom called his father "both the protagonist and victim of a long, punishing marriage to a beautiful, warm, but deeply troubled woman...."

Here was a woman who, beginning in her teenage years, longed to be an actress. She achieved that goal in her native land and then made the transition to America with relative ease. While the MGM contract was a dead end, Columbia seemed enthusiastic about giving her a shot. Marriage and motherhood stalled those plans and as the years passed, it would become harder for her to get back on track. A letter in *Photoplay* (December 1940) probably made Stradner happy (or frustrated): "Why isn't Rose Stradner given a chance to show that she can really act, act so well that only a few American actresses can compare with her?"

A tense moment as escaped convict Hal Wilson (Chester Morris) holds a family, including Doris (Rosa Stradner) and her son Davy (Scotty Beckett), captive in *Blind Alley* (1939).

It is uncertain when Stradner began to drink, but by the early 1940s she was a full-blown alcoholic exhibiting signs of mental illness. After Tom's birth, she was admitted to Kansas' Menninger Clinic, a stay that did little to curb her demons; she was there being treated for a "psychological disturbance so serious," wrote author Gerald Clarke, "that it had brought about a catatonic fit."

What was her husband doing while she was in Kansas? Mankiewicz was having affairs, notably with Judy Garland. Stradner came back to California not quite cured of her maladies, but she wasn't about to stop drinking. Increasingly resentful of her domestic role, she became despondent.

An intelligent woman, fluent in languages, she was extremely helpful to her husband and he relied on her to critique his screenplays because he respected her judgment. Yet, theirs was not a healthy relationship. Why did they stay together? "He was actually physically afraid of Rosa," Mankiewicz's friend Dr. Marc Rabwin (quoted by author Ronald L. Davis) explained. "[S]he could be violent. Joe is a very forceful person and can be pretty dominating. But where Rosa was involved, he would accede to anything just to keep peace."

She was always threatening to kill herself, using it as a sort of power play against her husband, whom she saw as the one person standing between her and film stardom. Mankiewicz was afraid that he would lose custody of his two boys. But he didn't want to publicly embarrass her by declaring her mentally incompetent, so he stayed with her—and they suffered together.

In 1941, when David O. Selznick acquired the rights to A.J. Cronin's novel *The Keys of the Kingdom*, Ingrid Bergman was set to play the part of the Reverend Mother Maria-Veronica. The project finally ended up (*sans* Selznick and Bergman) at 20th Century–Fox. Mankiewicz, who was now producing and had adapted the book for the screen with Nunnally Johnson, had promised the nun role to Stradner. Geraldine Fitzgerald was also up for the part but, per Johnson, Mankiewicz "practically got down on his knees" for his wife to be cast: "This will save or doom my marriage." Although Mankiewicz denied this, Stradner tested and won the role in his 1944 production *The Keys of the Kingdom* (billed as Rosa Stradner).

Many predicted a comeback, but Stradner none too convincingly told Robbin Coons before the movie's release that she was back but "[m]aybe not for long. I am acting again because I like the part. Perhaps there will be others, now and again. But I know I would be limited by my accent—and I am not a pin-up girl, only an actress."

The strong-willed, forbidding Reverend Mother of Cronin's book is described as possessing "both dignity and breeding. There was high breeding in the fine bones of her face and her wide heavy blue eyes." Her initial frostiness toward Father Francis Chisholm (played by an Oscar-nominated Gregory Peck) gradually gives way to admiration for his strength and faith. Stradner makes a quiet yet forceful showing, at her best in her affecting final scenes where her chilliness evaporates: when she asks Father Chisholm for forgiveness for her treatment of him; and then years later when they must say goodbye as he is going to leave the mission.

Most reviewers enjoyed the movie, the *San Francisco Examiner* calling it "rich in dignity, tolerance and understanding" and praising Stradner's "vivid characterization." The *St. Louis Post Dispatch* saluted Stradner as an "extraordinarily beautiful and capable actress."

"They had an affair, Gregory Peck and my mother, on that film," Tom Mankiewicz

The Rev. Mother Maria-Veronica (Rosa Stradner) and Father Francis Chisholm (Gregory Peck) clash in *The Keys of the Kingdom* (1944).

told Sam Staggs. Staggs concluded, "Perhaps Rosa Stradner's affair was in self-defense, for, in the words of her other son [Christopher], 'she was a woman who was continually betrayed. She was often institutionalized by my father, who was busy fucking Judy Garland at the time he was sending my mother away and calling her a very sick woman.'"

In November '44, the Mankiewiczes went through a very public separation, but reconciled. The following year, Sheilah Graham quoted Mankiewicz as saying that another columnist "printed on the morning of our reconciliation, and two days after Judy Garland had announced her engagement to Vincente Minnelli, that Judy and I were 'that' way about each other! When my brother [Herman] asked her why she printed it, she replied, 'Oh, I just don't like him!'"

Stradner's *Keys of the Kingdom* performance was so well-received by critics that it re-ignited her passion for acting. In January 1945, her management took a full-page *Variety* ad with all her glowing notices for *Keys of the Kingdom*. Fox wanted to put her under contract, and she was considered for parts in *Anna and the King of Siam*, *Forever Amber* and *Daisy Kenyon*. "If Leo McCarey can't get Ingrid Bergman for *Bells of St. Mary's*," wrote Hedda Hopper, "I suggest he look at Rosa Stradner in *Keys of the Kingdom*. She's outstanding and a great beauty." Bergman, of course, did get the role and, wrote Hopper in another column, "Now everybody's happy." Everyone but Stradner, who would have benefited from the break.

At the beginning of 1946, Edwin Schallert stated that Stradner had "decided in favor of pictures" and was still negotiating a 20th Century–Fox contract—which didn't happen. Hedda Hopper reported in April that Stradner "will have three plays to choose from when she returns to New York in mid–Summer. I suppose, after giving that delightful performance in *Keys of the Kingdom*, she'll have to prove all over again what a good film actress she is before getting the parts here she deserves." In August, Stradner was still "shopping for a play to do on Broadway" (Sheilah Graham). Louella Parsons asked in a May '48 column, "What goes with the Joe Mankiewiczes? One hears many, many disturbing rumors."

Tom Mankiewicz, who had a complex relationship with his mother, remembered how her "mental condition, a form of schizophrenia usually triggered by alcohol, [made her] absolutely terrifying at times." She was a Jekyll and Hyde personality; "nights of terror" with her would be tempered by a mother who was "warm, intelligent and caring."

Stradner desperately wanted to act. "Actresses never really quit, you know," remarked Tom. "Over the years, Mother always thought about returning to it." From time to time, columnists Louella and Hedda voiced their opinion that Stradner was a fine actress and should be working.

In 1948, Stradner finally got a role in a stage play, the headed-for-Broadway *Bravo!* It was written by Edna Ferber (her last) and George S. Kaufman (who also directed) and produced by Max Gordon. When she auditioned, both Ferber and Kaufman were so impressed by her cold reading that they applauded.

When it opened in Boston in October, critics were unkind and referred to it as a sort of Viennese *You Can't Take It with You*—but loved Stradner. Soon it was announced that she would be replaced by Hungarian-born Lili Darvas (wife of playwright Ferenc Molnár). There were conflicting reasons for the switch. Dorothy Kilgallen claimed that star Oscar Homolka didn't like Stradner's better reviews. Producer Gordon said that Homolka had nothing to do with her dismissal, and simply stated that Stradner was not suited to the part. Louella Parsons explained that Gordon wanted to soothe Lili Darvas' "ruffled feelings," as it was thought that the play was based on her life. Another version: Stradner was "too young and beautiful for the role." Her son Tom surmised, "I can only assume her mental illness must have flared up one night and it scared the hell out of them."

She got little consolation when the play flopped on Broadway. Losing the show was a "crushing disappointment" and a "bitter blow to her," Tom said. One she never truly got over.

It was clear to many that her drinking and mental state were interfering with her considerable ability. She was still reading play scripts in the early '50s, but it never went beyond that. Her last screen role came on a 1953 episode of TV's *Suspense* called "Reign of Terror," a somewhat ironic title given her vitriolic temper.

Her health rapidly deteriorating, Stradner was being treated by a psychiatrist. At the time, there was little they could do drug-wise for her mood swings, so basically she was prescribed sedatives.

On the night of September 26, 1958, at their summer home in Mt. Kisco, New York, Stradner and Mankiewicz had a terrible fight and he immediately left for New York City. The following day, she was found lying dead on the bedroom floor near a writing desk. In her hand was an "indecipherable note" saying she was "tired." She had overdosed on sleeping pills. Stradner was only 45.

She was interred for many years at Kensico Cemetery in Valhalla, New York. Christopher and Tom later made the decision to remove her and have her cremated, her ashes to be scattered in Europe at a later date.

Although sad about her death, Tom said, "My overwhelming feeling at the time was truly one of relief for Mother. She led such a tortured life. Thank God she was finally at peace. That's why, at the time, I never cried. I tried to, but I couldn't."

Rosa Stradner Filmography

1933: *Ein gewisser Herr Gran, Hochzeit am Wolfgangsee.*
1934: *So endete eine Liebe.*
1935: *Hundert Tage, Nacht der Verwandlung, Der Mann mit der Pranke.*
1936: *Der König lächelt–Paris lacht, Diener lassen bitten, Campo di maggio, Stadt Anatol.*
1937: *The Last Gangster.*
1939: *Blind Alley.*
1944: *The Keys of the Kingdom.*

Judy Tyler

Nineteen fifty-seven was to have been 24-year-old Judy Tyler's breakout year, coming to Hollywood to play lead roles in *Bop Girl Goes Calypso* and the Elvis Presley vehicle *Jailhouse Rock*. She had previously appeared on television on *The Howdy Doody Show* (as Princess Summerfall Winterspring), on Broadway in Rodgers and Hammerstein's *Pipe Dream*, and on the cover of *Life*, and now it seemed stardom was not going to be a mere pipe dream.

But before those two movies premiered, tragedy struck.

She was born Judith Mae Hess on October 9, 1932, in Manhattan, and grew up in Queens and Teaneck, New Jersey. Her father Julian Hess, who played trumpet with Benny Goodman and Paul Whiteman, later became a building contractor. Inspired by her mother, Lorelei Kendler, a former Ziegfeld Girl and understudy for Marilyn Miller, Judy took voice, dancing and acting lessons and performed in school productions.

Judy quit school in her high school junior year. In preparation for a show biz career, she changed her surname to Tyler. Being named "Miss Stardust of 1949" led to a modeling contract with Harry Conover. In October '49, she became a singing-and-dancing regular on WOR-TV's *Al Siegel's Song Shop*. "I was born with show business in my blood," she later told Karl Kohrs. Although there were stories that her maternal grandmother Cora had pushed Judy's mom onto the stage and was doing the same to Judy, Tyler was adamant that she went into it on her own.

Comedian Dayton Allen found Judy Tyler to be "a tough cookie. She knew everyone, and she'd been around the room a few times" (courtesy C. Robert Rotter/Glamour Girls of the Silver Screen).

According to Tyler, at age 16 she played several bit parts for 20th Century–Fox and Universal-International—really not a possibility since she lived on the East Coast at that time. Later, pressed about these mysterious credits by Steven H. Scheuer, she remarked, "I made some pictures, but I refuse to talk about them. As far as I'm concerned, my movie career is still ahead of me."

She auditioned at the Copacabana, telling Earl Wilson, "I just walked over there and they said, 'Do you dance?' and I said, 'Yes, I'm a dancer!' So they said, 'Oh,' and threw somebody else out. Of course, to call it dancing was entirely ridiculous. It was hardly walking."

Tyler met 26-year-old pianist Colin Romoff. "As a vocal coach, there ain't nobody better!" she later said. "I went to him as a pupil. He told me I was the worst singer he ever heard. He said, 'I won't take you on as a pupil. But I'll take you to cocktails.'" Two months after they met, on December 21, 1950, they married. "I always tell him I got free vocal lessons that way. Every offer I get comes to him before it comes to me."

With Romoff's help, Tyler started to perform in such New York nightclubs as Bill Miller's Riviera and Le Ruban Bleu. On the small screen, she appeared for 13 weeks on *The Milton Berle Show*, and guested on *The Colgate Comedy Hour* and *All-Star Revue*. "I detest people who are always taking credit for me," she later told Earl Wilson. "If anybody's responsible for me, it's me! I've broken down more doors in New York City than anybody in this room, I'm here to bet. I have the distinction in my agency of getting any job I auditioned for." Everyone who ever came in contact with Tyler remarked on her supreme self-confidence.

In late 1951, she got the role of Princess Summerfall Winterspring on the beloved kiddie program *The Howdy Doody Show* (both the radio and TV versions). When the series started, Princess was represented as a hand puppet, but the decision was made to transform her into a real person, thereby spiking the merchandising sales. The switch turned out to be a popular choice, not only with children but with some of the grown-ups in the audience.

According to cast members, the wholesome and pure character was a contradiction of the "real" Judy Tyler. Author Stephen Davis wrote that *Howdy Doody* producer Roger Muir initially felt that he needed to protect Tyler from the show's "foul-mouthed

Anchors aweigh! (courtesy C. Robert Rotter/Glamour Girls of the Silver Screen).

and twisted cast," especially the "un-controllable" comedian Dayton Allen. Muir told Davis, "I was worried that the group would corrupt this young and innocent performer. But soon, at least in terms of foul language and corruption, I learned I had to be concerned the other way." An attempt to tone down bad language in front of her ended after one rehearsal when an irritated Tyler let loose with some expletives and Muir found that the 20-year-old "could swear with the élan of a fishwife." Host Buffalo Bob Smith got a kick out of her behavior and encouraged it.

Dayton Allen (who played several characters on the series) told Davis he found Tyler to be "a tough cookie. She knew everyone, and she'd been around the room a few times. When she came on, I was cynical at first because they had a big hype for the papooses now there was a girl on the show. But she was honest and open, and we got along great."

Spring publicity portrait of Judy (courtesy C. Robert Rotter/Glamour Girls of the Silver Screen).

Actor Allen Swift remembered Tyler to Davis in slightly less glowing terms: "Judy Tyler always felt that the show was a little beneath her. So she was always a tough chorus-girl broad until the red light came on. She'd bad-mouth the Peanut Gallery kids and swear like a stevedore, but when the red light came on, she was all big eyes and sweet as candy."

Author Davis' father Howard was one of *Howdy Doody*'s directors and noted to his son that Tyler loved to shock. Backstage she would say things like, "Jesus Christ, if that kid in the second row coughs again while I'm singing, I swear I'll slug the little shit!"

Two reasons were given for Tyler leaving *Howdy Doody* in November 1953: She was considering film roles and was awaiting the birth of her first baby. (Neither of which materialized.) Producer Martin Stone told Davis that the truth was that he had to fire Tyler because her outrageous language and sexual escapades were potentially harmful to the show. He was afraid there would be a scandal if the public got wind of her drinking, dancing naked on nightclub tables, acting up on personal appearances tours, and being, as director-producer Bob Rippen described, a "sexed-up little thing." Stone remarked that the princess was "our symbol of purity, beauty, loveliness, good behavior, and all that. After a while, the symbol wasn't matched by the person.... Judy was problems, problems, problems. But we loved her because she was tremendous! She had guts! She was sensational!" Regarding Tyler's promiscuity, the show's prop man Scott Brinker stated, "Anybody who wanted to, could have. And did."

Whatever the reason for Tyler's dismissal, it coincided with her own desire to move on. Although they replaced Tyler, *The Howdy Doody Show* would never find a suitable or equally popular actress to portray the princess.

Tyler claimed to have turned down the opportunity to play the lead in the Broadway show *By the Beautiful Sea* (1954). Nightclubs continued to be her forte. On April 14, 1954, she filled in for Tony and Sally De Marco at the Mocambo in Hollywood. Going on cold, she impressed many, notably *Variety*:

> Not more than a dozen or so of the jam-packed room knew much about her or who she is, but 15 minutes later they not only knew but left the Mocambo completely captivated.
>
> No great shakes as a singer, no pretense at being an entertainer, *per se*, and no tricks of stage-craft. Just a determined kid not many weeks out of NY's Copa line of girls who won over as tough an audience as she'll ever face with an ease and composure that would have been the envy of a seasoned trouper. A looker with a personality to charm the dressed-up first nighters, she belted out six songs in a quarter-hour, smiled prettily and thanked everybody as she strolled off stage without a twitch of nervousness. The applause was deafening, not so much for her singing but her pluck and confidence in making the gay crowd like her.

She turned down the chance to play another Indian maiden in the Paramount film *The Far Horizons*. From July 11 to 16, 1955, Tyler was at the Valley Forge Music Fair head-lining the musical *Annie Get Your Gun*, directed by actor-singer Wilbur Evans. "[E]ven with a string of sure-fire songs, it takes an actress who will lend conviction to a difficult role, and the current production has just that in Judy Tyler," wrote the *Philadelphia Inquirer*'s Samuel L. Singer, who added, "She makes you think she really can shoot that gun. And she can put over a song."

In 1955, she was a regular on TV's *Caesar Presents*, a summer replacement show.

Judy as Princess Summerfall Winterspring on TV's *Howdy Doody Show.*

There were many offers, including the starring role of Daisy Mae in the Broadway production of *Li'l Abner*, which was then still in the works. (When it premiered in 1956, Daisy Mae was played by Edie Adams.)

She attracted the attention of Oscar Hammerstein's brother Reginald and was called in to audition for an upcoming Rodgers and Hammerstein stage musical, *Pipe Dream*, which was based on the John Steinbeck novel *Sweet Thursday*. Tyler described the audition to Karl Kohrs: "Was I nervous? Oh, horribly. But when I finished, Mr. Hammerstein applauded. Then I knew. After that, the whole stage could have caved in on top of me and I still would have been happy. That's the only way I can describe how I felt."

Tyler nabbed the role of the Cannery Row prostitute over first choice Julie Andrews (who wisely decided to do *My*

Fair Lady, which made her a star) and an unavailable Janet Leigh. Among those who auditioned was a young Barbara Cook, who told Matt Weinstock, "They had me work with the director [Harold Clurman], and I think I did fine. But you know, I had this little-girl look, and I think they wanted a more womanly look. Which is what they got with Judy Tyler. It was not a very good show."

True, Rodgers and Hammerstein's score was not considered one of their best, but there were some good songs, especially "All at Once You Love Her" and "Everybody's Got a Home But Me," the latter Tyler's big number.

Reviewing the Boston tryouts, the *Boston Globe*'s Cyrus Durgin mentioned what some would echo when the show hit Broadway, that Tyler was "weak upon the vocal side": "Her speaking voice is low; the songs given her range too high for her present capabilities. I dare say a vocal coach could narrow the gap between her chest and head resonances in singing." He was, however, impressed by her "magnetic stage personality," and thought her "portrayal of the fiercely proud Suzy, a girl down on her luck, is perhaps the most substantial dramatic performance of all." The *Cincinnati Enquirer*'s Carl Jacobs didn't think Tyler had a "particularly good natural voice," but her singing was "intense" and "handled with skill."

To many, her acting was her strongest asset, and she earned a Tony nomination. *Pipe Dream*, which ran from November 30, 1955, to June 30, 1956, was not the hoped-for hit, but it was still Rodgers and Hammerstein and therefore considered a big deal. When it closed, Tyler said (per Leonard Lyons), "Oh, Lord—will I ever get a role like this again?" (Her leading man, William Johnson, died young of a heart attack, age 41, in 1957.)

Tyler took advantage of her high-profile participation in *Pipe Dream* by working at various clubs and making appearances on *The Ed Sullivan Show*. She screen-tested at various studios, but there were no takers. She did get a regular spot as a panelist on TV's *Pantomime Quiz*; starred in *Anything Goes* at the Warwick Music Theatre in Rhode Island; and guested on *Circus Time* with ventriloquist Paul Winchell and his dummy Jerry Mahoney.

Right before *Pipe Dream*

Music promoter Judy Tyler takes ex-convict rock-and-roller Elvis Presley under her wing in *Jailhouse Rock* (1957).

opened, there were rumblings of trouble in the Romoffs' marriage: "Young Judy Tyler … has just one big problem, according to the Sardi Set: a stage husband" (Dorothy Kilgallen). She divorced Romoff in 1956.

In March '57, she was cast in her first film role, *Bop Girl Goes Calypso*, portraying the title character. The story had to do with a sociology student (Bobby Troup) proving that rock'n'roll is out and calypso is in. Along the way, Tyler sang in a rather robust fashion "Rovin' Gal," "Calypso Boogie," "Way Back in San Francisco," "Oo Ba Loo" and "De Rain." Considering the slim premise, Tyler was able to inject a sense of fun and a surprising talent for one-liners.

On March 17, 1957, just after her divorce from Romoff became final, Tyler wed Earl Gregory Nisonger, Jr., at the Balmoral Hotel in Miami, where she was fulfilling a singing engagement. Patti Page was her matron of honor. Tyler had met Nisonger, who went by the stage names Gregg Champlain and Gregory LaFayette, in acting class. It was widely reported that Nisonger was 24 (like Tyler), but he was actually 19. Nisonger's father disapproved of the relationship, and Gregory was disinherited.

Her second movie is her most famous: *Jailhouse Rock* with Elvis Presley. Tyler played his love interest, a record promoter who sees possibilities in the ex-convict. "Starring with Elvis is a turning point in my career," she told Vernon Scott. "I have a deal to make more

pictures for Metro. And I've learned a lot about acting from Elvis."

Nisonger-LaFayette just finished playing a supporting part in his first film, *Under Fire* with Rex Reason. That and *Jailhouse Rock* wrapped around the same time and Tyler and her new husband went to Laramie, Wyoming, for a brief honeymoon. Tyler had to be back in New York to appear on the game show *Pantomime Quiz* and they were going to do a stock version of *Desire Under the Elms* together.

They decided to drive back instead of taking a plane because they were traveling with their poodle and a kitten she was going to give her agent in New York.

On July 3, 1957, as they were driving on U.S. 30, three miles north of Rock River, Wyoming, a car pulled out in front of them; Nisonger, swerving to avoid it, smashed into a car in the oncoming lane. The 24-year-old Tyler was killed instantly. (There were rumors later that she'd been cut in half, but this wasn't true.) Nisonger later died in the hospital. Both of their

Publicity portrait from *Bop Girl Goes Calypso* (1957) (courtesy C. Robert Rotter/Glamour Girls of the Silver Screen).

pets were also killed, as well as a passenger in the other car. Before help arrived at the accident scene, the bodies of Tyler and Nisonger were looted of money, and her furs and jewelry were stolen.

Army Archerd: "Milton Sperling among those saddened yesterday by the auto death of Judy Tyler. Sperling and Irving Rapper had just looked at her *Jailhouse Rock* footage and were gonna use her in *Marjorie Morningstar sans* test."

Both of her films (and Nisonger's *Under Fire*) were released posthumously. Her episode of *Perry Mason* ("The Case of the Fan Dancer's Horse") was broadcast six months after her death.

Elvis Presley was especially upset by the news of Tyler's death and told reporters that he cried. "Nothing has hurt me as bad in my life," he said. "All of us boys really loved that girl. She meant a lot to all of us. I don't believe I can stand to see the movie we made together, now." He was unable to go to her funeral. Her ex Romoff said he was "heartsick about her, and that boy, too."

Tyler's ashes were interred in Ferncliff Cemetery in Hartsdale, New York. As a tribute, rockabilly singer Kenny Baker recorded a song in 1959 dedicated to her memory, "Goodbye Little Star."

Judy Tyler Filmography

1957: *Bop Girl Goes Calypso, Jailhouse Rock.*

Karen Verne

In the 1930s, Karen Verne escaped the Nazis and made it to the United States. A rough early life gave way to the possibility of becoming a movie star. She was under contract to MGM and then Warner Brothers and was given the top spot with Humphrey Bogart in *All Through the Night* (1942). Another lead, this time opposite Errol Flynn, loomed. But it was not to be. Like many actresses, she chose her husband, in this case Peter Lorre, over her career. It was easier than enduring her man's disapproval. By all accounts, Lorre was very jealous.

But, ultimately, it was Verne's own personal problems which stalled a career that held so much promise.

The older of two daughters, she was born Ingeborg Greta Katerina Marie-Rose Klinckerfuss on April 6, 1918, in Berlin. Her family was involved with music on both sides. Her grandmother (the mother of Ingeborg's father Erich), concert pianist Johanna Klinckerfuss, was Franz Liszt's last student. Johanna's daughter Margarete Klinckerfuss also became a pianist. (An outspoken anti–Nazi, Margarete was arrested by the Gestapo in 1937 and admitted to the Psychiatric Clinic Christophsbad in Göppingen.)

Ingeborg's mother Ella was born into the internationally famous Bechstein family, manufacturers of pianos. In 1904, when Erich married Ella, he was the company's franchise manager in the United Kingdom; after World War I, he became its general director. (Karen's Hollywood publicity included the false claim that Karen's real name was Kathleen Bechstein and that her father owned the company.)

Ella wanted Ingeborg to play piano, but acting was the child's main interest. In 1934, the 16-year-old dropped out of school and joined Berlin's Staatstheater where she appeared in a few small roles. She flunked her politically oriented final exam. It was required that Staatstheater members sign a loyalty oath to Hitler, and Ingeborg refused.

A young, dewy-eyed portrait of Karen Verne.

175

Ingeborg's parents divorced because of political incompatibility: One side of the family leaned toward Nazism, the other toward what columnist Dugal O'Liam called "old German ideology."

Ingeborg met Scottish-born Englishman Arthur Young, a pianist with Jack Hylton's orchestra. "He was a kindly man," Frederick C. Othman later wrote. If Ingeborg "were the wife of an Englishman, she could leave Germany. He proposed marriage. She accepted." On August 30, 1936, Ingeborg, 18, eloped to Denmark with Young, 31. Shortly after returning to Berlin from touring with her husband, she gave birth to a son, Alastair (1937–2015).

In England, separated from Young and their son, Ingeborg worked as a model. In January 1939, she was signed by 20th Century–Fox, but the association was brief (she didn't even make it to the U.S.) because of a dispute over money, and she made no films for that company.

Producer Irving Asher saw her Fox test and put her under personal contract. Her name changed to Karen Verne, she was cast opposite Rex Harrison in the British-made *Ten Days in Paris* (1939), which the *New York Times* called "one of the giddiest spy melodramas of the season" and "rattling good fun." Verne portrayed a woman in love with an amnesiac who gradually realizes he was a spy during the ten days he cannot account for. Many thought first-time screen actress Verne showed promise; *Motion Picture Herald* called her "easy on the ear as on the eye." Later, revealing her insecurities, she remarked to Dee Lowrance, "I saw [the film] in Hollywood. I didn't much like myself. I looked so fat and blond...."

Asher talked her up to MGM and, in March 1940, Verne arrived in Hollywood to do a screen test. Louella Parsons reported her "tough luck," that "she had no more than finished her first American test at MGM than she collapsed and had to be rushed to a hospital for an appendectomy.... The operation came right on top of a dangerous crossing from England on a tramp steamer."

The stay in the hospital kept her out of action, but MGM announced she would make her Hollywood debut in the musical *Bitter Sweet* (1940). When it started filming, however, her intended part was taken by Veda Ann Borg.

A glam Karen poses for Warner Bros.' publicity.

In July '40, Verne finally got

her first Metro assignment: In the Nick Carter mystery *Sky Murder* (1940), she played a German-born model protected from fifth columnists by the famous detective (Walter Pidgeon).

Adolf Hitler and the Nazi Party's bloody rise touched the U.S. during the beginning stages of Karen's career in America. Hollywood publicists needed to explain the German-born actress' family connections in a way palatable to the public. The Berlin–based Bechsteins were close to Hitler and helped him personally and politically. This bit of information wouldn't do. Instead, Frederick C. Othman wrote this in 1941: "The Bechstein fortune is no more and members of the Bechstein family are dead or exiled. They hated the Nazis and said so. That was the end of the Bechsteins as leaders in the world of music, or as citizens of Germany. In 1935, the Nazis started clamping down on the Bechsteins because they wouldn't heil Hitler. Their money was confiscated. Their factories were taken over." (In reality, in 1934, Helene Bechstein, wife of the owner of the Bechstein company, was awarded the Golden Party Badge by Hitler. The company's reputation and sales suffered because of their close association with him.)

Othman continued that in the aftermath of the Bechstein company's supposed collapse, "blonde, blue-eyed [Karen was] suddenly penniless. Her father had died, of grief as much as anything else." (He had really died of tuberculosis.)

Dramatically, Othman wrote that when Verne was a teenager in Germany, she feared that a concentration camp was in her future. "She still hated the Nazis and didn't care who knew it. She was desperate. She even contemplated suicide."

Edwin Schallert claimed that Verne would have a prominent part in *The Wild Man of Borneo* (1941) but what she got was an uncredited bit as an actress projected on a movie screen (alongside Tom Conway and William Tannen). We see them only in a long shot, and all three are unrecognizable.

During the short time Verne had been in Hollywood, she had appendicitis and suffered from anemia and tonsillitis. Although she was promised more roles at MGM, her option was dropped.

In a February 1942 interview with Hubbard Keavy, Verne made statements about why she left MGM that were more in line with today's #MeToo movement than 1940s Hollywood: "If I had known what was in store for me here, I wouldn't have come [to the U.S.].... I wouldn't play ball with the wolves. I mean, I was expected to attend social functions with men in the studio and I refused. I was told, 'Play ball or else.' I couldn't believe such things could happen in America. I chose 'or else.'"

A meeting with director Vincent Sherman led to a role in Warner Bros.' *Underground* (1941) as a café violinist involved with anti–Nazi Germans. She followed that with a small but charming performance as Robert Cummings' love interest in *Kings Row* (1942).

Verne was now under contract to Warners and the studio set about making the German girl more accessible to American film fans. Wrote Carlisle Jones:

[Her] sense of humor is distinctly American. Even as a child in Germany, she says, she always played Indian and never played with dolls. She is a chatterbox and doesn't stop talking when she is alone. She didn't wear orange blossoms at her wedding. Instead she wore, she says, a bathing suit. She likes rainy weather, cut-rate drug stores, and colored Easter eggs.... She doesn't write poetry or paint china or keep shoe trees in her shoes. She doesn't like to hear a clock tick but the sound of the wind intrigues her. She likes to sit on the floor or the ground. She follows murder cases in the papers, eats onion soup, and likes the smell of fresh paint. But she never will bait a fish hook, use scented stationery, or sign letters more affectionately than she really means them to be.... She likes roller coasters, Christmas trees, and relies on first impressions of the people she meets.

Verne first met Peter Lorre while visiting the set of *The Maltese Falcon* (1941). A month later, they went before the cameras together for Vincent Sherman's *All Through the Night* (1942); she was Humphrey Bogart's leading lady, Lorre a fifth columnist. It was the first film in which she was billed with the first name of Kaaren; Verne thought the double "a" sounded Scandinavian. "Kaaren Verne, blonde and with just enough accent, was believable and nicely adequate as the romantic foil of the plot," wrote *Variety*. She was the third choice for the assignment, after Olivia de Havilland and Ingrid Bergman weren't available. Verne made a likable foil for Bogart.

She and Lorre, who was 14 years older, fell in love during filming. They were an unlikely pair: Verne was a tall glamourpuss and he was a short, bug-eyed actor known for his menacing screen roles. The press was amazed that these two seemingly disparate individuals had found each other. "Peter Lorre and Karen Verne are a new, and strange looking couple," wrote columnist Barney Oldfield. "Peter Lorre isn't scaring Karen Verne," added Ed Sullivan. In fact, quite unlike his screen image, the Hungarian-born Lorre was an intelligent, charming and witty man who was fond of pranks.

"He was like a different person when he was with Kaaren," observed Vincent Sherman. "He was a romantic young man then. I'll never forget that when he came on the set, he was wearing a little slipover sweater and his hair was neatly combed and he was very well dressed.... I thought, my God, how attractive he looks, very dapper. He was obviously very happy."

Before *All Through the Night* wrapped, Verne announced she would go to Reno for a divorce from Arthur Young. This would develop into an arduous task and take a few years, as Young would not cooperate. Lorre also had a spouse to shed, actress Celia Lovsky, but she proved agreeable, befriended Verne and stayed close to the couple.

Warners announced that Verne would appear with Errol Flynn in *Desperate Journey* (1942) but she was replaced by Nancy Coleman. The reason Verne was dropped by Warners, according to *Modern Screen*'s Sylvia Kahn, was because "the studio wanted to give her a glamour buildup, and she preferred the company of a movie horror man."

This comment jibes with Verne's friend Rhoda Riker's statements to author Stephen D. Youngkin that Lorre was against Verne's career: "He resented her directors—and anybody who looked at her—and would suggest that they were trying to get her in bed. Everything they did was wrong.

Good-natured gambler Gloves Donahue (Humphrey Bogart) protects nightclub singer Leda Hamilton (Karen Verne) from fifth columnists in *All Through the Night* (1942).

He killed her whole Hollywood career out of pure and simple jealousy. Oh, he was vile about it."

At Universal, Verne had a supporting part as a baroness, part of a Nazi espionage ring, in *The Great Impersonation* (1942). She didn't have much to do except be jealous of Ralph Bellamy's interest in Evelyn Ankers. At the same studio, she had the nominal female lead in *Sherlock Holmes and the Secret Weapon* (1942) as the love interest of a Swiss scientist (William Post, Jr.). "She's blonde. Five foot six, full-lipped and very affectionate," Holmes deduces after questioning Post about his recent activity.

Karen and her second husband, actor Peter Lorre.

In MGM's *The Seventh Cross* (1944), set in 1936 Germany, Verne had two brief scenes as Spencer Tracy's sweetheart Leni. She is first seen in a romantic flashback lying in a field with Tracy. He is subsequently sent to a concentration camp. In letters, Leni had promised to wait for him, but when he escapes and seeks her assistance, she is now married and coldly refuses to help him. The scene where she rebuffs him is a stark contrast to their earlier scene, especially in her appearance. For *The Seventh Cross*, she reverted to the "Karen" spelling and would continue this until the end of her career.

On May 25, 1945, in Las Vegas, shortly after she obtained her divorce from Young, she and Lorre married.

"Karen had quite a nice movie career a few years ago," wrote Sheilah Graham in September '45, "I can't think why it ever stopped." She had quit to become the housewife Lorre wanted her to be. The following year, Graham quoted Lorre as saying, "One face-maker in the family is enough."

Before Rhoda Riker met Verne, actress Helene Weigel (second wife of Bertolt Brecht) told Riker to be nice to Verne. Weigel called Verne a "poor, forlorn, lost soul. Everyone thinks she's sitting on the top of the heap in Hollywood, but she isn't. She's absolutely miserable."

Feeling stifled by her lonely life and Lorre's infidelities and controlling attitude, Verne became an alcoholic and suffered from depression. Lorre, then struggling with morphine addiction, was frequently hospitalized. "I think both were very bitter about the other person," Verne's sister Barbara told author Youngkin, "because they felt the other party was the one who drove them to their afflictions. They never saw themselves as the guilty person."

In February 1947, Louella Parsons reported that Verne was in a New York hospital "suffering from a nervous condition." The following month, Dorothy Kilgallen added that Verne was "still ailing. Her condition is baffling the doctors."

George (Spencer Tracy) and Leni (Karen Verne) during a brief idyllic moment in *The Seventh Cross* (1944).

The Lorres were unable to have children, and Verne felt it was her fault. This, combined with the continuing guilt of giving up her only child years before, caused her much anguish and led to several suicide attempts.

Lorre left her in March 1950. Verne later said she was forced to sell most of her wardrobe and earned her living as a $30-a-week salesgirl in a dress shop. Poor health dogged her, she lost her job, and for a few months she resided at the Motion Picture Home.

"Karen Verne, Lorre's wife, has had the going a bit rough," wrote Edith Gwynn at the beginning of 1951. "But she's a good actress and we're glad to report that parts are coming her way again." Not really, and she was back working as a saleswoman.

When Verne finally filed for divorce from Lorre in December 1952, she asked for $250 a week, a pittance, she said, because he was earning an annual salary of $50,000 a year. "[The] Peter Lorre-Karen Verne asundering is complicated because of money she thinks he has, and he says he hasn't."—Sheilah Graham.

Verne said that she gave up her career for him but now she was unable to find work as an actress and was "living on a hand-to-mouth basis, and has eaten most irregularly during the last two years," wrote Alfred Albelli. When the divorce became final in June '53, Verne got a cash settlement of $13,750. (Two days before the Verne-Lorre divorce was final, Lorre's girlfriend Annemarie Brenning gave birth to his daughter Catherine. Lorre married Annemarie the following month.) Despite the unhappiness of their marriage and their lives in general, Verne and Lorre remained on fairly amicable terms after the split.

On November 25, 1953, Verne married Harold Susman, a manufacturer's agent. In June '54, she filed for divorce, asking for $877 a month in alimony. She charged that Susman was so possessive and "unreasonably jealous" that when he was out of town, "he'd call her almost hourly day and night." She added that when he was home, he would follow her around, never giving her any privacy, and he would open doors after she closed them. "I just couldn't sleep, ever," she stated.

In the meantime, she tried to pick up the pieces of her film career. But the still-troubled actress' years of drinking had altered her looks considerably. The movie roles she did get were inconsequential: a blink-and-you-miss-her party guest in *The Bad and the Beautiful* (1952); Steven Geray's wife in *The Story of Three Loves* (1953), who has one line: "Yes. Anton, your stomach"; bad guy Peter van Eyck's wife who calls Audrey Totter to the phone three times in *A Bullet for Joey* (1955); and Maurice Doner's wife in *Outside the Law* (1956).

In *The Juggler* (1953), one of the Jewish refugees at the King David camp in postwar Israel is a former world-renowned juggler (Kirk Douglas) haunted by the death of his wife and their children. At one point, Douglas mistakes Verne for his wife; it is a brief scene but a moving one and she conveys much with just her facial expressions.

She should have found more work as a character actress, but her weakened mental stability likely got in the way. These films all gave her little dialogue and it's sad that an actress of her caliber would have so few opportunities. An "important comedy role" (Edwin Schallert) in *Silk Stockings* (1957) was actually a quick, uncredited one as a mail lady; her ex Lorre had a major supporting part in the same picture.

Verne was reasonably busy on television in roles of varying size (*Fireside Theatre, Crusader, The Gale Storm Show: Oh! Susanna, The Californians, General Electric Theater, Bronco,* etc.). On stage, she did *Survival* (1956) and she played Mrs. Frank in a Players Ring production of *The Diary of Anne Frank* (1958). *The Los Angeles Times* praised her performance in the latter, noting that she "sustains throughout with warmth and understanding."

On August 10, 1955, James Powers became Husband #4 in Carson City, Nevada. He was a reporter turned editor who worked at *Variety* and *The Hollywood Reporter*. According to author Stephen D. Youngkin, they had met in Alcoholics Anonymous.

Peter Lorre died on March 23, 1964. His ex, Celia Lovsky, worried what would happen to his daughter Catherine, as Catherine's mother Brenning was now an alcoholic and unable to care for her. (Brenning ended up at Synanon, a drug treatment facility in Santa Monica.) Verne and her husband adopted Catherine. Youngkin explained to this author:

Peter and Celia lived in a house on Crescent Heights Drive just off Sunset and Laurel Canyon. Celia told Jim [Powers] and Karen that she would turn over the house if they would adopt Cathy. I don't think they wanted Celia's house. Jim and Karen weren't completely on board with the idea of adopting Cathy, who was, by that point, a young teen and they were older and both recovering alcoholics. Moreover, Cathy was

Publicity photo for *Underground* (1941).

a diabetic, one more thing to manage. Celia was desperate at this point. I suspect that maintaining the house (taxes and all) on Crescent Heights strained her limited budget. The easy solution was to offer Jim and Karen the house if they would adopt Cathy. A pretty attractive offer, but with a downside. In that way, Celia kept her home (the basement part of it) and found surrogate parents for Cathy. Cathy's first husband, Richard, the would-be bounty hunter, actually showed me correspondence which, sadly, documented the fact that no one wanted Cathy. And by this, I mean other family friends. Celia was like a grandmother to Cathy, hence, she felt it was incumbent upon her to find a home for her "granddaughter."

The 1960s saw Verne get a bit of TV work (*Michael Shayne, The Twilight Zone, The Untouchables, Kraft Suspense Theatre*) and small roles in the movies *Ship of Fools* (1965), *Torn Curtain* and *Madame ×* (both 1966).

Her last acting assignment was as a refugee on an episode of *12 O'Clock High*. When it aired on December 23, 1966, she had exactly one year to live. Life did not get better for her and she made more attempts to kill herself, finally succeeding on December 23, 1967. *Variety* didn't mention that the wife of its former staffer Powers took her own life, simply reporting that the 49-year-old "died suddenly in her Hollywood home ... following hospitalization earlier in week at Jules Stein Eye Clinic of the UCLA Medical Center." She is interred in the Powers family plot at Calvary Cemetery in St. Paul, Minnesota.

Karen Verne Filmography

1940: *Ten Days in Paris, Sky Murder.*
1941: *The Wild Man of Borneo* (uncredited), *Underground.*
1942: *All Through the Night, Kings Row, The Great Impersonation, Sherlock Holmes and the Secret Weapon.*
1944: *The Seventh Cross.*
1952: *The Bad and the Beautiful* (uncredited).
1953: *The Story of Three Loves* (uncredited), *The Juggler* (uncredited).
1955: *A Bullet for Joey.*
1956: *Outside the Law.*
1957: *Silk Stockings* (uncredited).
1965: *Ship of Fools.*
1966: *Torn Curtain* (uncredited), *Madame X.*

Helen Walker

How quickly things can go awry in Hollywood. New Year's Eve 1946, Helen Walker gave a lift to three hitchhikers. The ride turned tragic. Reportedly, she had been drinking and the car was totaled, leaving one passenger dead. It was an incident that would foreshadow the rest of her short life. While it didn't have an immediate impact on her career, it put her on an emotional path that severely curtailed it.

Of Irish ancestry, she was born Helen Marion Walker in Worcester, Massachusetts, on July 17, 1920, the second of three daughters to a grocery store manager. Life was difficult, and would get even more so: "We were very poor," Walker wrote in 1943. "Father

died when I was six years old and left nothing but a small insurance policy. When this was gone, Mother went to work in a department store." Helen and her sisters were sent to live on a farm in Upton, Massachusetts. After her mother had a nervous breakdown, the family was reunited and applied for Soldiers Relief.

"I came up the hard way," Helen remarked, but she credited her mother for her perseverance—and her cynicism. "She has always accepted fate, and has never counted on anything, so she has never been disappointed. Long ago she passed that philosophy on to me."

Walker began acting in high school and studied dramatics with John W. Oates. She won a scholarship to Boston's Erskine School of Dramatics, but believed herself so bad in her first play there that she dropped out. Oates helped her by getting her a spot in a local stock

Helen Walker as a 1940s Paramount contractee (courtesy C. Robert Rotter/Glamour Girls of the Silver Screen).

company, the first in a succession of Massachusetts companies where she picked up experience.

Notably, Walker toured with Helen Twelvetrees in a production of *Personal Appearance* and in stock appeared with Ruth Chatterton in *The Constant Wife*. In the latter, *The Boston Globe* thought she established herself as "an actress of sterling qualities," adding that she brought to the role "a convincing and complimentary interpretation that adds to the sparkle and savor."

Walker did more stock (*The Gorilla* with Buster Keaton and *Dear Brutus* with Henry Hull), played small roles in at least two New York–made Soundies, and understudied Dorothy McGuire in the Broadway hit *Claudia* (1941). She never went on for McGuire, but the play's author, Rose Franken, introduced her to playwright Samson Raphaelson, who cast her in his 1942 play *Jason*. Walker not only got good notices, she was seen by a Paramount scout and given a screen test and ultimately a contract. Early reports were that she had an "acting talent to compare with Katharine Hepburn" (Edwin Schallert).

Walker film-debuted opposite popular new star Alan Ladd in *Lucky Jordan* (1942), a Lucky Break for her. She and Ladd were going to be immediately reteamed in *Salty O'Rourke*, but when that finally started filming in '44 it was with Gail Russell. Walker was also considered for the lead in *The Uninvited*, but Russell got that role too. (According to Yvonne De Carlo, it was "good-natured but tough-talking" Walker who took insecure newcomer Russell "under her wing and introduced her to the tranquilizing benefits of vodka.")

On November 19, 1942, in Tijuana, Mexico, Walker wed Paramount attorney Robert Blumofe. They kept the union a secret a full year before disclosing it to the press.

Between 1943 and '45, Paramount gave her the leads in the Bs *The Good Fellows* ("May it rest in peace," she remarked in 1943) and *The Man in Half Moon Street*; in two loanout assignments to producer Edward Small (*Abroad with Two Yanks* and *Brewster's Millions*); and one of the films she is best known for today, the zany comedy *Murder, He Says* with Fred MacMurray.

Paramount, impressed by her beauty, charm, poise and sophistication, was grooming her, but Walker got impatient. When they gave her another loanout job, she refused to do it. In response, the studio dropped her option. ("I expected Paramount to suspend me. But they didn't. They fired me.") She later looked back on her stay at Paramount as one of missed opportunities, complaining that she was passed over for important roles and got the "routine" stuff. "I wasn't really an actress,

Helen made her feature film debut with Alan Ladd in *Lucky Jordan* (1942).

just a reactress, a reactor, to comedians like William Bendix and Dennis O'Keefe." Philip K. Scheuer wrote:

> There is really nothing remarkable about what she wants. As close as she could to expressing it, the simple desideratum is "grown-up parts." They keep casting her as ingénues—and Miss Walker, who is quite tall, who has a low, fascinating contralto and who is forthright as all get-out, is anything but. When she tries to simper, it turns into a grimace.

For most of their brief marriage, she and Blumofe were apart because he was in the Army. When he got out of the service, their reunion was anything but happy. In July '45, Walker announced she would file suit for divorce because "our careers don't go together." In court the following year, she remarked that Blumofe "was very unpleasant to my friends, belittled me, my acting, my clothes and my cooking and caused me great embarrassment." (Blumofe later married and divorced Doris Dowling and Joan Benny.)

As a freelancer, Walker was back at Paramount for the Pine-Thomas production *People Are Funny* (1946); supported Vera Ralston in Republic's mystery gem *Murder in the Music*

"I wasn't really an actress, just a reactress, a reactor, to comedians like William Bendix [*right*] and Dennis O'Keefe [*left*]," Helen said about movies like *Abroad with Two Yanks* (1944).

Hall (1946); and paired again with Dennis O'Keefe in Universal's *Her Adventurous Night* (1946).

Fox thought she did a good job replacing Peggy Cummins in Ernst Lubitsch's *Cluny Brown* (1946) and signed her. In *The Homestretch* (1947) starring Cornel Wilde and Maureen O'Hara, she had a third-billed supporting role as a sort of Other Woman. Walker would date the film's director, H. Bruce "Lucky" Humberstone, for a few years. History repeated itself: When Fox assigned her another supporting part, in *Moss Rose* (1947), Walker turned it down and asked for her release—and got it.

According to premier film historian Doug McClelland, Walker's performance opposite Nils Asther in *The Man in Half Moon Street* (1945) was more proof "that she was one of the forties' most beguiling heroines" (courtesy Tom Weaver).

In December 1946, she started filming the indic *Heaven Only Knows*, where she was portraying a dance hall girl called "The Copper Queen." She wasn't playing the love interest, but it was a meaty part.

New Year's Eve, 1946: Walker picked up three hitchhikers on Highway 99: Pfc. Robert Lee, Joseph Montaldo and Philip Mercado. Varying reports said that she was driving between 80 and 100 m.p.h. when the vehicle slid into the division strip in the center of the highway and rolled over six times; everyone was ejected. Lee, 18, stationed at March Field, was killed instantly; the two other men suffered multiple injuries. Walker came away with a broken pelvis and collarbone and some fractures.

At the inquest, Montaldo and Mercado said they begged Walker to slow down but she wouldn't. Redlands policeman Glen Solberg testified that he "smelled alcohol" on her breath at the scene, but "couldn't say" if she was intoxicated. The coroner's jury determined that the accident was a result of Walker's "negligent driving."

She remained in the hospital and was facing manslaughter charges. She was replaced by Marjorie Reynolds in *Heaven Only Knows*, which required reshooting to the tune of $100,000. Walker was in no shape to stand trial, so her lawyer obtained a continuance for March 25, 1947.

As if she didn't have enough troubles, a separate civil suit was filed against her by Philip Mercado, who charged that the speedometer "broke" at 100 m.p.h. and that Walker was driving "while under the influence of intoxicating liquor." Not long after this, Mercado was booked on a charge of possessing marijuana. The other passenger, Joseph Montaldo, had been convicted on a narcotic charge in 1944. And when he testified against Walker at the inquest, cops identified him as half of the duo that had recently held up a theater; he and a pal, armed with knives, severed the pinkie of the owner before fleeing with $5000 in cash.

At the preliminary hearing, Walker's defense successfully blocked mention of the fact that she might have been drinking that night. She claimed that during the war, she had given servicemen rides all the time, but nothing like this had ever occurred. This particular incident, she remarked, "was one of those terrible things that happen."

Walker was ordered to stand trial for manslaughter. But in April '47, the charges against her were dismissed due to "insufficient and uncertain evidence."

Contrary to other sources, the car accident did not have an immediate ruinous effect on her career. In fact, 20th Century–Fox signed her to a new contract. She was given important back-to-back assignments in two of Fox's best films of 1947, *Nightmare Alley*, where she was cast in her best-known role as the duplicitous and calculating Dr. Lilith Ritter, and *Call Northside 777*, as James Stewart's loving wife. The two parts were as unalike as parts could get and it appeared as though things were on the upswing. Fox claimed they were grooming her (again) for stardom and were going to test her and Gregory Peck for *Down to the Sea in Ships*.

By January 1948, she was gone. "Helen Walker being dropped by 20th Century–Fox was a surprise after her performances in *Nightmare Alley* and *Call Northside 777*," wrote Hugh Dixon. "Maybe just talent doesn't count anymore." In reality, according to *Variety*, "[f]uture roles at the studio had been announced, but actress and 20th execs were unable to get together on terms in new option."

She and John Beal starred in an excellent radio adaptation of the Cornell Woolrich story "Deadline at Dawn" for *Suspense* (May 15, 1948). Movie-wise, producer Harry M. Popkin came through with parts for her in *My Dear Secretary* (1948) and *Impact* (1949). They were both supporting roles, but she handled them expertly, especially the latter

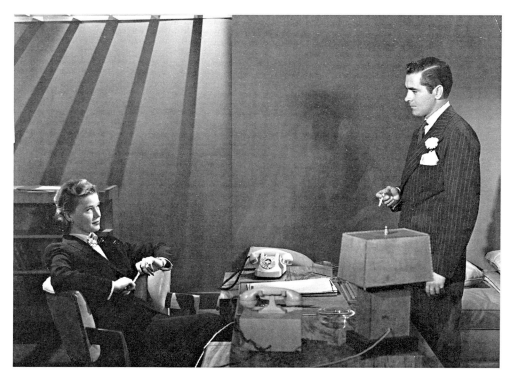

One of Helen's best roles was as the duplicitous Dr. Lilith Ritter with Tyrone Power in the noir classic *Nightmare Alley* (1947).

where she plots to kill her husband Brian Donlevy. (She was given the option to play the nice-girl lead, but she found the murderous wife more interesting.) It was announced that she signed for more with Popkin, but she never made any further pictures with him. In 1949, she acted in a Masquers Club stage production of *The Front Page* with Dane Clark and Taylor Holmes.

"No wonder so many actors are out of work, considering all the lousy scripts the agents hand you ... with such big buildups," she said to Gene Handsaker. "They're nearly all tripe. The dialogue is always the same. Everything's been done before. I've read 13 or 20 scripts in the last three weeks, and only one was any good." At a time when she should have been keeping busy and being cooperative, this may not have been the right approach.

She was sought for the lead opposite George Raft in the British-made *I'll Get You for This* (aka *Lucky Nick Cain*) and to headline the indie *One Too Many* (1950), but both were no-gos. The latter, in which she was replaced by Ruth Warrick, about a concert pianist and her career being sidetracked by alcoholism, perhaps had a plot that hit too close to home. Columnist Louella Parsons mentioned sympathetically that "the scars of the experience" (her car accident) would "always remain in her heart," which would explain why Walker's drinking got worse.

On April 29, 1950, Walker, 29, wed businessman Edward du Domaine, 41, at the Palm Springs home of Frank Morgan's widow. They had supposedly met eight months earlier on a street corner and he asked her to the beach. The two had something in common: In November 1938, when du Domaine was working as Morgan's chauffeur, he fell asleep

Helen as Brian Donlevy's homicidal wife in *Impact* (1949).

at the wheel and his vehicle jumped the curb, crashed into three orange trees and plowed into a grove. Morgan suffered minor injuries and du Domaine was arrested on a reckless driving charge.

Her new husband did not approve of her acting, so Walker worked sparsely: the radio drama "Dear Doctor" for *Hollywood Theater*; the lead in the Mickey Rooney–directed movie *My True Story* (1951); an unsold ABC radio pilot; print ads for Rheingold Beer (what was she thinking?); and a Sombrero Playhouse production of *Dinner at Eight* (1951) in Phoenix. In July 1951, Harrison Carroll wrote that Helen was "under observation at St. John's Hospital," but gave no hint of what was wrong with her.

On June 10, 1952, Walker received a divorce from du Domaine, alleging that he resented her friends, her career and the movie industry in general and she was "forced to give up all her connections with the acting profession because of [his] attitude." She was awarded $50 a month alimony for two years.

Walker was top-billed in the low-budget exploitation feature *Problem Girls* (1953). She was good as the rotten-to-the-core headmistress of the Manning School for Girls, Miss Dixon—"evil incarnate" (*Variety*). The school caters to troubled rich girls, troubles made worse by the domineering and shady Walker and her staff. Mara Corday, who played a young arsonist, told interviewer Tom Weaver that Walker was "drinking all through the picture," which would explain some of Walker's slurred words and her bloated appearance. Walker tried to make her character at least interesting and she succeeded. This was probably difficult for her; according to Corday, Walker hated the director, E.A. Dupont, and when he would shout "Quiet on the set!" she would yell "Fuck you!" back at him. Cast member Tandra Quinn told Weaver: "She may have been drinking through the whole shoot. And cuss everybody out? My *God*! They'd say, 'Miss Walker, we need you here,' and she'd tell 'em to go you-know-what themselves! 'I'll come when I'm goddamn *ready*. Shut up! Leave me alone!' A real caustic mouth. But she could be nice."

Her next film was another low-budgeter, but one that now has a cult following and a reputation as a classic noir, *The Big Combo* (1955). Her role wasn't large but her character of Alicia is important and talked about for most of the film, the police (headed by Cornel Wilde) trying to figure out her connection to big boss Mr. Brown (Richard Conte). Imbuing her portrayal of a pathetic lush with a sensitivity, Walker added an undercurrent of sadness and fear that makes her sympathetic. It showed that with the right material, she could deliver a sterling performance. "[There is] a particularly neat stint from Helen Walker," wrote *Variety*, while *The New York Times* added a hearty "welcome back" to the actress in their review. Unfortunately, it would be Walker's last film role.

Acting gigs became harder to come by. She did a *Dragnet* episode and played one of the leads in *The Children's Hour* (1956) on stage at the Players Ring Theater. "Anne Barton and Helen Walker, as the harried schoolteachers, are fine, displaying sensitive skill and a genuine understanding of their roles," wrote *Variety*.

The following year she appeared in a TV pilot with Glenda Farrell (*The Marriage Broker*) and was contracted to play Cliff Robertson's agent in *Career* at the Ivar Theater. She told Edwin Schallert she was "quite delighted by the assignment" and welcomed "the change it represents from the parts I formerly did." But on opening night, she did not go on; she had broken her ankle in a "bad accident" and was replaced by Mary James, who had been in the New York production.

Walker was seen in a La Jolla Playhouse production of *Once More with Feeling* (1959), co-starring and directed by Fernando Lamas. She also did some local television.

"One of Helen Walker's one-time movie directors snafu'd her chance to answer erroneous rumors about her 'alcoholic problem' on *This Is Your Life*," wrote Mike Connolly in his syndicated November 1959 column. "He bum-rapped the actress when Ralph Edwards' researchers called to question him about her."

That December, her Laurel Canyon home burned down. Friends Dinah Shore, Hugh O'Brian, Vivian Blaine, Ruth Roman and others staged a benefit to help her out. In 1960, she got her last acting roles in two episodes of the series *Lock Up*; typically, she gave good performances.

For the rest of the decade, she was ill from cancer and had multiple surgeries. In January 1962, Army Archerd mentioned in his "Just for *Variety*" column that she was going back to Cedars for her "fourth surgery session."

Walker was 47 years old when she died on March 10, 1968, in North Hollywood of jaw cancer. She is interred at Oak Hill Cemetery in Sterling, Massachusetts.

After her passing, a longtime friend, columnist Mel Heimer, paid tribute to her:

> When you are nonsensical, as she and I were, you latch on tightly to your brother nuts. Over the years we kept in touch, and when I traveled to California I'd look her up and we would start laughing again as if it had been only yesterday. Neither of us took much of anything seriously, which I suppose some would say was terrible, but it was a gas, anyway.
>
> I remember driving with her down Hollywood Boulevard in a convertible, as she waved a glass of booze in one hand, and drove with the other, reciting some of the great limericks of our time. I was sure we were going to end up busting into a telegraph pole, but I still couldn't help laughing. Maybe we were worthless, but there was, in all, a certain charm to it.
>
> Helen's career never really got where it should have, and bluenoses can sniff and say "Too busy having fun, humph!" and they were probably right. But she did a lot of good work and she acted with Boyer and James Stewart and so on and she bought a little house and life was a glorious cycle of song.
>
> It turned out she needed that ability to laugh. She made a couple of marriages that didn't pan out, she once gave a soldier a lift from Palm Springs and they got into a crash and the soldier got killed, her career slipped ... and at last she picked up cancer. Over the last few years, she would write me now and then—maybe telling me exactly where I went wrong in fashioning one of my books—and filling page after page with songs, dances and funny sayings. Then ... the letters stopped coming. I don't know what happened at the end, but I would suspect strongly that, in the great tradition of wise/foolish people such as ourselves, she exited laughing.

Helen Walker Filmography

1941: *Please Take a Letter, Miss Brown* (Soundie), *There's Something About a Soldier* (Soundie).
1942: *Lucky Jordan.*
1943: *The Good Fellows.*
1944: *Abroad with Two Yanks.*
1945: *The Man in Half Moon Street, Brewster's Millions, Murder, He Says, Duffy's Tavern.*
1946: *People Are Funny, Murder in the Music Hall, Cluny Brown, Her Adventurous Night.*
1947: *The Homestretch, Nightmare Alley.*
1948: *Call Northside 777, My Dear Secretary.*
1949: *Impact.*
1951: *My True Story.*
1953: *Problem Girls.*
1955: *The Big Combo.*

Constance Worth

In the 1930s, Jocelyn Howarth—the future Constance Worth—was one of Australia's most popular film actresses, although she made only two films there, producer-director Ken G. Hall's *The Squatter's Daughter* (1933) and *The Silence of Dean Maitland* (1934). Her countrymen were excited when she decided to transplant her talents to the U.S., and she became known as "Australia's Gift to the Screen."

But quite often, beauty and talent are just not enough.

A well-publicized divorce from a big American movie star, George Brent, tainted her reputation, and it seemed to go downhill from there.

The youngest of the three daughters of a wholesale grocer turned importer, she was born Enid Joyce Howarth in Sydney, Australia, on August 19, 1911. Throughout her life, she would prefer the first name Joy.

Constance Worth in the 1940s.

Her parents had a stormy relationship. In 1916, Moffatt Howarth sued his wife Mary Ellen for divorce alleging she was having an affair with boxer Gordon Coghill. They reconciled, but in 1921, Mrs. Howarth charged her husband with "misconduct" with a woman who worked as his typist. This time it did end in divorce.

After graduating from Ascham School, Enid, now alternating between the names Jocelyn and Joy, joined the Pickwick Theatre Group. In 1932, while she was appearing in the play *Cynara*, she was noticed by director Ken G. Hall, who asked her to screen test for his movie *The Squatter's Daughter*. Hall said that her test showed "light and shade, good diction, no accent" and that "she undoubtedly could act with no sign of the self-consciousness which almost always characterized the amateur." It didn't hurt that actress Mary Marlowe, who had played the lead in *The Squatter's Daugh-*

ter on stage in London, had recommended Howarth. Also up for the role was Mona Barrie (then known as Mona Barlee), who would soon go to Hollywood.

Given the lead in her film debut (billed as Jocelyn), Howarth was signed by Cinesound Productions Ltd.; they publicized the newcomer as "Australia's first movie star" based on this movie and *The Silence of Dean Maitland*, released the following year. Howarth made a series of personal appearances which boosted her popularity among the country's film fans. For J.C. Williamson Ltd., she appeared on stage in *The Wind and the Rain* (1934) and *Ten Minute Alibi* (1934–35).

The grass is always greener on the other side: In 1936, Howarth decided it was time to crash Hollywood. Her first three months in the film capital were discouraging and she got no roles. That August, she attempted suicide by gassing herself in her apartment. She was saved by her neighbor, actor Tyrone Power, who rushed to her rescue after receiving an "incoherent telephone call" from her. Three days after news of this appeared in American newspapers, the *Australian Women's Weekly* quoted a letter they received from Howarth where she claimed she was "stepping high and wide" in Los Angeles, "going places and seeing things" and "having the time of her young life."

If we are to believe some Australian newspapers, Howarth was being "cruelly" exploited by the "sensational methods of certain American newspapers" and a "young actor who probably saw a chance to get some publicity" (*Smith's Weekly*). Howarth was "distressed" that anyone thought she had tried to kill herself; she was merely making a cup of tea when the gas heater "blew up." It was claimed that Howarth, "a defenseless Australian girl in a strange land," was "fair game" for yellow journalists.

She did profit from the attention: Universal and Selznick tested her, and there were reports that she would star in two pictures with Paul Lukas. Ken G. Hall offered her a movie back in Australia (*It Isn't Done*), but Howarth decided to stick it out in Hollywood.

Producer Edward Small signed her to a contract with the promise of at least three movies, including one with Robert Donat. Nothing came from her Small association except losing a Broadway show (because of the contractual ties) and a chance for a test with MGM.

She was signed at RKO and her first for the company was the lead in the second feature *China Passage* (1937), which she thought

Happier times between Constance and first husband George Brent (courtesy of Scott O'Brien).

was "very bad." Because her leading man was Vinton Haworth, the RKO powers-that-be changed her name. "I pleaded to keep the last syllable of my name—and got 'Worth,'" she told *The Daily Telegraph*. "'Constance' was because [RKO's head of production] Sam Briskin had never known a film 'Constance' who was a failure." (Subsequently, she has often been confused with a 1920s stage actress named Constance Worth.) *China Passage* was followed by another leading lady part in *Windjammer* (1937) with George O'Brien.

Things were on the rise for Worth: leads in her first two American movies. Then fate stepped into her life in the form of actor George Brent. After a six-week courtship, they eloped to Mexico on May 10, 1937. She later told *The Daily Telegraph*, "George did not want me to be under contract to any studio. I kept on refusing parts."

Wedded bliss came to a screeching halt on June 14 when Brent decided that he no longer wanted to be married. "He said he was unhappy, and had been thinking over things," Worth said. "I asked him if he wanted a divorce, and he replied that it would be unnecessary because the marriage was illegal. He said his attorney had told him so a fortnight after the marriage."

Brent claimed that they did not fulfill the legal requirements necessary to go through with a marriage in Mexico and he pressed for an annulment; Worth sought to remain wedded to him. The court case was big news and both actors got some unwanted publicity. Brent alleged that he was "pressured" into marrying her. "If Brent is a gentleman," Worth said, "he will explain what he meant by pressure on him to marry. I do not see where pressure comes in when a man repeatedly proposes and a woman finally consents." Brent replied rather nastily, "I had hoped to confine the trial to technicalities, but if Miss Howarth wants mudslinging we will give her all the dirt she wants." The public never did get the dirty details. At one point, Worth collapsed in court due to the assertions that Brent "fought against the marriage, but yielded to Miss Howarth's repeated urgings." She also broke into sobs and rushed out of the courtroom.

In Australia, the press wanted a ban on all of Brent's films, and it was even discussed in the House of Representatives. Aussie newspapers were not amused by his conduct. "I hope Australians in general will show their contempt for a cad of his caliber by staying away from any theatre where there is a film in which he figures being shown in future," wrote the *Sunday Times*. "There have been some pretty cheap things done by some people in American film circles at times in the past, but in recent years Brent's conduct towards one of our Australian girls stands out

George O'Brien romances Constance Worth in *Windjammer* (1937).

as the rottenest on record…. Brent's name here smells like a skunk and that no one wants to see him in another picture as long as he lives." (Jeez.) Worth responded to the talk of boycotting by telling *The Mail*,

> I'd do everything in my power to stop it! After all, picture-making is his living. An attempt to damage that would do no good. Nothing that can be said or done to hurt him can make me feel any better. Besides, I'm not vindictive…. I don't want revenge, and I don't want to hurt anyone. I'd rather the whole thing were forgotten, and I'm making every effort to get it cleared up without any further publicity.

The trial lasted until September 1937, when it was ruled that the marriage was legal. When Worth finally filed for divorce, Brent got off easy: She asked for no alimony or community property.

Worth's RKO contract was terminated because, she would imply later, of all the publicity with Brent. She turned down a lucrative offer to do a personal appearance tour because the promoter wanted to bill her as "The Ex–Mrs. George Brent." She claimed to have had a nervous breakdown after the divorce. "I really was in an emotional state in those days," she told Guy Austin. "I had little faith in myself and still less money."

With no substantial acting offers from the major studios, she accepted the exploitation flick *The Wages of Sin* (1938). While she gave a sincere performance as a girl who gets into prostitution, it was obviously a step down.

In April '38, she was in the hospital recuperating from an unspecified illness. *The Mail* wrote, "In spite of the remarkable run of bad luck that has followed her during her stay in Hollywood, the Australian lass is still in fine spirits. Luckily, she has a grand sense of humor that enables her to see the funny side of almost anything—and she needs it." Two days after Worth entered the hospital, director George Cukor wanted to test her for an "important role" in *Holiday* with Katharine Hepburn, but she couldn't do it because she was still recovering.

She also lost a role in *Mr. Smith Goes to Washington* (1939) to Astrid Allwyn because Worth's "coloring" was almost the same as star Jean Arthur's. Another missed opportunity: *Broadway Serenade* (1939) at MGM. Worth instead did radio. One report said that she appeared uncredited in MGM's *Let Freedom Ring* (1939), but this has not been verified.

After she played a supporting part at Universal in *Mystery of the White Room* (1939), the studio wanted to sign her, but she turned them down; she thought *White Room* would lead to better roles at other studios. You have to wonder who was advising her.

In the summer of 1939, she returned to Australia to see her family. She was "farewelled" by her friend, actress Anna Sten, who was not acting at the moment. Wrote the *Maryborough Chronicle, Wide Bay and Burnett Advertiser*, Sten's career "was killed by the wrong kind of publicity. She preferred to play poker and look after her lovely garden," to which Worth replied, "I think that is a happier life."

While in Sydney, she appeared in P.G. Wodehouse's play *Good Morning, Bill* (1939) with the husband-and-wife team of Henry Mollison and Lina Basquette. In a first act scene, Worth had to break crockery in a rage and then faint. During one performance, this went horribly wrong when she fell on a broken cup which, related the *West Australian* newspaper,

> inflicted several deep gashes in her right thigh. She was carried from the stage by Mr. Henry Mollison and another member of the cast, but as this was part of the play no one in the audience knew

that anything was wrong. There was a great deal of blood from the wounds and as Miss Howarth had to appear again in three minutes she stemmed the flow of blood with a roll of toweling, which she hid from the audience with a fur. She was in considerable pain, but insisted on playing her part, so Dr. R.A. Eakin plugged the wounds until after the performance, when he inserted several stitches. Miss Howarth's pain was increased by the fact that she plays a boisterous part and had on occasions to run across the stage.

At the end of July '39, Basquette left the show after a disagreement with management and Worth was given top billing. "This is the first time I have ever seen my name in big lights outside the theater," she remarked to *The News*.

Worth was injured again in August, when she hurt her arm falling off a platform at a fashion show. ("Bad luck seems to be following the footsteps of Miss Joy Howarth, the Australian film star, since her return from Hollywood."—*Sydney Morning Herald*.) "I think there must be a hoodoo on me," she told the *Newcastle Sun*.

In Sydney, she acted in another play, *A Kiss from Kiki* (1939), before sailing back to the U.S.

Small parts on radio kept her fairly busy. A friend, actor Robert Coote, reportedly tried to help her get jobs. "She's on a strict diet and studying hard," wrote *The Mail*'s J.M. Ruddy, "so her chances should be better."

In mid–1940, she signed a two-picture deal with Columbia. She had long hated the name Constance Worth, considering it bad luck, but could not go back to Howarth since Columbia had Rita Hayworth under contract. Both films, *Angels Over Broadway* (1940), where she coolly played the ex-mistress of Thomas Mitchell, and *Meet Boston Blackie* (1941), as an international agent, were smallish parts she handled well. Bad luck continued to dog her: A sprained ankle took her out of the cast of Paramount's *The Night of January 16th* (1941).

Freelancing, she landed parts at the Poverty Row outfits PRC (as spies in *Criminals Within* and *The Dawn Express*) and Monogram (a society girl in *Borrowed Hero*). There was also a small part as a society woman in Hitchcock's *Suspicion* (1941). But this activity was not enough for her to make ends meet: "It is true I worked as a waitress in a Beverly Hills drive-in, where I carried trays to customers in cars," Worth revealed to *Australian Women's Weekly*'s Viola MacDonald. "I worked night duty for several weeks, while I spent my days hunting work around the studios. I hoped nobody recognized me while I was a waitress, as I did not want my family in Australia to worry. Many times I was tempted to catch the first boat for Australia, but something made me carry on."

Constance did two Boston Blackie series films with Chester Morris, *Meet Boston Blackie* (1941) and *Boston Blackie Goes Hollywood* (1942).

Nazi spy Constance Worth (posing as a Polish refugee) looks on as chemist Michael Whalen and Anne Nagel embrace in PRC's *The Dawn Express* (1942).

Her luck changed when Columbia came calling again. "It was not a star's contract, by any means," she admitted to Lon Jones, "but I grabbed it very gratefully." She worked in supporting and bit parts, and had the top female roles in *Boston Blackie Goes Hollywood* (1942), the Charles Starrett westerns *Cyclone Prairie Rangers* (1944) and *Sagebrush Heroes* (1945) and (on loanout to Republic) the serial *G-Men vs. the Black Dragon* (1943).

G-Men director William Witney wrote in his autobiography that Worth turned out to be one of the best actresses he'd ever worked with "and was as pretty as any blonde in pictures."

But, Witney continued, "Unfortunately she drank."

According to Witney, one day he was shooting a fight scene in a lumberyard when Worth disruptively sashayed onto the scene swinging a whiskey bottle like a bell, planted herself in his director's chair and insisted, "Come on, let's all have a party!" And when the *G-Men* troupe was on location in Santa Barbara, Worth came knocking at Witney's hotel room door in the middle of the night in a sheer nightgown, drink in hand, saying, "I'm lonesome" and trying to push her way in—which panicked Witney, as his wife was asleep in the bed! Fortunately for Witney, *G-Men* cameraman Bud Thackery happened to come along, assessed the scene, got Worth up into his arms and carried her away (and into his own room, Witney noted). Witney said he felt like one of his own serial heroes, saved from death by a sidekick.

On the set of *Klondike Kate* (1943), Worth met writer William A. Pierce, who was married with two children, and was about ten years her senior. Flash-forward two years:

At midnight on June 18, 1945, Pierce's wife Wilma arrived at a hideaway apartment with a private detective and two policemen in tow. Pierce opened the door wearing only a bathrobe and holding a hammer. A naked Worth was hiding in the bed; Wilma claimed that it was just "one of a series of trysts too numerous to recall." In the Pierce divorce case, Worth was named co-respondent, but denied any wrongdoing—she and William were merely good friends, she said. His divorce became final in January 1946.

In 1945, Worth was optimistic talking to writer Lon Jones about the state of her movie career: "I have no desire to play romantic leads anymore, though I do think I still look good enough for such roles. I'm now concentrating on character parts, similar to those that have made Claire Trevor famous. I think I can do them, and I feel they'll offer me a longer screen life than romantic leads. At least the competition won't be so stiff."

After her Columbia pact expired, Worth freelanced, mostly at the Poverty Row studios. A promised good part in RKO's *Deadline at Dawn* (1946) did not amount to much and some reported that a few of her scenes were cut. Worth always felt there was a curse on her because of several behind-the-scenes mishaps on movie sets where she was hurt, but these could well be attributed to her drinking.

Around March 1947, she and William Pierce married. A few days before she was to start playing a part in *Forever Amber* (1947), she and her husband (in the driver's seat) were on the Coast Highway in Malibu when they were hit by another vehicle. "I put my hand across my husband's face to protect him but I myself got my face smashed against the rear-view mirror and then was tossed through the windshield," Worth told the *Sydney Morning Herald*'s Guy Austin. The accident kept her in the hospital for several months and her scarred face required extensive plastic surgery.

A noirish portrait of Worth from *Deadline at Dawn* (1946).

After parts in two 1949 films, *The Set-Up* ("And here's an odder footnote: one of the minor characters at the ringside looks remarkably like Joy Howarth"—*Daily Telegraph*'s Josephine O'Neill) and *Western Renegades*, Worth became a TV bit player.

In May 1950, a return to Australia to introduce her husband to her family was postponed. "That reason," Worth told Louella Parsons, "is motherhood. We expect a baby in the late summer." She had a miscarriage.

Her mother told the *Sydney Morning Herald* in October 1952, just after visiting her, "I saw her in a number of small pictures [on TV], playing all sorts of roles—comedy, drama, and 'the other woman.' And just as I left, she was negotiating with a big producing company for a new TV serial." She added that her daughter was "well and happy" and "looked younger than ever."

In the mid–1950s, Worth was not acting anymore and she and her husband lived in Memphis where Pierce did some writing. Director Ken G. Hall said that Worth had become an "ordinary housewife" and endured an unhappy existence as an alcoholic.

After a bout of illness and a stay with her family in Australia, she professed a desire to return to movies. She told Guy Austin in 1961 that she felt she had "every chance to pick up my career where I left off. I am going to have my name put back in the Players' Directory and get in touch with the producers and directors who have often asked why I don't work." Nothing happened.

On October 18, 1963, the 52-year-old was suffering from cirrhosis of the liver and anemia when she died at her home in Los Angeles.

Constance Worth Filmography

1933: *The Squatter's Daughter.*
1934: *The Silence of Dean Maitland.*
1937: *China Passage, Windjammer.*
1938: *The Wages of Sin.*
1939: *Mystery of the White Room.*
1940: *Angels Over Broadway.*
1941: *Meet Boston Blackie, Criminals Within, Suspicion* (uncredited), *Borrowed Hero.*
1942: *The Dawn Express, Boston Blackie Goes Hollywood, When Johnny Comes Marching Home* (uncredited).
1943: *City Without Men, G-Men vs. The Black Dragon, Let's Have Fun, She Has What It Takes, Crime Doctor* (uncredited), *Appointment in Berlin* (uncredited), *Dangerous Blondes* (uncredited), *My Kingdom for a Cook* (uncredited), *The Crime Doctor's Strangest Case, Klondike Kate, Who's Hugh?* (short).
1944: *Cover Girl* (uncredited), *Jam Session* (uncredited), *Frenchman's Creek* (uncredited), *Cyclone Prairie Rangers.*
1945: *Sagebrush Heroes, The Kid Sister, Dillinger* (uncredited), *Why Girls Leave Home, Sensation Hunters.*
1946: *Deadline at Dawn.*
1949: *The Set-Up* (uncredited), *Western Renegades.*

References

Lynne Baggett

"Actress Charged with Hit-Run Death of Boy, 9." *Los Angeles Times*, July 10, 1954.
"Actress Gets 60 Days for L.A. Hit-Run Death." *Press Democrat*, December 1, 1954.
"Actress Lynne Baggett Dies, Pills By Her Side." *Los Angeles Times*, March 23, 1960.
"Actress Takes Overdose of Sleeping Pills." *Honolulu Star-Bulletin*, June 8, 1959.
Archerd, Army. "Just for Variety." *Variety*, March 24, 1960.
"Divorce Granted to Lynne Baggett." *Daily Press*, April 1, 1955.
Dixon, Hugh. "Hollywood." *Pittsburgh Post-Gazette*, August 24, 1942.
"Former Actress in Mental Ward." *Journal News*, August 25, 1959.
Fraser-Cavassoni, Natasha. *Sam Spiegel*. New York: Simon & Schuster, 2003.
"Hit-Run Actress Found Dead in Bed." *Democrat and Chronicle*, March 24, 1960.
"Hit-Run Driving Lands Actress in Jail for 60 Days." *Corsicana Daily Sun*, December 2, 1954.
"Lynne Baggett Held in Hit-Run Death of Child." *Morning Call*, July 10, 1954.
"Lynne Baggett, 32-Year-Old Actress, Dies." *Baytown Sun*, March 23, 1960.
Mosby, Aline. "No Lavish Eve Party for Hit-and-Run Actress." *Pittsburgh Press*, December 31, 1954.
Parsons, Louella. *Anderson Daily Bulletin*, October 28, 1959.
"Pill Death Claims Actress Baggett." *Pasadena Independent*, March 23, 1960.
Soanes, Wood. "Curtain Calls." *Oakland Tribune*, October 20, 194.

Suzan Ball

"Actress Suzan Ball Falls, Breaks 'Jinxed' Leg." *Democrat and Chronicle*, November 30, 1953.
Ames, Walter. "Suzan Ball in TV Show to Walk Minus One Leg." *Los Angeles Times*, May 26, 1954.
Bacon, James. "Suzan Ball Discards Crutches to Walk Down Church Aisle." *Asbury Park Press*, April 12, 1954.
Ball, Suzan, as told to Aline Mosby. "Suzan Ball Worried About How Leg Loss Would Upset Others." *The Town Talk*, January 29, 1954.
_____, as told to Aline Mosby. "Suzan Says Artificial Leg Like Owning False Teeth." *The Times*, February 2, 1954.
_____, as told to Julian Hartt. "Suzan Ball Tells of Her Plans for Future After Leg Amputation to Halt Bone Cancer." *San Francisco Examiner*, January 24, 1954.
_____, as told to Julian Hartt. "Suzan Ball Tells of Getting Break in Films Before Amputation of Leg." *San Francisco Examiner*, January 25, 1954.
_____, as told to Julian Hartt. "Suzan Ball Describes Decision to Amputate." *San Francisco Examiner*, January 26, 1954.
Crivello, Kirk. *Fallen Angels*. Secaucus, NJ: Citadel Press, 1988.
"Death Ends Suzan Ball's Heroic Battle with Cancer." *Los Angeles Times*, August 6, 1955.
"Fire Hits Shop Owned By Dad of Suzan Ball." *Daily News*, July 17, 1955.
Kilgallen, Dorothy. "Voice of Broadway." *The Tennessean*, March 5, 1953.
Morrell, Warren. "Thru the Hills." *Rapid City Journal*, July 13, 1954.
Mosby, Aline. "Plucky Suzan Ball Loses Leg—Not Career Hopes." *Long Beach Independent*, January 13, 1954.
_____. "Suzan Ball Not Bothered By Amputation." *Great Bend Tribune*, January 21, 1954.
_____. "Suzan Ball May Have to Use Crutches to Attend Wedding." *The Town Talk*, April 7, 1954.
_____. "Suzan Ball Dying of a Lung Cancer." *Akron Beacon Journal*, July 14, 1955.

Quinn, Anthony, with Daniel Paisner. *One Man Tango*. New York: HarperCollins, 1996.
"Santa Maria's Daughter Wins Film Star Contract." *Santa Maria Times*, November 21, 1951.
Schallert, Edwin. *Los Angeles Times*, November 13, 1951.
_____. *Los Angeles Times*, March 10, 1952.
Scheuer, Steven H. "TV Keynotes." *Brooklyn Daily Eagle*, May 25, 1954.
Scott, John L. "No Cheesecake, Just Chocolate Aided Suzan." *Los Angeles Times*, March 23, 1952.
Smith, Cecil. "Producer Cal Kuhl Says Play's the Thing in Television Drama." *Los Angeles Times*, July 26, 1954.
"Starlet Reveals She Almost Lost Leg Because of Cancer." *Des Moines Register*, August 5, 1953.
"Suzan Ball Faces $11,174 Damage Suit." *Santa Maria Times*, March 9, 1954.
"Suzan Ball Married in Santa Barbara Church." *Los Angeles Times*, April 12, 1954.
"Suzan Ball Paid Star's Tribute at Final Rites." *Los Angeles Times*, August 10, 1955.
Tannen, Lee, via Michael Karol. Email to Author, September 10, 2018.
Thomas, Bob. "Actress Tells How She Was Saved from Amputation, Threat to Life." *Oakland Tribune*, August 4, 1953.
_____. "Hope Alone Is Keeping Actress Suzan Ball Alive." *Boston Globe*, July 27, 1955.
Weaver, Tom. *Wild Wild Westerners*. Duncan, OK: BearManor Media, 2012.
What Is Ewing's Sarcoma https://www.webmd.com/cancer/ewings-sarcoma#1.
Wilson, Earl. "It Happened Last Night." *Winona Republican Herald*, September 24, 1952.

Helen Burgess

"Actress Dies of Pneumonia." *Albuquerque Journal*, April 8, 1937.
Burgess, Helen. "Anything But School, Says New Movie Actress." *San Mateo Times*, October 31, 1936.
Carroll, Harrison. "Behind the Scenes in Hollywood." *Evening News*, April 24, 1937.
"Given Decree of Annulment." *Los Angeles Times*, March 6, 1937.
"Helen Burgess Laid to Rest." *Los Angeles Times*, April 11, 1937.
"Hollywood News." *Clovis Evening News Journal*, April 10, 1937.
"Hollywood Tragedy." *Photoplay*, June 1937.
Packer, Eleanor. "Homeliness is Only Skin Deep, New Star is Uncovered." *Fresno Bee*, January 3, 1937.
Von Blon, Katherine T. "Clark Group Gains New Favor in New Play." *Los Angeles Times*, February 15, 1935.

Susan Cabot

Adams, Marjory. "Susan Cabot, Native of Boston, Never in American Girl Role." *Boston Globe*, April 8, 1952.
_____. "Boston-born Susan Cabot No Kin to Lodge or Lowell." *Boston Globe*, September 18, 1959.
Barker, Mayerene. "Defendant May Be Son of Hussein, Lawyer Says." *Los Angeles Times*, April 13, 1989.
Carroll, Harrison. "In Hollywood." *Vidette Messenger of Porter County*, April 4, 1959.
_____. "Behind the Scenes in Hollywood." *Wilkes Barre Times Leader*, June 21, 1968.
Cook, Ben. "Hollywood Film Shop." *Shamokin News Dispatch*, September 4, 1951.
Des Barres, Pamela. "The Agony and the Ecstasy—A Rare Interview with Christopher Jones." *Movieline*, August 1996.
Doctoroff, Andrew S., and Gabe Fuentes. "Susan Cabot, B Movie Star of '50s, Slain." *Los Angeles Times*, December 12, 1986.
"Former Movie Actress Slain; her son, 22, is arrested." *Des Moines Register*, December 12, 1986.
Garver, Jack. "Hollywood Gets Actors to Meet Public." *The Times*, January 1, 1952.
Goldstein, Carl. "*Kismet* Cast and Music Pace Show." *Asbury Park Press*, July 17, 1956.
"Here in '26 Supporting Role, Geer Star of TC Playhouse Final Show." *Press and Sun Bulletin*, August 27, 1956.
Hopper, Hedda. *Chicago Tribune*, May 20, 1943.
_____. *Los Angeles Times*, December 2, 1950.
Johnson, Erskine. "In Hollywood." *San Bernardino County Sun*, November 8, 1951.
Klein, Patricia. "Actress in Deep Despair on Day She Was Slain, Psychologist Says." *Los Angeles Times*, October 5, 1989.
Klunder, Jan. "Son Sets Up Possible Insanity Defense in Slaying of Actress." *Los Angeles Times*, February 24, 1987.
_____. "Bizarre Lives Bared of Star, Son Accused of Her Murder." *Los Angeles Times*, June 7, 1987.
Lerner, Patricia Klein. "Son Convicted of Killing Actress Mother." *Los Angeles Times*, October 11, 1989.
Locker, Ray, and Ed Brackett. "JFK Files: CIA Lined Up Actress for Date with Jordan's King Hussein During Visit to United States." *USA Today*, January 8, 2018.
Lozano, Carlos. "Actress' Son Admitted Killing Her, Attorney Reveals." *Los Angeles Times*, May 17, 1989.
_____. "Man Who Killed Actress Mother Gets Probation." *Los Angeles Times*, November 30, 1989.

Lyons, Leonard. "Best of Broadway." *Philadelphia Inquirer*, January 7, 1963.
Mabbott, Lucille. "Rising Young Actress Prefers Bad Girl Roles." *Rapid City Journal*, June 11, 1950.
Manners, Dorothy. *Philadelphia Inquirer*, June 10, 1966.
McHenry, Charles. "On the Town." *Daily News*, April 26, 1967.
Metro Digest. *Los Angeles Times*, April 13, 1989.
Parsons, Louella. *Albuquerque Journal*, May 10, 1959.
Quinn, James. "Judge Grants Mistrial in Susan Cabot Slaying Case." *Los Angeles Times*, May 23, 1989.
"Rapid City and Hollywood Entertainers in Spotlight." *Rapid City Journal*, June 5, 1950.
Richardson, John H. "The Wasp Woman Stung." *Premiere*. April 1991.
Roman, Michael. Interview with Tom Weaver. September 2, 2018.
Royal, Don. "Meet Susan Cabot." *Paducah Sun*, May 29, 1959.
"Son Testifies on Actress' Death." *Los Angeles Times*, October 6, 1989.
Steinberg, Lynn. "Patients Who Took Growth Hormone Live in Terror of Deadly Disease." *Los Angeles Times*, February 21, 1988.

Mary Castle

"Actor Ordered to Pay Despite Lack of Work." *Tampa Times*, February 15, 1958.
"Actress Explains Her Overdue Bill." *Daily Oklahoman*, December 12, 1959.
"Actress Has Near Brush with Death." *Amarillo Globe Times*, September 14, 1959.
"Actress Mary Castle Arrested Three Times." *Marshfield News-Herald*, April 22, 1960.
"Actress Tries Suicide After Arrest as Drunk." *Pasadena Independent*, November 14, 1959.
Bustin, John. "Show World." *Austin American*, January 24, 1956.
Carroll, Harrison. "Behind the Scenes in Hollywood." *Lancaster Eagle Gazette*, April 9, 1954.
"Despondent Over Divorce." *Pittsburgh Post-Gazette*, November 14, 1959.
Fidler, Jimmie. "Jimmie Fidler in Hollywood." *Nevada State Journal*, June 9, 1950.
Graham, Sheilah. "In Hollywood." *Tampa Times*, April 16, 1954.
Gwynn, Edith. "Hollywood." *The Mercury*, August 15, 1951.
"Harvey in Hollywood." *Council Grove Republican*, August 1, 1950.
Hyatt, Wesley. *Emmy Award Winning Nighttime Television Shows, 1948–2004*. Jefferson, NC: McFarland, 2006.
Johnson, Erskine. *The Daily Times*, October 4, 1951.
_____. *The News Herald*, December 4, 1951.
_____. *The Daily Times*, June 9, 1952.
_____ "Movie & TV-Views." *Elmira Advertiser*, May 8, 1954.
Lee, Cynthia. Emails to Author, January 4 and 5, 2019.
Magers, Boyd. Do You Remember? *Stories of the Century*. http://www.westernclippings.com/remember/storiesofcentury_doyouremember.shtml.
Marsh, Maralyn. "Hollywood Unveils Luscious Redhead to Replace Rita." *Lebanon Daily News*, August 3, 1950.
"Mary Castle Files Separation Suit." *Independent*, January 17, 1958.
"Mary Castle, Husband in Divorce, Property Tiff." *Los Angeles Times*, January 20, 1958.
"Mary Castle Shells Out $50 to Court for Traffic Case." *Salt Lake Tribune*, April 27, 1960.
"Mary Castle Too Ill to Continue in *Good*." *Variety*, July 26, 1955.
Mosby, Aline. "Columbia Finds New Glamour Girl, Double for Rita." *Terre Haute Star*, August 3, 1950.
"Movie Actress is Served with Debt Warrant." *The Bee*, April 21, 1960.
Padgitt, James. "In Hollywood." *The Herald*, March 29, 1951.
Parsons, Louella. *Cincinnati Enquirer*, April 17, 1953.
_____. *Pittsburgh Post-Gazette*, September 3, 1960.
Ryon, Art. "About with Art Ryon." *Los Angeles Times*, March 10, 1963.
Stearn, Jess. "The Burden of Beauty." *Daily News*, July 12, 1953.
"Telepix Review." *Variety*, November 8, 1951.
"TV Actress Arrested as Drunk." *Pasadena Independent*, December 25, 1957.
Wilson, Barbara L. Mary Gains Own Identity. *Philadelphia Inquirer*, November 9, 1952.
Wilson, Earl. *San Francisco Examiner*, June 3, 1953.
Winchell, Walter. *Wilkes Barre Times Leader*, March 23, 1960.
Witney, Jay Dee. Email to Author, November 8, 2018.

Mae Clarke

"Actress Betrothed to John McCormick." *Los Angeles Times*, November 27, 1930.
"Any Queen in Deck Better Than Wife." *Bismarck Tribune*, January 2, 1930.

Archerd, Army. "Just for Variety." *Variety*, October 9, 1953.
Belser, Emily. "In Hollywood." *El Paso Herald Post*, August 8, 1955.
Biederman, Patricia Ward. "Actress Savors Film Career Sweetened By Grapefruit." *Los Angeles Times*, July 22, 1985.
Blaker, John. "The Newsreel." *Province Sun*, July 24, 1932.
Carroll, Harrison. "Behind the Scenes in Hollywood." *Bristol Daily Courier*, March 7, 1934.
_____. "Behind the Scenes in Hollywood." *Evening News*, June 25, 1934.
Clarke, Mae, with James Curtis. *Featured Player*. Metuchen, NJ: Scarecrow, 1996.
Connolly, Mike. "Just for Variety." *Variety*, August 7, 1950.
Coons, Robbin. "Comeback Hard for Player Who Has Been Ill." *Decatur Daily Review*, November 5, 1932.
_____. "Grapefruit Massage Still Brings Fame to Mae Clarke." *Asbury Park Press*, December 7, 1936.
_____. "In Hollywood." *Chillicothe Gazette*, June 7, 1938.
Fawcett, Captain Roscoe. "Screen Oddities." *The Times*, October 2, 1933.
"Former Actress Visits Hollywood." *Los Angeles Times*, August 29, 1939.
"Former Movie Actress Obtains Reno Divorce." *Evening News*, January 6, 1940.
Gloss, Edward E. "German Star Makes American Film Bow." *Akron Beacon Journal*, January 15, 1932.
Graham, Sheilah. "Many Former Stars Glad to Get Small Roles." *Dayton Daily News*, June 22, 1941.
"'Grapefruit Scene' Pursues Mae Clarke." *Cumberland Sunday Times*, December 20, 1936.
Green, Jesse. "You Must Remember This." *Premiere*, March 1991.
Kingsley, Grace. "Hobnobbing in Hollywood." *Los Angeles Times*, May 24, 1933.
Lamparski, Richard. *Whatever Became Of ...?* Fourth Series. New York: Crown, 1973.
Lusk, Norbert. "Good Acting Marks Films." *Los Angeles Times*, September 15, 1929.
"Mae Clarke, Film Actress, to Wed." *San Francisco Examiner*, September 15, 1937.
"Mae Clarke Injured." *Fresno Bee The Republican*, March 2, 1933.
"Mae Clarke Seeking $1 Million Over Show." *San Bernardino County Sun*, October 17, 1957.
"Mae Clarke Sues Actor in Accident." *Los Angeles Times*, August 25, 1933.
"Mae Clarke Tells Shock at Seeing Portrayal on TV." *Independent*, July 17, 1958.
Mank, Gregory William. *Women in Horror Films, 1930s*. Jefferson, NC: McFarland, 1999.
Michaelson, Judith. "Where They Live the Last Picture Show." *Los Angeles Times*, August 28, 1983.
Miller, Frank, and Molly Haskell. *Leading Men: The 50 Most Unforgettable Actors of the Studio Era*. San Francisco: Chronicle Books, 2006.
Morris, Ruth. "Uncommon Chatter." *Variety*, May 20, 1931.
Muir, Helen. "The Madding Crowd." *Miami News*, December 19, 1938.
Parsons, Louella. *Fresno Bee*, July 9, 1934.
Pearson, Drew. "The Washington Merry-Go-Round." *Advocate Messenger*, May 19, 1944.
Schallert, Edwin. "*Flying Tigers* Compelling Saga of Intrepid Airmen." *Los Angeles Times*, September 23, 1942.
Schallert, Eliza. "Mae Clarke, Ex-Star, Suffers Breakdown." *Los Angeles Times*, January 28, 1950.
Schroeder, Mildred. "Culture Begins at 40 for Mae Clarke." *San Francisco Examiner*, September 3, 1964.
Shaffer, George. Flowers. "Flowers Everywhere But Jean Bought 'Em." *New York Daily News*, July 17, 1934.
Thomas, Bob. "Actress Mae Clarke Looks Back on Her Movie Career." *Miami Daily News Record*, October 25, 1953.
_____. "Art Is Shown by Mae Clarke." *Bridgeport Post*, October 28, 1963.
Thomas, Dan. "Mae Clarke Gets a Break in the Movies." *News Herald*, June 15, 1931.
_____. "Gossip from Hollywood." *Pensacola News Journal*, January 14, 1935.
_____. "Mae Clarke to Abandon Jinx Siren Roles." *Decatur Daily Review*, January 18, 1935.
Tildesley, Alice L. New Coiffures Often Change Personalities. *Courier Journal*, April 29, 1934.
Tinee, Mae. "Expert Player Saves Movie Despite Flaws in Production." *Chicago Tribune*, April 9, 1933.
Wilson, Earl. "It Happened Last Night." *Columbus Telegram*, January 31, 1974.
Winchell, Walter. *Courier Post*, June 18, 1934.

Dorothy Comingore

"Actress Declines Answer to Query of Red Activities." *Town Talk*, October 22, 1952.
"Actress Tells of Picket Line at Red Inquiry." *Los Angeles Times*, October 31, 1952.
"Attorneys Clash in Comingore Custody Contest." *Los Angeles Times*, October 23, 1952.
Carson, James. "They're Not All Perfect!" *Modern Screen*, November 1940.
Ciment, Michel. *Conversations with Losey*. New York: Methuen, 1985.
Communist Activities Among Professional Groups in the Los Angeles Area, Hearings Before the Committee on Un-American Activities, House of Representatives, Eighty-Second Congress, Second Session, October 3, 6, and 7, 1952. https://archive.org/stream/communistactivit04unit/communistactivit04unit_djvu.txt.
Coons, Robbin. "Associate Producers Hollywood's Buffoons Even in Pre-Guild Days." *The Record*, August 9, 1938.

_____. "Movie Side Lights from Hollywood." *Palladium-Item*, February 6, 1944.
"Dorothy Comingore to Enter Mental Hospital." *Los Angeles Times*, May 29, 1953.
Feeney, F.X. "How a Little Known Writer Became the Inspiration for a Writers Guild Award Honoring Courage." https://www.writtenby.com/webexclusives/our-unknown-soldier.
Fidler, Jimmie. "Hollywood Roundup." *Evening Standard*, April 16, 1942.
"Former Screen Star Seized on Vice Charge." *Los Angeles Times*, March 20, 1953.
Harker, Milton. "In Hollywood." *Kane Republican*, August 9, 1938.
_____. "In Hollywood." *The Dispatch*, June 3, 1939.
Heffernan, Harold. "Hollywood Highlights." *Hartford Courant*, August 1, 1941.
Hoberman, J. *An Army of Phantoms: American Movies and the Making of the Cold War.* New York: The New Press, 2011.
"Kin of Hoosiers in Film Role." *Indianapolis News*, April 23, 1941.
"New Leading Lady? Yes, No Chaplin Says." *San Francisco Examiner*, March 18, 1938.
Othman, Frederick C. "Ex-Oakland Girl Denies She's Chaplin Protege." *Oakland Tribune*, April 29, 1938.
_____. "Dorothy Chooses Her Parts." *Wisconsin State Journal*, August 12, 1941.
_____. "3 Years of 'No' Cost Dorothy 3 Years' Work." *New York Daily News*, February 11, 1944.
"Red Issue Raised in Fight Over Actress' Children." *Los Angeles Times*, October 22, 1952.
Scott, John L. "Miss Comingore to Come Back." *Los Angeles Times*, April 1, 1945.
Sharp, Kathleen. "Destroyed by HUAC: The Dorothy Comingore Story." *Los Angeles Review of Books*, September 13, 2013.
Stanfield, Audrey. "Down the Aisle." *Dayton Daily News*, July 21, 1944.
"Star-Find of *Citizen Kane* Has Temper to Match Tresses." *Boston Globe*, August 29, 1941.
"Third Chance Wins for Her in Hollywood." *Press and Sun-Bulletin*, April 18, 1941.
Vaughn, Thomas. "The Boy Grows Older." *Hollywood*, December 1940.
"Welles's Find Is Making Good." *The Record*, April 18, 1941.

Patricia Dane

Carroll, Harrison. "Behind the Scenes in Hollywood." *Daily Journal*, December 10, 1940.
_____. "Behind the Scenes in Hollywood." *Wilkes-Barre Record*, January 31, 1941.
Cohen, Harold W. "Drama Desk." *Pittsburgh Post-Gazette*, March 28, 1940.
"Did Pat Dane Wield Knife? She Has Chance to Answer." *Pittsburgh Press*, August 15, 1944.
Dixon, Hugh. "Hollywood." *Pittsburgh Post-Gazette*, December 24, 1943.
"Dorsey Case Thrown Out of Court." *Tampa Tribune*, December 8, 1944.
"Dorsey's Marriage Shocks Ex-Bride." *Fresno Bee*, March 28, 1948.
Fidler, Jimmie. "Jimmie Fidler in Hollywood." *Sioux City Journal*, December 19, 1939.
Graham, Sheilah. "Hollywood Today." *Indianapolis Star*, June 3, 1941.
_____. "Hollywood Today." *Indianapolis Star*, June 18, 1941.
Hopper, Hedda. *Minneapolis Star*, May 7, 1941.
_____. *New York Daily News*, August 4, 1942.
"I've Been Drunk for 25 Years, Actor Tells Police." *Mt. Vernon Register-News*, October 22, 1948.
"Judge Dismisses Assault Charges Against Dorseys." *Daily Times*, December 7, 1944.
Kilgallen, Dorothy. "Broadway." *Star Gazette*, August 28, 1943.
_____. "The Voice of Broadway." *The Tennessean*, January 24, 1957.
Levinson, Peter. *Tommy Dorsey: Livin' in a Great Big Way, A Biography.* New York: Da Capo Press, 2006.
Lindstrom, Andy. "The Stories She Can Tell." *Tallahassee Democrat*, May 29, 1988.
Parsons, Louella. *Philadelphia Inquirer*, January 12, 1940.
_____. *Fresno Bee*, March 6, 1941.
"Quiz Pat Dane in Hall Battle." *San Mateo Times*, August 12, 1944.
"Sultry-Eyed Pat Dane to Tell About Passes." *San Mateo Times*, August 15, 1944.
Todd, John. "Patricia Dane to Spurn Love for Movie Career." *The Times*, September 19, 1947.
Truesdell, John. "Pat Dane Has Capacity to Become Star—Maybe." *Courier-Journal*, August 28, 1941.
_____. "The 'Late' Pat Dane." *Cincinnati Enquirer*, October 12, 1941.
"Widow of Tommy Dorsey is Broke." *The Times*, September 1, 1959.

Dorothy Dell

Black, Shirley Temple. *Child Star.* New York: McGraw-Hill, 1988.
Coons, Robbin. "Hollywood Sights and Sounds." *Greenwood Commonwealth*, June 15, 1934.
Denhoff, Alice. "Re-Glorifying the Old-Fashioned Hips and Legs." *Hamilton Evening Journal*, June 13, 1931.
Gray, Mrs. Benjamin. "Society." *Shreveport Times*, August 4, 1931.
Keavy, Hubbard. "Screen Life in Hollywood." *Morning News*, December 4, 1933.

Kilgallen, Dorothy. "Voice of Broadway." *The Mercury*, April 14, 1942.
Krug, Karl. "The Show Shop." *Pittsburgh Press*, February 24, 1931.
Merrick, Mollie. *Lincoln Evening Journal*, March 2, 1934.
"Mississippi Girl in *Wharf Angel* at Paramount." *Greenwood Commonwealth*, May 23, 1934.
"New Orleans Lass Dislikes Housework; Keen for Stage." *Evening Independent*. August 9, 1930.
"Shots from Eastern Studios." *The Film Daily*, August 1, 1932.
Sobol, Louis. "The Voice of Broadway." *Minneapolis Star Tribune*, November 4, 1931.
Star Foresaw "Early Death." *Altoona Tribune*, June 9, 1934.
"Stars Avoid Disaster Hall As Unlucky Movie Omen." *Oakland Tribune*, December 10, 1936.
"What Never Was Told About the Tragic Crash of Lovely Dorothy Dell." *Salt Lake Tribune*, August 12, 1934.
Winchell, Walter. "On Broadway." *Reading Times*, September 27, 1932.

Sidney Fox

"Actress Sidney Fox Asks Decree, Means It." *Los Angeles Examiner*, October 11, 1940.
Ager, Cecelia. "Going Places." *Variety*, March 13, 1934.
Atkins, Rick. *Guest Parking 2: Ian Wolfe, Carl Laemmle, Jr., Alan Napier, David Manners*. Duncan, OK: BearManor, 2016.
Carroll, Harrison. "Behind the Scenes in Hollywood." *Evening News*, May 16, 1932.
"Chemists in Death Case." *Miami Daily News Record*, November 17, 1942.
Fidler, Jimmie. *Salt Lake Tribune*, September 12, 1936.
"Film Star's WPA Dad Dies Scorning Her Aid." *New York Daily News*, December 3, 1936.
Glad, Gladys. "Flicker Star Exercises to Keep Figure." *San Bernardino County*, June 2, 1932.
Hall, Mordaunt. "The Screen." *New York Times*, November 11, 1931.
"Hollywood Marriage." *Des Moines Register*, August 5, 1934.
"Hurt in Auto." *Chicago Tribune*, May 11, 1932.
James, Rian. *Brooklyn Daily Eagle*, December 22, 1933.
_____. *Brooklyn Daily Eagle*, January 11, 1934.
Kingsley, Grace. "Universal Signs Sidney Fox." *Los Angeles Times*, November 7, 1930.
_____. *Los Angeles Times*, November 15, 1933.
Lost Sheep Review. *New York Times*, May 6, 1930.
"L.U.K. What to Do, See and Hear." *Harrisburg Telegraph*, July 28, 1937.
Morris, Ruth. "Uncommon Chatter." *Variety*, May 20, 1931.
"Movie Biographies: Sidney Fox." *Brooklyn Daily Eagle*, March 24, 1932.
Parsons, Louella. *Fresno Bee*, December 25, 1933.
"Reconciliation of Short Duration." *Sedalia Democrat*, February 21, 1934.
Seymour, Deming. "Weak Play Wins Hand at Opening." *Akron Beacon Journal*, May 24, 1930.
"Sidney Fox, Actress, Visits Here." *Elmira Star-Gazette*, October 16, 1941.
"Sidney Fox Changes Mind." *Indiana Gazette*, March 31, 1934.
"Sidney Fox Files for Divorce." *Piqua Daily Call*, February 21, 1934.
"Sidney Fox, Film Player, Discovered Dead in Bed." *Los Angeles Times*, November 16, 1942.
"Sidney Fox Says She Feared Spouse." *Akron Beacon Journal*, April 20, 1934.
Stine, Whitney. *Mother Goddam*. New York: Hawthorn Books, 1974.
Sullivan, Ed. *St. Louis Star and Times*, June 19, 1934.
"Universal Signing Youthful Actress." *Los Angeles Times*, June 27, 1930.
Whitaker, Alma. "Sidney Fox Returns to Film Spotlight." *Los Angeles Times*, February 9, 1934.
Winchell, Walter. *Wilkes Barre Times Leader*, August 2, 1935.

Charlotte Henry

Carroll, Harrison. *Tampa Tribune*, September 23, 1933.
_____. *Tyrone Daily Herald*, October 28, 1933.
"Ex-Stars, Still Young, Are Extras at $10 a Day Now." *Pittsburgh Post-Gazette*, June 4, 1940.
"Forbidden Heaven. Capsule Guide." *Hollywood*, November 1935.
Fraser, Harry. *I Went That-a-Way: The Memoirs of a Western Film Director*. Metuchen, NJ: Scarecrow, 1990.
Heffernan, Harold. "Stage and Screen." *Winnipeg Tribune*, May 22, 1940.
Hopper, Hedda. *Chicago Tribune*, May 20, 1943.
_____. *Los Angeles Times*, May 26, 1943,
Keavy, Hubbard. "Screen Life in Hollywood." *Deadwood Pioneer Times*, September 24, 1933.
_____. *Central New Jersey Home News*, November 21, 1937.
Kilgallen, Dorothy. "Voice of Broadway." *Cincinnati Enquirer*, January 7, 1949.
_____. "Voice of Broadway." *News Journal*, February 3, 1950.

Kingsley. Grace. "New Revue Offered at Beaux Arts." *Los Angeles Times*, July 25, 1942.
Lamparski, Richard. *Whatever Became Of...? Giant 1st Annual*. New York: Bantam Books, 1976.
"*Lena Rivers* Victory Next." *Salt Lake Telegram*, April 29, 1932.
Monahan, Kaspar. "Show Shops." *Pittsburgh Press*, December 22, 1933..
Parsons, Louella. *The Courier*, June 10, 1941.
Rhodes, Robert J. "Alice Finds That Wonderland Proved Just a Myth, After All." *The Times*, July 20, 1939.
Scheuer, Philip K. "A Town Called Hollywood." *Los Angeles Times*, September 24, 1933.
_____. "A Town Called Hollywood." *Los Angeles Times*, October 1, 1933.
Shaffer, George. "Alice Begins Movie Career All Over Again." *Detroit Free Press*, February 5, 1935.
Shaw, Len G. *Detroit Free Press*, March 1, 1934.
Stafford, M. Oakley. "Informing You." *Hartford Courant*, January 12, 1949.
"Star of 1933 Working Now as an Extra." *Lansing State Journal*, August 4, 1940.
"To Play Carroll's Alice." *Salt Lake Tribune*, October 22, 1933.
"What the Picture Did for Me. L.A. Irwin, Palace Theatre. Penacook, NH." *Motion Picture Herald*, February 8, 1936.

Rita Johnson

"Around the World." *Star Tribune*, March 27, 1947.
"Boyer-Sullavan Film Illustrates Importance of Voices for Screen." *The Gazette*, December 23, 1941.
Carroll, Harrison. "Behind the Scenes in Hollywood." *Republican and Herald*, August 30, 1948.
Clary, Patricia. "Rudy, the Vagabond Lover, Now a Character Actor." *Pittsburgh Press*, June 16, 1945.
Cohen, Harold W. "The Drama Desk." *Pittsburgh Post-Gazette*, May 28, 1940.
Fidler, Jimmie. "Fidler in Hollywood." *News Press*, November 13, 1948.
Graham, Sheilah. "Hollywood Day By Day." *Calgary Herald*, January 6, 1949.
_____. "Hollywood." *Pittsburgh Post-Gazette*, March 23, 1949.
_____. "Hollywood Today." *Arizona Daily Star*, March 17, 1953.
Gwynn, Edith. "Hollywood." *The Mercury*, October 19, 1948.
_____. "Hollywood." *The Mercury*, October 28, 1948.
Handsaker, Gene. "Hollywood." *Rocky Mount Telegram*, May 17, 1948.
Harker, Milton. "In Hollywood." *Press Democrat*, November 4, 1938.
Johnson, Erskine. "In Hollywood." *Dixon Evening Telegraph*, November 25, 1953.
Kilgallen, Dorothy. "The Voice of Broadway." *Star Gazette*, November 1, 1948.
Martin, Boyd. "Boyd Martin's Show Talk." *Courier Journal*, September 28, 1954.
Moore, Charles R. "Hollywood Film Shop." *McAllen Daily Press*, September 28, 1941.
Mosby, Alice. "Rita Johnson Battles for Comeback Movie Roles." *San Mateo Times*, January 1, 1952.
"New Plan is Considered for Harlow Picture." *Post Star*, June 14, 1937.
Parsons, Harriet. *San Francisco Examiner*, June 27, 1940.
Parsons, Louella O. *Philadelphia Inquirer*, July 1, 1937.
Peak, Mayme Ober. "The Latest Cinderella—From Worcester." *Boston Globe*, July 15, 1937.
_____. "Reel Life in Hollywood." *Boston Globe*, June 27, 1938.
_____. "Rita Johnson, Planning Wedding, to Consider Stage, Radio Offers." *Boston Globe*, November 11, 1940.
"Rita Johnson, Former Actress, Dies at Age 52." *Philadelphia Daily News*, November 2, 1965.
"Rita Johnson Guarded by Mishap Policy." *Salt Lake Telegram*, October 9, 1939.
"Rita Johnson in Poor Condition." *Boston Globe*, September 10, 1948.
"Rita Johnson Near Death; Foul Play." *Clarion Ledger*, September 12, 1948.
"Rita Johnson Near Death, Mystery Blow Probed." *Miami News*, September 9, 1948.
Schallert, Edwin. *Los Angeles Times*. July 25, 1939.
_____. *Los Angeles Times*, June 8, 1940.
Tierney, Michael. Email to Author, October 10, 2018.
Weinstock, Matt. "The Booby-Trapped Life of Rita Johnson." *Los Angeles Review of Books*. August 13, 2013.
Winchell, Walter. "Walter Winchell on Broadway." *Courier Post*, June 17, 1937.
_____. Walter Winchell on Broadway. *Indianapolis Star*, January 11, 1938.
_____. "Walter Winchell on Broadway." *Nevada State Journal*, September 19, 1948.
_____. *Wilkes-Barre Times Leader*, November 10, 1948.
"Worcester Girl Gets Chance Today to Make Good in Jean Harlow Role." *Boston Globe*, June 11, 1937.

Mayo Methot

Arvad, Inga. "Hollywood Today." *Kingsport News*, January 3, 1945.
"Avenue Theater." *Vancouver Sun*, July 15, 1913.

Bacall, Lauren. *By Myself*. New York: Knopf, 1978.

Bogart, Mrs. Humphrey (Mayo Methot). "Bogy Bogart Doesn't Bogey at Home." *Des Moines Register*, April 5, 1942.

Bogart, Stephen. *Bogart: In Search of My Father*. New York: Dutton, 1995.

Brooks, Louise, *Lulu in Hollywood*. Minneapolis: University of Minnesota Press, 2000.

Brownlee, Earl C. "Spring Songs from Broadway; Easter Season's Newsy Notes." *Oregon Daily Journal*, March 27, 1921.

Cameron, Kate. "Menjou a Slick Detective in *The Night Club Lady*." *Daily News*, August 27, 1932.

Chapman, John. "*Torch Song* a Theatrical Mixture." *Daily News*, August 28, 1930.

"C.T.H. Play at Baker This Week 'Frenchy.'" *Oregon Daily Journal*, March 22, 1920.

"Descendant of Long Line of Play Folk." *Capital Journal*, September 18, 1912.

Dixon, Hugh. "Hollywood." *Pittsburgh Post-Gazette*, September 4, 1945.

"E.C.L. Glad Play at Baker; All Are Good." *Oregon Daily Journal*, December 1, 1919.

Fidler, Jimmie. "In Hollywood." *St. Louis Star and Times*, January 18, 1945.

_____. "In Hollywood." *The Mercury*, December 1, 1945.

"Geraldine Dare Has Premier at Baker." *Oregon Daily Journal*, September 22, 1919.

Graham, Sheilah. *Hartford Courant*, August 9, 1938.

_____. Different On and Off. *Baltimore Sun*, February 17, 1946.

"A Gruesome Tale." *Quad City Times*, February 28, 1938.

"Home, Stage Dispute Ends in Divorce for Actress." *Oakland Tribune*, February 23, 1937.

"John Methot Fined for Slapping Youth." *Oregon Daily Journal*, February 26, 1918.

Johnson, Erskine. "In Hollywood." *Miami Daily News Record*, January 11, 1944.

Lowrance, Dee. "Battling Bogarts." *Arizona Republic*, December 14, 1941.

Mantle, Burns. "*Strip Girl* Profanely Honest." *New York Daily News*, October 21, 1935.

Martin, Mildred. "Mrs. Bogart Frets Over Police Escort." *Philadelphia Inquirer*, January 6, 1941.

"Mashers Condemned by Court." *Oregon Daily Journal*, May 1, 1918.

"Mayo Methot Asks Divorce After Years of Separation." *Oakland Tribune*, October 5, 1927.

"Mayo Methot, Film Star, Becomes Bride." *The Times*, November 27, 1931.

"Mayo Methot Free of Marital Bonds." *Bakersfield Californian*, February 24, 1937.

"Mayo Methot Will Not Go into Movies." *Oregon Daily Journal*, December 26, 1917.

"*The Medicine Man*." *Brooklyn Daily Eagle*, October 25, 1927.

"News Briefs of the Nation." *Miami News*, February 24, 1937.

"Notes About the Players." *Boston Globe*, December 2, 1923.

"Portland Likes Show, To Be Here Thurs." *Statesman Journal*, September 18, 1912.

"President Writes Governor." *Statesman Journal*, June 22, 1913.

Scheuer. Philip K. *Los Angeles Times*, February 4, 1931.

"The Show Window." *Hartford Courant*, December 16, 1929.

Sperber, A.M., and Eric Lax. *Bogart*. New York: William Morrow, 1997.

Starr, Jimmy. *Barefoot on Barbed Wire*. Metuchen, NJ: Scarecrow, 2001.

Stuart, Gloria, with Sylvia Thompson. *I Just Kept Hoping*. New York: Little, Brown and Company, 1999.

Thompson, Lloyd S. "Mayo Methot Leaves East, But Her Original Role Pursues Her Here." *San Francisco Examiner*, January 4, 1931.

_____. "Play Tense Study of Human Actions." *San Francisco Examiner*, January 5, 1931.

"Verna Felton is New Star at Baker." *Oregon Daily Journal*, August 31, 1919.

Wells, Carol. "Troubled Film Stars Got Their Start at 23rd Avenue School." *NW Examiner*, January 2012. http://nwexaminer.com/wp-content/uploads/2014/05/01January2012.pdf.

"Will of Actor's Ex-Wife Probated." *Victoria Advocate*, August 2, 1951.

Winner, Vella. "Club Activities." *Oregon Daily Journal*, April 10, 1915.

Young, Nicholas. "Greet Day Show Bright and Sunny Opines Noted Critic." *Pittsburgh Courier*, September 28, 1929.

Marjie Millar

Ames, Walter. *Los Angeles Times*, September 17, 1954.

_____. "Bolger Yields Director Job to Stay on Toes." *Los Angeles Times*, October 19, 1954.

Belser, Emily. "Delectable Blonde Says She's a Fugitive from Cheesecake." *Lubbock Evening Journal*, April 13, 1953.

Devane, James. "Look and Listen." *Cincinnati Enquirer*, September 9, 1954.

"Dragnet Actress Wins Divorce from Director." *Long Beach Independent*, August 29, 1958.

Fidler, Jimmie. "Fidler in Hollywood." *Nevada State Journal*, December 12, 1953.

"Former TV, Film Star Dies." *Port Angeles Evening News*, April 19, 1966.

Johnson, Erskine. "In Hollywood." *Portsmouth Herald*, December 2, 1953.

Madigan Army Hospital Bedside Network (Fort Lewis). http://www.historylink.org/File/10416.

Mahony, Jim. "Behind the Scenes in Hollywood." *Wilkes-Barre Times Leader*, July 31, 1957.
"Marjie Millar Too Ill to Play Dead Role." *Variety*, April 19, 1957.
Maynard, John. "Look Who Wants to Steal a Yak." *Albany Times Union*, March 13, 1953.
"McCallum, Marjie Millar Here Working on Book." *Port Angeles Evening News*, April 21, 1961.
"Movie Aspirant Loses Arm, Leg." *Albuquerque Journal*, August 18, 1953.
"Night Club Singer Meets Industrialist in Adult Motion Picture, *About Mrs. Leslie*." *Bridgeport Telegram*, September 12, 1954.
Scheuer, Steven H. "Viewers Give Approval to Friday's Gal." *Des Moines Tribune*, February 14, 1956.
"Seek Jury Trial in Damage Case." *Port Angeles Evening News*, May 18, 1962.
Starr, Eve. "Inside TV." *Morning Call*, September 30, 1955.
_____. "Inside TV." *Morning Call*, December 9, 1955.
_____. "Inside TV." *Democrat and Chronicle*, March 13, 1956.
_____. "Inside TV." *Rochester Democrat Chronicle*, June 6, 1956.
_____. "Inside TV." *Morning Call*, April 25, 1961.
"Stars Shine Again on Tacoma's Marjie Millar." *Seattle Times*, January 14, 1962.
Torres, Marie, with Jack Webb. "Webb Will Not Drop *Dragnet*." *Oakland Tribune*, June 20, 1956.

Mary Nolan

"Actress Trying to Chase Jinx." *Morning Herald*, December 29, 1934.
Ankerich, Michael G. *Dangerous Curves Atop Hollywood Heels*. Duncan, OK: BearManor Media, 2010.
Bodeen, DeWitt. "The Hard Luck Girl." *Films in Review*, May 1980.
Brenner, L.C. "Memory Lane." *Salt Lake Tribune*, April 22, 1936.
"Death at Last Ends the Woes of Mary Nolan." *New York Daily News*, November 1, 1948.
"Dope, Operations Bring Hard Luck for Mary Nolan." *Fresno Bee*, June 4, 1937.
"Ex-Follies Star Mary Nolan Buried; Friend Brings Rosebuds as Tribute." *Los Angeles Times*, November 5, 1948.
Fidler, Jimmie. *Monroe News Star*, May 3, 1948.
Harrison, Dale. "Follies Girl of Yesteryear Fights for Life." *Central New Jersey Home News*, June 13, 1937.
Harrison, Paul. "In New York." *Pittsburgh Press*, August 3, 1934.
"Homes Not to Be Searched on Warrants." *San Bernardino County Sun*, August 1, 1930.
"Imogene Wilson Left U.S. Today." *Lebanon Daily News*, September 20, 1924.
"Imogene Wilson Loses Her Job." *Morning News*, August 7, 1924.
"Malnutrition Strikes Ex-Actress Mary Nolan." *Los Angeles Times*, April 21, 1948.
"Mannix Says He Paid Off Nolan." *New York Daily News*, March 31, 1936.
"Mary Nolan Again Enters Bellevue." *New York Daily News*, October 19, 1937.
"Mary Nolan Better, to Wed Her Manager as Future Brightens." *Evening News*, May 7, 1937.
"Mary Nolan, Ex-Follies Star, Dies." *Los Angeles Times*, November 1, 1948.
"Mary Nolan, Improving, Says Life Was Beautiful." *Los Angeles Times*, April 25, 1948.
"Mary Nolan Leaves Bellevue on Stretcher." *New York Daily News*, November 13, 1937.
"Mary Nolan Settles Mannix Suit, But Keeps Terms Secret." *Chicago Tribune*, October 18, 1936.
"Mary Nolan's Death Laid to Sleeping Pills." *Courier Journal*, November 23, 1948.
"Mary Nolan's Ex-Husband in Police Court." *Evening News*, August 19, 1937.
"Mary Nolan's Gone—So Is Agent's $2,000." *New York Daily News*, November 5, 1934.
"Mary Nolan's Husband Said It with Fists, Manicurist Charges." *New Daily News*, August 21, 1931.
"Mary Nolan Starts for New Comeback." *San Bernardino County Sun*, December 29, 1934.
"Mary Nolan Sues Paper for Libel." *Pittsburgh Courier*, August 14, 1937.
Mitchell, Joseph. "Mary Nolan, Night Club Queen, Has Hopes of Staging Comeback in Movies." *Pittsburgh Press*, January 6, 1935.
"Movies and Amusements." *St. Louis Star and Times*, September 14, 1938.
"No Mary Nolan, So No $25,000." *Daily News*, November 16, 1938.
Nolan, Mary. "Real Life Follies of Bubbles Wilson." *San Francisco Examiner*, October 12, 1941.
_____. "Real Life Follies of Bubbles Wilson." *San Francisco Examiner*, October 26, 1941.
_____. "Real Life Follies of Bubbles Wilson." *The Tennessean*, November 9, 1941.
_____. "Real Life Follies of Bubbles Wilson." *San Francisco Examiner*, November 30, 1941.
"Odds Are That Imogene Wilson Will Go Through With Love Damage Suit." *Oshkosh Northwestern*, May 30, 1924.
Parsons, Louella. *Fresno Bee*, April 23, 1948.
Ray, Ebenezer. "Dottings of a Paragrapher." *New York Age*, June 5 1937.
"Screen Actress Is Operated On." *New Castle News*, November 18, 1933.
"Screen Actress Sues Director." *Miami Daily News-Record*, July 9, 1935.
Tucker, George. "Seen and Heard in New York." *The Post-Crescent*. February 24, 1936.
"$25,000 Sought by Mary Nolan in Debt Arrest." *Daily News*, November 12, 1938.

Winchell, Walter. *Naugatuck Daily News*, April 17, 1944.

_____. *Courier Post*, May 17, 1944.

_____. *Wilkes-Barre Times Leader*, June 25, 1945.

"Ziegfeld Girls Send Mary Nolan to Home." *New York Daily News*, June 3, 1937.

Susan Peters

"Actress Susan Peters' Final Divorce Entered." *Los Angeles Times*, July 7, 1951.

"Blond Model, 27, 'Too Old,' Says Her Husband, 21." *Salt Lake Telegram*, October 30, 1942.

Carroll, Harrison. "Harrison in Hollywood." *Lancaster Eagle-Gazette*, September 17, 1940.

_____. "Behind the Scenes in Hollywood." *Wilkes Barre Record*, June 15, 1948.

_____. "Behind the Scenes in Hollywood." *Republican and Herald*, May 2, 1949.

Chapman, Frank. "Spotlight Finish of 'Dr. Peters.'" *Albuquerque Journal*, November 29, 1942.

Cohen, Harold V. "*Barretts of Wimpole Street* Stars Susan Peters at Nixon." *Pittsburgh Post-Gazette*, January 24, 1950.

Crowther, Bosley. "*The Sign of the Ram*, Marking Return of Susan Peters to Films, at Loew's State." *New York Times*, March 4, 1948.

"Death Held No Terror for Susan Peters." *Star Tribune*, October 26, 1952.

"Divorce and Tears for Susan Peters, Also Adopted Son." *St. Louis Post Dispatch*, September 11, 1948.

Fidler, Jimmie. *Monroe News Star*, January 17, 1946.

_____. "In Hollywood." *The Mercury*, June 22, 1946.

Graham, Sheilah. "Hollywood." *Pittsburgh Post-Gazette*, February 14, 1949.

Hart, Evelyn. "Down the Aisle." *Dayton Daily News*, June 15, 1942.

Heffernan, Harold. "Gossip from the Hollywood Studios." *Ottawa Citizen*, February 12, 1945.

"Hollywood Actress Seriously Shot in Hunting Accident." *Boston Globe*, January 2, 1945.

"Hunting Accident Shot Paralyses Susan Peters." *Los Angeles Times*, January 9, 1945.

Johnson, Erskine. "In Hollywood." *Dunkirk Evening Observer*, April 6, 1945.

_____. "In Hollywood." *Central New Jersey Home News*, February 21, 1952.

_____. "In Hollywood." *Dixon Evening Telegraph*, June 28, 1952.

Jones, Paul. "Susan Peters Pleases in *Glass Menagerie*." *Atlanta Constitution*, March 28, 1950.

Kirkley, Donald. "Two New Films." *Baltimore Sun*, May 10, 1945.

MacPherson, Virginia. "Susan Peters Defies Medics for First Show in Wheelchair." *Oakland Tribune*, September 5, 1945.

Morris, Mary. "Girl Fights for Career from Wheelchair." *Des Moines Register*, November 11, 1945.

Morse, Jim. "Susan Is Beautiful...and So's Vivian." *Star Gazette*, July 30, 1950.

Othman, Frederick C. "Behind the Scenes Hollywood." *Press Democrat*, June 21, 1942.

Parsons, Louella. *San Francisco Examiner*, February 2, 1943.

_____. "Producer about *The Song of Russia*." *Evening Courier*, June 11, 1943.

_____. *San Francisco Examiner*, March 27, 1944.

_____. *Courier Post*. April 29, 1944.

_____. *San Francisco Examiner*, January 4, 1945.

_____. *Fresno Bee*, February 2, 1945.

_____. *Democrat and Chronicle*, September 25, 1946.

_____. "Susan Peters, Husband Part." *San Francisco Examiner*, May 3, 1948.

_____. *Philadelphia Inquirer*, May 5, 1948.

Peak, Mayme Ober. "I Cover Hollywood." *Boston Globe*, November 18, 1944.

Peters, Susan. "Meet Susan Peters." *Boston Globe*, April 6, 1943.

_____. "Meet Susan Peters." *Boston Globe*, April 8, 1943.

_____. "A Girl Can Go Places Without Legs." *American Magazine*, December 1947.

"Practical Is the Word for Susan." *New York Times*, December 20, 1942.

Quine, Shannon. Email to Author, December 12, 2018.

Schallert, Edwin. *Los Angeles Times*, June 23, 1942.

_____. "Future Brightens for Susan Peters." *Los Angeles Times*, August 5, 1945.

"Seaman Weds Susan Peters After Film Studio Romance." *Los Angeles Times*, November 8, 1943.

Skolsky, Sidney. "She's No Longer 'Screen Test' Girl." *St. Louis Post Dispatch*, May 11, 1943.

"*Song of Russia* Review." *Variety*, December 29, 1943.

Starr, Peggy. "On with the Show." *Akron Beacon Journal*, November 15, 1949.

"Susan Peters and Husband Are Parted." *Des Moines Tribune*, May 3, 1948.

"Susan Peters Convalescing." *The Times*, January 25, 1945.

"Susan Peters Has Sudden Operation." *Los Angeles Times*, April 5, 1944.

"Susan Peters to Open Red Feather Drive." *Detroit Free Press*, October 26, 1948.

Thomas, Bob. "Susan Peters 'Couldn't Live' But She's Walking." *Evening Sun*, June 22, 1945.

_____. "Susan Peters Sparks Yule." *Decatur Daily Review*, December 26, 1946.

_____. "Paralyzed Two Years Ago Susan Peters Makes Comeback." *Ottawa Journal*, July 19, 1947.
_____. "Hollywood Comment." *Harrisburg Telegraph*, August 6, 1947.
_____. "Invalid Movie Actress Finds Her Best Future Is on Stage." *The Dispatch*, September 30, 1949.
Todd, John. "Susan Peters and Husband Anxious to Adopt Two Babies; Want Boy and Girl." *The Dispatch*, January 5, 1946.
Toomey, Elizabeth. "Start New Career Says Susan Peters." *Green Bay Press Gazette*, March 1, 1951.

Lyda Roberti

"Actress Paid Final Tribute." *Los Angeles Times*, March 16, 1938.
Cohen, Harold W. *Pittsburgh Post-Gazette*, October 14, 1933.
Ellis, Iola. "Minute Biography." *Pittsburgh Post-Gazette*, July 27, 1934.
"E.S.C., Conklin Peps T. & D. Patrons to Laughter." *Oakland Tribune*, November 14, 1927.
Graham, Sheilah. *Star Tribune*, August 12, 1936.
Keavy, Hubbard. "Movie Fan's Corner." *Valley Morning Star*, October 28, 1936.
Krug, Karl. "The Show Shops." *Pittsburgh Press*, October 31, 1930.
"Lyda Roberti Arrives Behind Dark Glasses." *Brooklyn Daily Eagle*, July 30, 1935.
"Lyda Roberti, Film Star, Dies After Heart Attack." *Philadelphia Inquirer*, March 13, 1938.
"Lyda Roberti, Find Who Stayed Found." *Brooklyn Daily Eagle*, March 6, 1932.
"Lyda Roberti Ill in Richmond." *Atlanta Constitution*, October 31, 1935.
"Lyda Roberti Is Featured at Fox." *Philadelphia Inquirer*, April 1, 1933.
"Lyda Roberti of Stage and Film Fame is Buried." *Quad City Times*, March 16, 1938.
"Lyda Roberti Trip Delayed." *Los Angeles Times*, July 4, 1935.
"Lyda Roberti Waitress in a Cafe of Shanghai." *Baltimore Sun*, March 20, 1932.
Mantle, Burns. "Old Theater Tradition Found Foolish." *Chicago Tribune*, February 1, 1931.
_____. "*Roberta*, With Handsome Gowns and Tunes." *Daily News*, November 20, 1933.
Merrick, Mollie. "Hollywood in Person." *Montana Standard*, March 4, 1932.
Miles, Margaret. "For Your Amusement." *Miami News*, August 13, 1936.
"Philip Barry Play Praised." *Los Angeles Times*, January 25, 1931.
Pollock, Arthur. "The Theaters." *Brooklyn Daily Eagle*, December 27, 1932.
_____. "The Theaters." *Brooklyn Daily Eagle*, November 20, 1933.
Sentner, David P. "Slim, Blonde Lyda Roberti Steals Show." *Tampa Times*, February 13, 1931.
Skolsky, Sidney. "About Broadway." *Daily News*, February 8, 1931.
Tinee, Mae. "*Nobody's Baby* Suggested for Movie Fans with the Blues." *Chicago Tribune*, May 30, 1937.
Winchell, Walter. *Tampa Times*, January 9, 1931.
_____. *Akron Beacon Journal*, January 23, 1931.
_____. *Wilkes Barre Times Leader*, August 2, 1935.
_____. *Wilkes Barre Times Leader*, August 26, 1935.
"You Said It." *Philadelphia Inquirer*, December 21, 1930.

Peggy Shannon

"Actor, Shot Last July, Marries Chorus Girl." *Joplin Globe*, February 27, 1926.
"Actress' Ex-Husband Jailed in Row with Present Mate." *Los Angeles Times*, March 11, 1941.
"Actress Peggy Shannon Says Mate Played While She Worked." *Los Angeles Times*, July 9, 1940.
Alan Davis Obituary. *Variety*, December 15, 1943.
"Blame Actress' Death on Excessive Alcoholism." *Daily Capital News*, May 13, 1941.
Coons, Robbin. *Monroe News Star*, August 27, 1931.
_____. "Peggy Shannon Says She Is Just Getting Started." *Decatur Daily Review*, June 25, 1932.
Gloss, Edward E. "Roman, Greek Gods Try Modern Gayety in Movie at Palace." *Akron Beacon Journal*, May 1, 1935.
Harker, Milton. "Young Movie Stars to Set Example for Others." *New Castle News*, February 13, 1939.
"How a Little Girl from Arkansas Conquered Broadway." *San Francisco Chronicle*, June 24, 1923.
"Husband Follows Beauty in Death." *San Bernardino County Sun*, May 31, 1941.
"In Hollywood." *Piqua Daily Call*, February 9, 1932.
Kish, Frances. "Peggy from Pine Bluff." *Photoplay*, December 1932.
Morris, Ruth. "Uncommon Chatter." *Variety*, March 22, 1932.
"Nasty Details Before Davis Acquittal." *Variety*, May 5, 1926.
"News from the Dailies." *Variety*, February 3, 1926.
Parsons, Louella. *Modesto News Herald*, February 9, 1932.
"Peggy Shannon, Actress, Injured." *Ardmore Daily Ardmoreite*, July 13, 1938.
"Peggy Shannon's Death Natural." *Los Angeles Times*, June 1, 1941.

Rosa Stradner

Balch, Jack. "The New Films." *St. Louis Post Dispatch*, February 9, 1945.
"Boos and Bouquets." *Photoplay*, December 1940.
Clarke, Gerald. *Get Happy: The Life of Judy Garland*. New York: Delta, 2001.
Coons, Robbin. "Hollywood Chatter." *Evening Review*, March 18, 1944.
Cronin, A.J. *The Keys of the Kingdom*. Boston: Little, Brown and Company, 1941.
Currie, George. "Theater." *Brooklyn Daily Eagle*, November 8, 1948.
Davis, Ronald L. *Hollywood Beauty: Linda Darnell and the American Dream*. Norman: University of Oklahoma Press, 1991 (second edition).
Graham, Sheilah. "Hollywood." *Miami News*, March 19, 1945.
_____. "Hollywood." *Indianapolis Star*, August 30, 1946.
Harrison, Paul. "Rose Stradner Leads Glamour Gal Parade from Vienna to Hollywood Studios." *Wausau Daily Herald*, February 22, 1938.
Heffernan, Harold. "Luise Rainer Too Fussy; Studios Cold Shoulder Her." *Star Tribune*, September 3, 1937.
Hopper, Hedda. *Daily News*, January 21, 1945.
_____. *Mansfield Advertiser*, February 14, 1945.
_____. *Daily News*, April 4, 1946.
Kilgallen, Dorothy. "The Voice of Broadway." *News Herald*, November 8, 1948.
Lyons, Leonard. "The Lyons Den." *Quad City Times*, November 19, 1947.
Mankiewicz, Tom, and Robert Crane. *My Life as a Mankiewicz: An Insider's Journey Through Hollywood*. Lexington: University Press of Kentucky, 2012.
Morton, Hortense. "Keys of the Kingdom Cast Gives Inspiring Performance." *San Francisco Examiner*, January 31, 1945.
"Movies' Universal Appeal Makes English World Tongue." *Detroit Free Press*, November 21, 1937.
Munn, Michael. *Gregory Peck*. London: Robert Hale, 1999.
Parsons, Harriet. *Camden Courier-Post*, August 25, 1937.
Parsons, Louella. *Courier Post*, October 20, 1938.
_____. *San Francisco Examiner*, May 17, 1948.
_____. *San Francisco Examiner*, August 11, 1948.
_____. *San Francisco Examiner*, November 5, 1948.
"Probe Death of Ex-Actress Stradner." *Chicago Tribune*, September 29, 1958.
Schallert, Edwin. *Los Angeles Times*, January 17, 1946.
Staggs, Sam. *All About All About Eve: The Complete Behind-the-Scenes Story of the Bitchiest Film Ever Made!* New York: St. Martin's, 2001.
"Star Offers Powerful Portrayal in New Story." *Kingsport Times*, December 12, 1937.
Tildesley, Alice L. "Another Foreign Invasion Under Way." *Lincoln Star*, January 9, 1938.
"Viennese Rose." *Orlando Sentinel*, August 31, 1932.
Wilcox, Grace. "Hollywood Reporter." *Detroit Free Press*, November 28, 1937.

Judy Tyler

Archerd, Army. "Just for Variety." *Variety*, July 5, 1957.
Davis, Stephen. *Say Kids! What Time Is It? Notes from the Peanut Gallery*. Boston: Little, Brown and Company, 1987.
Durgin, Cyrus. "Rodgers and Hammerstein's Pipe Dream Resounding Hit." *Boston Globe*, November 13, 1955.
Jacobs, Carl. "*Pipe Dream* Falls Off R. & H. Musical Peaks." *Cincinnati Enquirer*, December 4, 1955.
"Judy Tyler's Auto Looted, Family Hints." *Pasadena Independent*, July 8, 1957.
Kilgallen, Dorothy. "Voice of Broadway." *Daily Journal*, September 15, 1955.
Kohrs, Karl. "Judy Tyler: New Broadway Cinderella." *Honolulu Star-Bulletin*, November 12, 1955.
Lyons, Leonard. "The Lyons Den." *Pittsburgh Press*, July 8, 1956.
"Nitery Reviews." *Variety*, April 21, 1954.
Scheuer, Steven H. "TV KEYnotes." *Munster Times*, August 23, 1955.
Scott, Vernon. "Elvis' New Leading Lady Has Rock 'N' Roll Ideas." *Indianapolis Star*, June 14, 1957.
Singer, Samuel L. "Berlin Musical at Valley Forge." *Philadelphia Inquirer*, July 12, 1955.
"Starlet Dies in Accident." *News-Palladium*, July 5, 1957.
"Tuesday Set for Funeral of Judy Tyler." *New York Daily News*, July 6, 1957.
Weinstock, Matt. "Barbara Cook Talks about Working with Rodgers & Hammerstein." About New York City Center, October 25, 2014. https://www.nycitycenter.org/About/Blog/blog-posts-2014/barbara-cook-talks-about-working-with-rodgers—hammerstein/
Wilson, Earl. "Judy Tyler Is Her Own Discovery." *Tampa Bay Times*, December 16, 1955.

Karen Verne

"Actor Peter Lorre Divorced by Wife." *Daily Oklahoman*, June 21, 1953.
"Actress Karen Verne Is Awarded Divorce." *The News Journal*, January 19, 1955.
"Actress Wants Divorce." *Santa Ana Register*, September 13, 1941.
Albelli, Alfred. "Hungry Mrs. Lorre Seeks Alimony." *Daily News*, December 16, 1952.
"*All Through the Night* Review." *Variety*, December 2, 1941.
"C. Bechstein: The Legend Lives On." http://www.marksonpianos.com/bechstein-pianos/CarlBechstein_History.pdf.
"Close Watch on Actress." *Kansas City Times*, January 19, 1955.
"Ex-Wife of Film Actor to Shed Third Husband." *Marion Star*, June 4, 1954.
Graham, Sheilah. "Hollywood Gossip." *Ottawa Citizen*, September 1, 1945.
_____. "Hollywood Today." *Kingsport News*, July 6, 1946.
_____. "Hollywood Today." *Boston Globe*, August 9, 1952.
Gwynn, Edith. "Edith Gwynn's Hollywood." *Cincinnati Enquirer*, November 7, 1950.
_____. "Edith Gwynn in Hollywood." *Cincinnati Enquirer*, January 9, 1951.
Jones, Carlisle. "Refugee Actress Kaaren Verne Makes Sixth Bid for Stardom." *The Record*, April 29, 1941.
Kahn, Sylvia. "Good News." *Modern Screen*, July 1942.
Karen Verne Obituary. *Variety*, January 3, 1968.
Keavy, Hubbard. "As Exotic as LaMarr or Dietrich." *Pittsburgh Post-Gazette*, February 17, 1942.
Kilgallen, Dorothy. "The Voice of Broadway." *News Herald*, March 24, 1947.
Lowrance, Dee. "From Hitler to Hollywood." *The Missoulian*, March 8, 1942.
Oldfield, Barney. "Theater Topics." *Lincoln Star*, November 9, 1941.
O'Liam, Dugal. "Valiant Lady." *Hollywood*, February 1942.
Othman, Frederick C. "Daughter of Great Piano Maker Starts Life Anew." *Journal Herald*, March 28, 1941.
Parsons, Louella. *Morning News*, March 16, 1940.
_____. *Daily Times*, February 18, 1947.
Schallert, Edwin. *Los Angeles Times*, November 6, 1940.
_____. *Los Angeles Times*, January 22, 1957.
"The Screen; A Case of Amnesia." *New York Times*, April 21, 1941.
Sullivan, Ed. "Little Old New York." *Daily News*, November 8, 1941.
"Ten Days in Paris." *Motion Picture Herald*, October 28, 1939.
Warren, Geoffrey. "*Anne Frank* Well Staged." *Los Angeles Times*. October 24, 1958.
"Wife Asks $250 Week Bite from Gourmet Peter Lorre." *Vancouver Sun*, December 16, 1952.
"Wife Divorces Peter Lorre." *Los Angeles Times*, June 21, 1953.
Youngkin, Stephen D. *The Lost One: A Life of Peter Lorre*. Lexington: University Press of Kentucky, 2005.
_____. Emails to Author, February 12 and February 25, 2019, and March 7, 2019.

Helen Walker

"Actor's Driver to Face Trial." *San Bernardino County Sun*, November 29, 1938.
"Actress Absolved of Manslaughter Charge." *St. Louis Star and Times*, April 8, 1947.
"Actress Dies at 47 After Tragic Years." *San Francisco Examiner*, March 11, 1968.
"Actress Divorces Studio Attorney." *Los Angeles Times*, January 23, 1946.
"Actress Helen Walker Freed of Manslaughter Charges from Accident." *Freeport Journal Standard*, April 9, 1947.
"Actress Hurt as Car Upsets, Killing Soldier." *Los Angeles Times*, January 3, 1947.
Archerd, Army. "Just for Variety." *Variety*, January 16, 1962.
"*The Big Combo* Review." *Variety*, February 10, 1955.
Carroll, Harrison. "Behind the Scenes in Hollywood." *Wilkes Barre Times Leader*, July 30, 1951.
"*The Children's Hour* Review." *Variety*, October 11, 1956.
Connolly, Mike. "Mr. Hollywood." *Independent Star News*, November 29, 1958.
De Carlo, Yvonne, and Doug Warren. *Yvonne: An Autobiography*. New York: St. Martin's Press, 1987.
Dixon, Hugh. "Hollywood." *Pittsburgh Post-Gazette*, March 13, 1948.
"Film Actress Must Stand Trial." *San Bernardino County Sun*, March 26 1947.
"Film Actress to Sue." *Pittsburgh Press*, July 19. 1945.
Handsaker, Gene. "Hollywood." *St. Cloud Times*, July 28, 1948.
Heimer, Mel. "Glamour Girl Passes Out of Spotlight." *Evening Herald*, March 25, 1968.
"Helen Walker Gets Divorce." *New York Daily News*, June 10, 1952.
"Helen Walker to Face Charges in Auto Death." *Los Angeles Times*, January 5, 1947.
"Hitch-Hiker Says Actress Was Driving 100 Miles An Hour." *Dunkirk Evening Observer*, March 6, 1947.
"Hitchhiker Seeks Damages from Helen Walker." *Los Angeles Time*, February 6, 1947.

"Marijuana Charge Holds Youth, 18." *Wilmington Daily Press Journal*, March 19, 1947.
Parsons, Louella. *San Francisco Examiner*, January 6, 1947.
_____. "Helen Walker Turns Cynical About Future in Hollywood." *El Paso Times*, June 5, 1949.
Problem Girls Review. *Variety*, March 11, 1953.
Schallert, Edwin. *Los Angeles Times*, August 24, 1942.
_____. "*Career*, Story of Actor's Fight for Success, to Open at Ivar." *Los Angeles Times*, October 27, 1957.
_____. "Actor's Life in Theater Well Probed." *Los Angeles Times*, October 29, 1957.
Scheuer, Philip K. "Helen Walker Clings to Ideals." *Los Angeles Times*, November 4, 1945.
"Screen: *The Big Combo*; Crime Drama Is New Feature at Palace." *New York Times*, March 26, 1955.
"Summer Stage: *The Constant Wife*." *Boston Globe*, July 23, 1941.
Walker, Helen, as told to Mayme Ober Peak. "Freckled-Faced Worcester Girl Tells How She Became a Hollywood Star." *Boston Globe*, October 3, 1943.
"Walker, 20th Sever." *Variety*, January 21, 1948.
Weaver, Tom. *It Came from Horrorwood: Interviews with Moviemakers in the Science Fiction and Horror Tradition*. Jefferson, NC: McFarland, 2004.
_____. *I Talked with a Zombie: Interviews With 23 Veterans of Horror and Sci-Fi Films and Television*. Jefferson, NC: McFarland, 2008.
"Witness Against Actress Identified in Theater Holdup." *San Bernardino County Sun*, March 28, 1947.
"Worcester's Helen Walker Steps into Star Film Roles." *Boston Sunday Post*, October 18, 1942.

Constance Worth

"Actress Is Revived After Hollywood Suicide Attempt." *Fresno Bee*, August 5, 1936.
"American Papers Victimise Australian Film-Actress." *Smith's Weekly*, September 26, 1936.
Austin, Guy. "I'll Rebuild My Life as an Actress." *Sydney Morning Herald*, November 5, 1961.
"Australian on U.S. Television." *Sydney Morning Herald*, October 9, 1952.
"Ban Brent." *Sunday Times*, September 19, 1937.
"Brent's Action for Annulment Miss Howarth's Evidence." *Tweed Daily*, August 23, 1937.
"Brent's Wife Denies She Put Heat on Him." *Courier-Journal*, August 19, 1937.
"Constance Worth Claims Good Faith in Wedding Brent." *Times Herald*, August 21, 1937.
"The Courts." *Daily Telegraph*, September 22, 1921.
"Film Star's Return." *Maryborough Chronicle, Wide Bay and Burnett Advertiser*, June 12, 1939.
"Former Wife Does Not Wish Boycott." *The Mail*, January 22, 1938.
Hall, Ken G. *Directed by Ken G. Hall: Autobiography of an Australian Film Maker*. Melbourne: Lansdowne Press, 1977.
Howarth, Joy. "What Happened in Hollywood." *Daily Telegraph*, June 26, 1939.
"The Howarth Case: Boxer as Co-Respondent." *Evening News*, August 29, 1916.
"Intimate Jottings." *The Australian Women's Weekly*, August 8, 1936.
Jones, Lon. "The Girl Who Came Back." *The Australasian*, August 25, 1945.
"Joy Howarth as Mannequin." *Sydney Morning Herald*, August 16, 1939.
"Joy Howarth Claims to Have Hoodoo." *Newcastle Sun*, July 15, 1939.
"Joy Howarth in Hospital." *The Mail*, April 20, 1938.
"Judge Decides Against Brent." *The Age*, September 15, 1937.
MacDonald, Viola. "Sydney Girl's Luck Has Changed." *Australian Women's Weekly*, December 12, 1942.
"Mrs. Pierce Divorces Movie Producer." *Dunkirk Evening Observer*, January 10, 1946.
"Name in Lights Was Dream Come True." *The News*, July 28, 1939.
"Numerous Trysts Get Divorce for Producer's Wife." *Medford Mail Tribune*, January 13, 1946.
O'Neill, Josephine. "Josephine O'Neill's Reviews." *Daily Telegraph*, June 12, 1949.
Parsons, Louella. *San Francisco Examiner*, May 6, 1950.
"The Play Goes On." *West Australian*, July 15, 1939.
Ruddy, J.M. "How Hollywood Treats Australian Favorites." *The Mail*, May 25, 1940.
"Sidney's Talking About." *Sydney Morning Herald*, August 7, 1947.
Sloan, Amber. "Jocelyn Howarth." BONZA National Cinema and Television Database, RMIT University, 1998.

Index

Numbers in **bold italics** indicate pages with illustrations

213